MALAY
PHRASEBOOK

Susan Keeney

Malay phrasebook
2nd edition – February 2002
First published – November 1996

Published by
Lonely Planet Publications Pty Ltd, ABN 36 005 607 983
90 Maribyrnong St, Footscray, Victoria 3011, Australia

Lonely Planet Offices
Australia Locked Bag 1, Footscray, Victoria 3011
USA 150 Linden St, Oakland CA 94607
UK 10a Spring Place, London NW5 3BH
France 1 rue du Dahomey, 75011 Paris

Cover illustration
Malay Family Watch'n Telly by Patrick Marris

ISBN 1 74059 175 5

text © Lonely Planet Publications Pty Ltd 2002
cover illustration © Lonely Planet Publications Pty Ltd 2002

Printed by The Bookmaker International Ltd
Printed in China

ABOUT THE AUTHOR

Having lived in Malaysia on and off for 16 years, Susan Keeney first started to learn Malay in the kitchens and back rooms of obscure places like Kajang and Serdang. She wound up teaching communication courses (in both Malay and English) at various universities and colleges in Malaysia. She is now teaching elementary school (in English) in California.

FROM THE AUTHOR

Many thanks to my three children, Johan (without whom this book would never have been finished on time), Sarah and Sabrina, for their help, advice and patience while I worked on this project. I would also like to thank my one and only *guru tatabahasa*, Awang Sariyan, who was a wonderful teacher and who certainly shared my love of grammar; and most of all, to my father, Bob Keeney, for all his love and support.

FROM THE PUBLISHER

The *Malay phrasebook* was edited by first time kite-fighter Meg Worby, who learned the rules from Senior Editors, Master of Games Karin Vidstrup Monk and Chief Top Spinner Karina Coates. Quizmaster Ben Handicott proofed the book and designer Patrick Marris painted the award-winning front cover and finished the maze of layout in record time. His layout relay team mate, champion 'Rubex cuber' Belinda Campbell, was also the creator of the beaut illustrations, and they were both encouraged from the sidelines by vocal Senior Designer Fabrice Rocher. Natasha Velleley provided the competition map and Emma Koch expertly coached the steps of the traditional 'dance of the dictionary'; medals must also go to Karin Vidstrup Monk, Sophie Putman, Ben Handicott and Karina Coates for their unbeatable expertise and assistance at the crucial stages. Tam Yewming and Kusnandar answered every question right. Publishing Manager Jim Jenkin left his competent fingerprint on the final layout and had the box seat for all the fun and games.

CONTENTS

INTRODUCTION 9

How to Use This Phrasebook .. 12
Abbreviations Used in
   This Book 12
Legend 13

PRONUNCIATION 13

Stress 15
Transliteration System 15
Vowels 16
Consonants 17

GRAMMAR 19

Word Order 19
Articles 19
Nouns 20
Pronouns 20
Adjectives 23
Adverbs 25
Verbs 26
To Be 29
To Have 30
Modals 30
Imperatives 32
Questions 32
Question Words 34
Answers 35
Negatives 35
Classifiers 36
Prepositions 37
Conjunctions 38

MEETING PEOPLE 39

You Should Know 39
Greetings & Goodbyes 40
Forms of Address 41
First Encounters 42
Making Conversation 42
Nationalities 46
Cultural Differences 47
Age 47
Occupations 49
Religion 50
Body Language 53
Feelings 54
Breaking the Language
   Barrier 55
Staying in Touch 56
Homestays 57

GETTING AROUND 59

Finding Your Way 59
Directions 60
Addresses 61
Buying Tickets 62
Air 63
Bus 65
Train 66
Taxi 68
Boat 69
Car 70
Bicycle 74
Local Transport 76

6   Contents

ACCOMMODATION 77

Finding Accommodation 77
Booking Ahead 78
Checking In 79
Requests & Complaints 82
Checking Out 85
Longer Stays 85

AROUND TOWN 87

Looking For 88
At the Bank 89
At the Post Office 91
Telecommunications 93
Sightseeing 96
Paperwork 97

GOING OUT 99

Invitations 100
Dating & Romance 101

FAMILY 105

Questions 105
Replies 106
Family Members 107

INTERESTS 109

Common Interests 109
Sport 111
Writing Letters 113
Social Issues 114
Politics 115
Music 116
Crafts 116
Performing & Martial Arts .. 118

SHOPPING 119

Looking For 119
Making a Purchase 120
Bargaining 121
Essential Items 122
Souvenirs 123
Clothing 124
Materials 125
Colours 126
Toiletries 127
For the Baby 128
Music 128
Stationery & Publications .. 129
Photography 130
Smoking 131
Sizes & Comparisons 132
Weights & Measures 133

FOOD 135

Breakfast 135
Vegetarian &
  Special Meals 136
Eating Out 138
Typical Dishes 141
Menu Decoder 141
Self-Catering 146
At the Market 146
Drinks 152

IN THE COUNTRY 155

Camping 155
Hiking 157
At the Beach 160
Weather 161
Geographical Terms 163
Fauna 164
Flora & Agriculture 165

HEALTH 167

At the Doctor 167
Ailments 170
Women's Health 172
Special Health Needs 174
Alternative Treatments 175
Parts of the Body 175
At the Chemist 176
At the Dentist 178

SPECIFIC NEEDS 179

Disabled Travellers 179
Gay Travellers 180
Travelling with the Family ... 181
On Business 182
Film & TV Crews 183
Pilgrimage & Religion 184
Tracing Roots & History 186

TIME, DATES & FESTIVALS 187

Telling the Time 187
Days 188
Months 189
Dates 189
Present 190
Past 190
Future 191
During the Day 192
Seasons 192
Holidays & Festivals 193
Weddings 197
Funerals 198

NUMBERS & AMOUNTS 199

Cardinal Numbers 199
Ordinal Numbers 200
Fractions 200
Quantity 201

EMERGENCIES 203

Dealing with the Police 204
Health 207

ENGLISH – MALAY DICTIONARY 209

MALAY – ENGLISH DICTIONARY 257

INDEX 301

MALAY

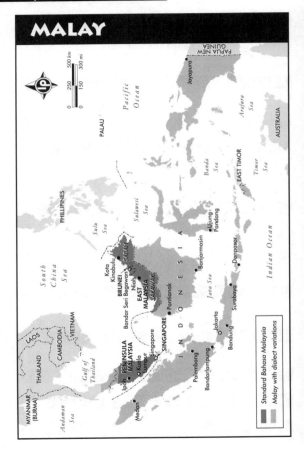

INTRODUCTION

The national language of Malaysia is Malay. Malaysians refer to it as *Bahasa Malaysia* (Language of Malaysia) or *Bahasa Melayu* (Language of the Malays). It's been the language in government and schools since the early '70s, so nearly every Malaysian speaks it, either as their first or second language.

Don't be confused by the terminology. 'Malays' are those who are racially considered Malay, usually Muslim, who also speak the language Malay. Malaysians are, of course, anyone who is a Malaysian citizen.

Malay is a member of the Western Austronesian language family and is spoken with slight variations throughout Malaysia and some parts of southern Thailand, Singapore and Brunei. In Malaysia, it's by no means the only language. Multiracial Malaysia is of course multilingual. Chinese Malaysians, who form approximately one third of the population, belong to many different dialect groups, including Cantonese, Hakka, Hokkien, Teochew and Hainanese, and many also speak Mandarin. Indian Malaysians have linguistic backgrounds in Tamil and Malayalee; other groups speak Punjabi, Gujerati and Bengali. They account for about 10% of the population.

Wherever you go in Malaysia you will see shop signs in a rainbow of languages and scripts. Malay uses the Roman alphabet, but was originally written in *jawi,* an adaptation of Arabic script created during the introduction of Islam in the 14th century. You might notice the *halal* sign in *jawi* script, which shows food is kosher for Muslims. At the crossroads of many trade routes, Malaysia's language has a potpourri of influences. In addition to Arabic (*mahkamah,* 'court'), there's Portuguese (*garfu,* 'fork'), Sanskrit (*istana,* 'palace'), Chinese (*mee,* 'noodles'), and English, (*elektrik,* 'electric').

Classical Malay was almost lost during British colonisation. It was the traders and merchants who kept the language alive during these times. 'Bazaar Malay' became a lingua franca and was the basis for the *Bahasa Melayu* we know today.

Bahasa Melayu also forms the basis for *Bahasa Indonesia*, but while Indonesian has been influenced by Dutch, Malaysian has adopted more English words, making it a dream of a language to learn for English speakers. English is Malaysia's second tongue, and is a compulsory subject in schools from the age of seven. Words such as 'clinic' and 'antibiotic' are incorporated into Malay through a change of spelling (*klinik* and *antibiotik*) and educated Malays often tend to mix languages in their daily conversations. English is commonly spoken in urban areas and it's not difficult to find someone who speaks some, even in rural areas.

While standard Malay is spoken in Kuala Lumpur, other regions of Malaysia have their own dialects that vary in pronunciation and accent. Regional accents can be strong, with variations in vocabulary. In Kelantan, *Apa khabar?*, 'How are you?' becomes *Guano demo?*. But never fear, your attempts at standard Malay will definitely be understood!

BAHASA MALAYSIA OR BAHASA MELAYU?

In this country where racial tensions still bubble under the surface of every decision, the difference between these two terms is loaded with meaning.

After the race riots of 1969 the government made many moves to address economic inequities, including a declaration that Malay should become the national language and the medium of instruction in all schools. But what to call the language?

Bahasa Malaysia, 'the language of Malaysia', was considered a unifying name, implicitly for Malaysians of all origins. In 1989 however, the members of the *Dewan Bahasa dan Pustaka* (The Hall of Language and Publishing), who are predominantly Malay, decided to change it back to *Bahasa Melayu,* 'the language of the Malays'. This move was seen by some to be a racially possessive, 'our language, not yours' move. It remains the official name.

Bahasa Melayu is an easy language to learn to speak. The spelling is largely phonetic; tenses are simple to use and you don't have to worry about gender in grammar. This makes for fast progress and plenty of communication. You'll get a kick out of learning Malay, and remember that, even a simple *terima kasih*, **te-**ree-**muh** *kah*-si(h), 'thank you', will please the people you meet. *Selamat belajar*, se-*lah*-**maht** be-*lah*-jar, 'happy learning' and now *jumlah!* , *joom*-lah(h)! – 'let's get to it!'

MALAY & INDONESIAN

Bahasa Melayu and *Bahasa Indonesia* have only a few differences in vocabulary and pronunciation. The structure and other aspects of grammar remain the same in both languages. This means that this book could stay in your bag for travels further south, and the same goes for our *Indonesian phrasebook* – a great read – in Malaysia. The differences in vocabulary include some of the most common words:

ENGLISH	MALAY	INDONESIAN
after	*selepas*	*sesudah*
afternoon	*petang*	*sore*
beef	*daging lembu*	*daging sapi*
brother	*abang/adik*	*kakak/laki-laki*
can (as in 'I can')	*bisa*	*boleh*
car	*boleh*	*kereta*
city	*bandar*	*kota*
cold (adj)	*sejuk*	*dingin*
cute (eg, baby)	*manis/cun*	*lucu*
invite	*menjemput*	*mengundang*
Mr	*Tuan/Encik*	*Bapak*
Mrs	*Puan*	*Ibu*
office	*pejabat*	*kantor*
room	*bilik*	*kamar*
shoes	*kasut*	*sepatu*
shop	*kedai*	*toko*
toilet	*tandas/toilet*	*WC; kamar kecil*

INTRODUCTION

HOW TO USE THIS PHRASEBOOK
You *Can* Speak Another Language

It's true – anyone can speak another language. Don't worry if you haven't studied languages before, or that you studied a language at school for years and can't remember any of it. You just need to start speaking. Once you start, you'll be amazed how many prompts you'll get to help you build on those first words. You'll hear people speaking, pick up sounds from TV, catch a word or two from the local radio, see something on a billboard – all these things help to build your understanding.

Plunge In

There are a few everyday words you could learn right away. The general greeting is *Selamat pagi*, se-*lah*-maht *pah*-gee. For other hellos and goodbyes, see page 40. If you are moving though a crowd or trying to get past people it is polite to say *Maafkan saya*, mah-*ahf*-kahn *sai*-yuh, which means 'Excuse me'. For tips on civilities and body language, see page 53. Two easy words to remember are *Tidak*, tee-dah(k), 'No' and *Ya*, ya, 'Yes'. If you're having trouble understanding someone, just say *Saya tidak faham*, *sai*-yuh tee-dah(k) fah-hahm, 'I don't understand'. 'How much is it?' is *Berapa harganya ini?*, be-*rah*-puh *hahr*-guh-nyuh ee-nee?. If you find yourself in an emergency situation, turn to page 203 for some handy phrases.

ABBREVIATIONS USED IN THIS BOOK

adj	adjective	lit	literal translation
col	colloquial	n	noun
excl	exclusive	pl	plural
incl	inclusive	pol	polite
inf	informal	v	verb

INTRODUCTION

LEGEND

The following notation is used throughout this phrasebook:

( ) parentheses

- indicate words can be replaced with words of your choice:

> Let's meet at (6 o'clock) at ...
> *kee*-tuh ber-*te*-moo *pah*-duh   *Kita bertemu*
> (*poo*-kool e-*nahm*) dee ...   (*pukul enam) di ...*

- indicate the words are optional:

> Can you show me (on the map)?
> *to*-long *toon*-joo(k)-kahn   *Tolong tunjukkan*
> (dee *pe*-tah)?   (*di peta)?*

- indicate one of the following:
  - meaning, eg, demonstration (protest)
  - usage, eg, date (time)
  - aspect of grammar, eg, masculine (m) and feminine (f)
  - literal translation, eg, (lit: I already eat)

/ forward slash

- indicates when single words on either side of the slash are interchangeable:

> To the left/right.   ke *ki*-ree/*kah*-nahn   *Ke kiri/kanan.*
>
> denotes:
>
>   To the left.   ke *ki*-ree   *Ke kiri.*
> and   To the right.   ke *kah*-nahn   *Ke kanan.*

- indicates when single words are synonyms – or different forms of the same word (typically masculine, or feminine, singular or plural, informal or polite):

> I'm a student.   *sai*-yuh *moo*-rid/   *Saya murid/*
>   pe-*lah*-jahr   *pelajar.*
>
> I'm not a Muslim.   *sai*-yuh boo-*kahn*   *Saya bukan*
>   moos-*lee*-meen/   *Muslimin/*
>   moos-*lee*-mah(h) (m/f)   *Muslimah.*

This denotes:

I'm not a (male) Muslim.	*sai*-yuh boo-*kahn* moos-*lee*-meen (m)	*Saya bukan Muslimin.*

and

I'm not a (female) Muslim.	*sai*-yuh boo-*kahn* moos-*lee*-mah(h) (f)	*Saya bukan Muslimah.*

; semicolon

- separates two (or more) alternative words where one (or more) consists of <u>more</u> than one word:

chilli sauce	*sam*-bahl; sos *chi*-lee	*sambal; sos cili*

denotes:

chilli sauce	*sam*-bahl	*sambal*

and

chilli sauce	sos *chi*-lee	*sos cili*

- **bullet points**
- are used in the dictionary only to separate alternative words (synonyms):

painter	pe-*loo*-kis • *ahr*-tis • se-*nee*-mahn	*pelukis • artis • seniman*

If it is necessary to clarify the difference between alternatives, this is indicated in parentheses after each word.

PRONUNCIATION

Malay is a breeze to pronounce. Unlike English, Malay is spoken as it's written, in Roman script, so getting your tongue around the correct way to say things isn't difficult. The Malay alphabet is the same as the English alphabet. You can hear little seven-year-olds reciting the 'ABC' song in schools, when they are beginning their English lessons.

There are some regional differences regarding how the language is spoken in the north-east and north-west of Malaysia, but standard Malay, *Bahasa Baku*, **bah-***hah***-suh** ***bah***-**koo**, is what's taught in schools and understood everywhere.

Malays will be thrilled to assist you with correct pronunciation, so be sure to ask. The following pronunciation tips will help you to speak Malay and be understood.

STRESS
Most syllables have reasonably equal stress in Malay, but a good rule of thumb is to put more emphasis on the second-last syllable.

TRANSLITERATION SYSTEM
To help you understand the relationship between the letters and their corresponding sounds, a simple phonetic transliteration has been used throughout this book. All transliterations are in purple. We use a hyphen to indicate when a new syllable begins. The syllable to be stressed is written in italics, eg, **tranz-li-te-***ray***-shuhn**

PRONUNCIATION

VOWELS

Malaysian vowel sounds are much more standard than in English.
The following should help you to pronounce things correctly.

a	ah	as the 'a' in 'father'
	uh	as the 'u' in 'cup'
	ai	as the 'i' in 'aisle'

Sometimes, in the words borrowed from other languages, the 'a'
sounds like 'ay' in day or the 'a' in cat – these will be transliterated
as ay and a.

e	e	as the 'e' in 'water'
	eh	as the first 'e' in 'enter'
i	ee	as the 'ee' in 'teen'
	i	as the 'i' in 'bit'
o	o	as the 'o' in 'no'
u	oo	as the 'oo' in 'zoo'
	u	as the 'u' in 'put'

Diphthongs (Vowel Combinations)

Malay has four vowel combinations.

ai	ai	as the 'ai' in 'aisle'
au	ow	as the 'ow' in 'cow'
oi	oy	as the 'oy' in 'toy'
ua	wah	as the 'wa' in 'swan'

GET TO THE POINT

Adding -*lah* to a word gives it emphasis. Put a forceful
-*lah* on the end of any phrase to really get your point
across. You can liven up the dinner table when all you
savour is *sedaplah!*, se-*dahp*-lah(h)!, (totally
delicious!), or prevent near death when you tell your
taxi driver to *Berhenti di sinilah!*, ber-*hen*-tee dee
see-nee-lah(h)!, 'Stop here!'.

CONSONANTS

Some consonants that fall at the end of a word in Malay are not pronounced as clearly as they would be in English. It's as though the speaker starts to say the letter and then swallows it. This is shown in the transliteration system by brackets, eg, **boo-***soo(k)*, 'smelly'. You will see it applied in particular to **h** and **k**.

Words ending in h have some rules all of their own. An (**h**) indicates a breathy h sound at the end of a syllable, and a slight lengthening of the vowel sound, which can indicate a different meaning. Don't get caught out! *Dadah*, *dah-***dah(h)**, means 'illegal drugs' and *dada*, *dah-***duh**, means 'breast'. It's not unusual for tourists ordering a nice bit of chicken in a restaurant to accidentally ask for narcotics! Ask a Malay to pronounce some of these sounds for you and see if you can hear (and repeat) the difference. Most consonants are pronounced as they are in English, and the few exceptions are listed below.

c	ch	as the 'ch' in 'chair'
g	g	as the 'g' in 'garlic'
gh	gh	a throaty 'g' sound, as if you are clearing your throat
h	h	always pronounced. Stressed a little more strongly than in English, as if you were sighing. This heavy pronunciation is especially evident for words of Arabic origin, when the 'h' appears between two vowels that are the same;
	(h)	at the end of a word, in brackets, a breathier, slightly prolonged version of the preceding vowel sound
k	k	as the 'k' in 'king';
	(k)	at the end of a syllable, in brackets, as a glottal stop — the sound made between the words 'uh-oh'
kh	kh	as the 'ch' in the Scottish *loch*
ny	ny	as the 'ny' in 'canyon'
ng	ng	as the 'ng' in 'singer'
r	r	always trilled clearly and distinctly
sy	sh	as the 'sh' in 'ship'

ABBREVIATED TALK

Many common words are abbreviated when you're speaking in a casual or intimate way. Sometimes the second syllable is used alone; sometimes a middle portion is dropped.

PRONUNCIATION

I (inf)	*aku/ku*	ah-koo/koo
you (inf)	*kamu/mu*	kah-moo/moo
you (inf)	*engkau/kau*	eng-kow/kow
near/at	*dekat/kat*	de-*kaht*/kaht
already/finished	*sudah/dah*	soo-dah/dah(h)
not/isn't it?	*bukan/kan*	boo-kahn/kahn
no/not	*tidak/tak*	tee-dah(k)/tah(k)
want	*hendak/nak*	hen-dah(k)/nah(k)
this/these	*ini/ni*	ee-nee/nee
that/those	*itu/tu*	ee-too/too
a little bit	*sedikit/sikit*	se-*dee*-kit/*see*-kit
a little while	*sekejap/jap*	se-ke-*jahp*/jahp
only	*sahaja/saja*	sah-*hah*-juh/*sah*-juh

So, the question:

How long have you
been in Malaysia?

   soo-dah(h) be-*rah*-puh   *Sudah berapa*
   lah-muh *eng*-kow   *lama engkau*
   de-*kaht* mah-*lay*-see-ah?   *dekat Malaysia?*

would become:

   dah(h) be-*rah*-puh *lah*-muh   *Dah berapa lama*
   kow kaht mah-*lay*-see-ah?   *kau kat Malaysia?*

GRAMMAR

Many aspects of Malay grammar make it an easy language to learn. Verbs don't change according to subject or tense, nouns don't have to have plural forms, and there are no gender-related rules to remember. Like any other language, there are nuances to be learned, but for the purpose of basic communication, the grammar is quite straightforward.

WORD ORDER

The structure of a Malay sentence is the same as in English: subject-verb-object.

> I'm climbing the tree.
> *sai*-yuh me-*mahm*-jaht *po*-ko(k)   *Saya memanjat pokok.*
>   (lit: I to-climb tree)

It's not unusual in Malay for the object to be mentioned first if it's being stressed. This causes some changes in verbs, so the beginner will find it easier to simply use the subject-verb-object construction.

ARTICLES

There's no word corresponding to 'the' or 'a/an'. Instead, they're understood from the context of a sentence. Alternatively, demonstrative adjectives *ini*, 'this/these', and *itu*, 'that/those' are placed after the noun.

this book	*boo*-koo *ee*-nee	*buku ini*
		(lit: book this)
that table	*meh*-juh *ee*-too	*meja itu*
		(lit: table that)

NOUNS
Plurals

Plural forms of nouns can be indicated by doubling the noun or by the use of quantity words such as *ramai*, 'many/numerous'.

those books	*boo-koo-boo-koo ee-too*	*buku-buku itu* (lit: books those)
many visitors	rah-*mai* pe-*lah*-waht	*ramai pelawat* (lit: visitors many)

PRONOUNS
Personal Pronouns

Saya, *sai*-yuh, is the Malay equivalent of 'I' in English. Referring to yourself as *saya* is considered polite. A more informal word for 'I' is *aku*, *ah*-koo, which is often abbreviated to *ku*. However, *aku* should only be used if you know the person you're speaking to very well, and if they're of roughly the same age and status. See the next page for polite ways of addressing people.

Malay pronouns can be a bit confusing, as Malaysians will often use a person's name, family status or title instead of the pronoun 'I' or 'you'. Malaysians also sometimes use their own names or titles when referring to themselves, rather than using 'I'. It might take a while to get used to an older Malay woman referring to herself as 'Auntie'.

Makcik boleh buat.
mah(k)-chi(k) bo-*leh(h) boo*-aht

Auntie can do it.
(lit: Auntie can do)

when the sense is:

Saya boleh buat.
sai-yuh bo-*leh(h) boo*-aht

I can do it.
(lit: I can do)

Other common age-related terms which Malaysians may use instead of 'I', even if there is no real familial relationship, include:

abang	ah-*bahng*	older brother; someone slightly older than the speaker
kakak	*kah*-kah(k)	older sister; someone slightly older
adik	ah-*di*(k)	younger brother or sister; slightly younger, or any child
pakcik	*pah*(k)-chi(k)	uncle; old enough to be the speaker's uncle or father
nenek	neh-*neh*(k)	grandmother; old enough to be the speaker's grandmother
datuk	*dah*-tu(k)	grandfather; old enough to be the speaker's grandfather

The pronoun 'you' causes problems for learners of Malay, because like 'I' there are hierarchical differentiations between various forms. The safest forms of 'you' to use when you want to make sure you are being polite are:

encik	en-*chi(k)*	mister
tuan	twahn	sir
puan	pwahn	ma'am or missus
cik	chi(k)	miss

Singular Pronouns

I/me	*sai*-yuh, ah-koo	*saya, aku*
you (inf)	*kah*-moo, *eng*-kow, ah-*wah*(k)	*kamu, engkau, awak*
you (pol)	*ahn*-duh, sow-*dah*-ruh	*anda, saudara*
he/she/her/him	*dee*-uh	*dia*
it	*ee*-uh	*ia*

Plural Pronouns		
we/us/our (excludes person spoken to)	*kah*-mee	*kami*
we/us/our (includes person spoken to)	*kee*-tuh	*kita*
you	*ahn*-duh, *ah*-wah(k) se-*moo*-uh	*anda, awak semua*
they/them/their	me-*reh*-kuh	*mereka*
they (inf)	*dee*-uh o-rahng	*dia orang*

Possessive Pronouns

Malay uses possessive pronouns *after* the noun. The first and second person, 'my' and 'your', as well as the third person plural, 'their', are separate words placed after the noun they modify:

my money	*doo*-it *sai*-yuh	*duit saya* (lit: money my)
your umbrella	*pai*-yung *ahn*-duh	*payung anda* (lit: umbrella your)
their car	ke-*reh*-tuh me-*reh*-kuh	*kereta mereka* (lit: car their)

In the third person singular, 'he' and 'she', the suffix *-nya* (lit: of him/her) is added to the thing that's possessed, or the word *dia*, 'his/her' is used after the noun; *-nya* can also be used in place of the plural possessive pronoun *mereka*, 'their'.

her watch	*jahm*-nyuh; jahm *dee*-uh	*jamnya; jam dia* (lit: watch-of-her; watch her)
his keys	*koon*-chee-nyuh	*kuncinya* (lit: keys-of-him)
their house	*roo*-mah(h)-nyuh	*rumahnya* (lit: house-of-their)

Relative Pronouns

The relative pronoun *yang* is used to mean 'who/which/that/the one which/that which'.

This is the book that I want to buy.

    *ee-*nee *boo-*koo **yahng**   *Ini buku yang*
    sai-yuh *mah-*hoo be-*lee*   *saya mahu beli.*
                             (lit: this book that I want
                                     to-buy)

The man who's big is crying.

    *lah-*kee-*lah-*kee **yahng**   *Laki-laki yang*
    be-*sahr ee-*too me-*nah-*ngees   *besar itu menangis.*
                             (lit: man who big that to-cry)

ADJECTIVES

Adjectives always follow the noun they're describing.

big	**be-***sahr*	*besar*
big car	ke-*reh-*tuh be-*sahr*	*kereta besar*
		(lit: car big)
clean	*ber-*si(h)	*bersih*
clean room	*bee-*li(k) *ber-*si(h)	*bilik bersih*
		(lit: room clean)

As there's no commonly used verb which means 'is/are', the above constructions can also translate as 'The car is big' and 'The room is clean'. In writing or formal speech, the verb *ialah*, ee-*ah-*lah(h), is used here.

The relative pronoun *yang*, 'which/who', is often used with an adjective, especially when you want to describe more than one thing about the noun.

the blue car with yellow tyres

    ke-*reh-*tuh *bi-*roo **yahng**   *kereta biru yang*
    ber-*tai-*yahr *koo-*ning   *bertayar kuning*
                             (lit: car blue which tyre yellow)

the big, white house

    *roo-*mah(h) *poo-*ti(h)   *rumah putih yang besar*
    yahng be-*sahr*   (lit: house white which big)

Comparatives

The words *lebih*, 'more', and *kurang*, 'less', are used to indicate comparisons. They're placed before adjectives. The word *daripada*, 'than', appears after adjectives to form the following constructions.

lebih/kurang + adj (+ *daripada*)
(lit: more/less ... (than))

bigger	le-*bi(h)* be-*sahr*	*lebih besar*
		(lit: more big)
slower than	*koo*-rang *che*-paht	*kurang cepat*
	dah-ree-*pah*-duh	*daripada*
		(lit: less fast than)

Daripada is also used if both objects being compared are mentioned.

Mangoes are more expensive
than bananas.

mahng-guh le-*bi(h)* mah-*hahl*   *Mangga lebih mahal*
dah-ree-*pah*-duh *pee*-sahng   *daripada pisang*
(lit: mango more
expensive than banana)

The way you compare quality in English, eg, 'as ... as', is indicated in Malay by the prefix *se-*.

as beautiful as   se-*chahn*-ti(k)   *secantik*
(lit: *se*-beautiful)

Superlatives

To form the adjectives that correspond to 'most ... ' or '-est' in English, the word *paling*, 'the most', is used.

noun + *paling* + adj

cheap	*moo*-rah(h)	*murah*
the cheapest	*pah*-ling moo-*rah(h)*	*paling murah*
		(lit: most cheap)
good	bah-*gus*	*bagus*
the best	*pah*-ling bah-*gus*	*paling bagus*
		(lit: most good)

ADVERBS

As in English, adverbs can appear at the beginning, at the end or within a sentence.

also	*joo*-guh/pun	*juga/pun*
always	se-*lah*-loo/	*selalu/*
	sen-tee-*ah*-suh	*sentiasa*
here	dee *see*-nee	*di sini*
immediately	se-ge-ruh;	*segera;*
	de-*ngahn* se-ge-ruh	*dengan segera*
in this way	be-*gee*-nee	*begini*
in that way	be-*gee*-too	*begitu*
just now	*tah*-dee	*tadi*
maybe	*moong*-kin	*mungkin*
never	*tee*-dah(k) *per*-nah(h)	*tidak pernah*
not yet	be-*lum;*	*belum;*
	be-*lum lah*-gee	*belum lagi*
often	ke-*rahp*/se-*ring*	*kerap/sering*
perhaps	*moong*-kin	*mungkin*
possibly	*moong*-kin/bo-*leh(h)*	*mungkin/boleh*
rarely	jah-*rahng*	*jarang*
really	*soong*-gu(h)/be-*gee*-too	*sungguh/begitu*
sometimes	kah-dahng-*kah*-dahng/	*kadang-kadang/*
	kah-dahng-*kah*-luh	*kadang-kala*
so that	soo-*pai*-yuh/*ah*-gahr	*supaya/agar*
there	dee *sah*-nuh	*di sana*
very	sah-*ngaht*	*sangat*

VERBS

Malay verbs are divided into a number of different classes, and are formed from a root word plus a suffix and/or prefix. The root word conveys the meaning, while adding suffixes and/or prefixes indicates that it's a useable verb – one you can use in a sentence. However, the bare root-word form can always be used in everyday speech and you'll still be understood.

1. The simplest type of verb stands alone and never requires a prefix. Fortunately, many of the most commonly used verbs fit into this category:

to bathe	*mahn*-dee	mandi
to eat	*mah*-kahn	makan
to go	*per*-gee	pergi
to laugh	ke-*tah*-wuh	ketawa
to sit	*doo*-du(k)	duduk
to sleep	*tee*-dur	tidur

2. The second type of verb requires the *me-* prefixes which include *meng-*, *mem-*, *men-* and *meny-* and *me-*. These are added to the root word.

me- is used with root words beginning with *l, m, n, ng, ny, r, w* or *y*. For example, the root word 'look' becomes useable: 'to look'.

look; to look	*lee*-haht/me-*lee*-haht	lihat/melihat
record; to record	*rah*-kahm/me-*rah*-kahm	rakam/merakam

meng- is used with words beginning with *g, h, k, q, a, e, i, o, u.* The *k* is dropped to make the verb.

change; to change	*gahn*-tee/ meng-*gahn*-tee	ganti/ mengganti
pardon; to pardon	*ahm*-poon/ me-*ngahm*-poon	ampun/ mengampun

mem- is used with words beginning with *b, v, p* or *f.* The *p* and *f* are dropped to make the verb and an *m* used instead.

buy; to buy	be-*lee*/mem-be-*lee*	beli/membeli
cut; to cut	*po*-tong/me-*mo*-tong	potong/memotong

GRAMMAR

men- is used with words beginning with *c, j, d, t,* or *z.*

search; to search	*chah*-ree/men-*chah*-ree	*cari/mencari*
climb; to climb	*dah*-kee/men-*dah*-kee	*daki/mendaki*

meny- is used with words beginning with *s.* The *s* is replaced by a *y*:

touch; to touch	*sen*-tu(h)/me-*nyen*-tu(h)	*sentuh/menyentuh*
rent; to rent	*seh*-wuh/me-*nyeh*-wuh	*sewa/menyewa*

3. The third type of verb requires the prefix *ber-* followed by the root word. For example, the root word *tanya*, 'ask', becomes *bertanya*, 'to ask'. If the root word starts with *r*, such as *renang*, 'swim', the prefix drops the *r* and the verb becomes *berenang*, 'to swim'.

walk; to walk	*jah*-lahn/ber-*jah*-lahn	*jalan/ berjalan*
get ready; to get ready	se-dee-*uh*/ber-se-dee-*uh*	*sedia/ bersedia*
speak; to speak	bee-*chah*-ruh/ ber-bee-*chah*-ruh	*bicara/ berbicara*

4. The fourth type of verb requires the prefix *me-* and the suffix *-kan*. With the addition of *-kan*, the verb must have an object.

witness; to witness	*sahk*-see/ me-*nyahk*-see-kahn	*saksi/ menyaksikan*
clean; to clean	ber-*si*(h)/ mem-ber-*si*(h)-kahn	*bersih/ membersihkan*

5. The fifth type of verb requires the prefix *me-* and the suffix *-i*. If the root word starts with *k*, it is replaced with a *g*.

enjoy; to enjoy	*nik*-maht/ me-*nik*-mah-tee	*nikmat/ menikmati*
love; to love	*kah*-si(h)/me-*ngah*-si-hee	*kasih/ mengasihi*

Don't be too concerned about these prefixes – you'll still be understood if you use the root word in a sentence. They mainly need to be used in formal settings or when writing.

GRAMMAR

GRAMMAR

Essential Verbs

to be able (can)	bo-*leh(h)*	*boleh*
to agree	ber-se-*too*-joo	*bersetuju*
to become	men-*jah*-dee	*menjadi*
to bring	mem-*bah*-wuh	*membawa*
to come	*dah*-tahng	*datang*
to cost	ber-*hahr*-guh	*berharga*
to depart (leave)	ber-*to*-lah(k)	*bertolak*
to do	mem-*boo*-aht	*membuat*
to give	mem-*be*-ree	*memberi*
to go	*per*-gee	*pergi*
to know (someone)	ke-*nahl*	*kenal*
to know (how to)	*pahn*-dai/*tah*-hoo	*pandai/tahu*
to like	*soo*-kuh	*suka*
to live	*hee*-dup	*hidup*

to make	mem-*boo*-aht	*membuat*
to meet	ber-*joom*-puh	*berjumpa*
to need	per-*loo*	*perlu*
to prefer	le-*bi(h)* *soo*-kuh	*lebih suka*
to return	*bah*-li(k)/	*balik/*
	poo-lahng	*pulang*
to say	ber-*kah*-tuh	*berkata*
to stay	*ting*-gahl	*tinggal*
to take	me-*ngahm*-bil	*mengambil*
to understand	*fah*-hahm	*faham*
to want	*mah*-hoo/	*mahu/*
	hehn-dah(k)/	*hendak/*
	nah(k)	*nak*

Tense

Luckily for the learner of Malay, verbs don't change their form according to tense. The tense of a verb can be easily worked out by context or by the inclusion of a time word such as *semalam*, 'yesterday', and *nanti* or *kemudian*, 'later'.

I went swimming yesterday.
se-*mah*-lahm *sai*-yuh
per-gee be-re-*nahng*

*Semalam saya
pergi berenang.*
(lit: yesterday I to-go to-swim)

I will eat later.
sai-yuh *mah*-kahn
ke-*moo*-dee-ahn/*nahm*-tee

*Saya makan
kemudian/nanti.*
(lit: I to-eat later)

Another way to indicate tense is by placing certain adverbs immediately before the verb. The most common are:

already	*soo*-dah(h)	*sudah*
currently	se-*dahng*	*sedang*
have just	bah-*roo*	*baru*
not yet	be-*lum*	*belum*
still	*mah*-si(h)	*masih*
will	*ah*-kahn	*akan*

I have already eaten
sai-yuh *soo*-dah(h)
mah-kahn

*Saya sudah
makan.*
(lit: I already eat)

TO BE

There's no direct equivalent of 'to be' in conversational Malay. The words 'is' and 'are' are implied in a sentence. In writing or formal speech, the verb *ialah*, ee-*ah*-lah(h), is used.

My name is Abu.
nah-muh *sai*-yuh
ee-*ah*-lah(h) *ah*-boo (pol)

*Nama saya
ialah Abu.*
(lit: name I is Abu)

GRAMMAR

I am here.
  sai-yuh dee *see*-nee   *Saya di sini.*
                                   (lit: I in here)

That baby is hungry.
  bai-yee *ee*-too *lah*-pahr   *Bayi itu lapar.*
                                   (lit: baby that hungry)

To say that something does or doesn't exist, the word *ada* 'there is/ are' (lit: to-exist) can be used in a sentence with no definite subject.

Is there a night bus?
  ah-duh bahs *mah*-lahm?   *Ada bas malam?*
                                   (lit: to-exist bus night?)

TO HAVE

Ada can also be used to mean 'has/have'.

I have a younger brother.
  sai-yuh *ah*-duh   *Saya ada adik lelaki.*
  ah-*di(k)* le-*lah*-kee   (lit: I have younger-sibling
                                        male)

MODALS

There are other auxiliary words that can be used with a verb to indicate modality. These include *boleh*, 'can', *suka*, 'like to', *hendak/nak*, 'want to' and *tahu*, 'know how to', and they always come before the other verb.

can; be able to	bo-*leh(h)*	boleh

I can climb trees.
  sai-yuh bo-*leh(h)* pahm-jaht   *Saya boleh panjat pokok.*
  po-ko(k)   (lit: I can to-climb tree)
Where can I buy ...?
  dee *mah*-nuh *sai*-yuh   *Di mana saya boleh beli ...?*
  bo-*leh(h)* be-*lee* ...?   (lit: in where I can buy ...?)

| like to | *soo*-kuh | suka |

I like to eat curry.
   sai-yuh *soo*-kuh *mah*-kahn
   kah-ree   *Saya suka makan kari.*
                             (lit: I like-to to-eat curry)
I like to play soccer.
   sai-yuh *soo*-kuh main
   bo-luh *seh*-pah(k)   *Saya suka main bola sepak.*
                             (lit: I like-to to-play
                             ball kick)

| want to | *hehm*-dah(k)/nah(k) | hendak/nak |

I want to dance.
   sai-yuh nah(k) me-*nah*-ree   *Saya nak menari.*
                             (lit: I want-to to-dance)
I don't want that one.
   sai-yuh *tee*-dah(k)
   hehn-dah(k) yahng *ee*-too   *Saya tidak hendak yang itu.*
                             (lit: I no want-to which/
                             that that)

| must; have to | hah-*roos*/mes-tee | harus/mesti |

What time do I have to be at
the airport?
   poo-kool be-*rah*-puh *sai*-yuh
   hah-*roos* *ah*-duh dee
   lah-*pahng*-ahn *ter*-bahng?   *Pukul berapa saya harus ada*
                             di lapangan terbang?
                             (lit: hour how-much I
                             have-to to-exist in
                             field-fly?)

| may/might/can | bo-*leh*(h) | boleh |

May I speak to ...?
   bo-*leh*(h) *sai*-yuh
   ber-*chah*-kahp de-*ngahn* ...?   *Boleh saya*
                             bercakap dengan ...?
                             (lit: can I to-speak with ...?)

May I take photos?
   bo-*leh*(h) *sai*-yuh *ahm*-bil
   gahm-bahr?   *Boleh saya ambil gambar?*
                             (lit: can I to-take photo?)

know how to	*tah*-hoo	*tahu*

I know how to swim.
  sai-yuh *tah*-hoo be-re-*nahng*   *Saya tahu berenang.*
                                        (lit: I know-how-to to-swim)

IMPERATIVES

If you're asking, insisting or demanding that someone does something, don't use the prefix on the verb.

  Look!   te-*ngo(k)!*   *Tengok!*

To make a more polite command, add *silakan*, 'please', before the
verb, in the context of offering someone something. *Tolong*, 'please'
or 'help', is used when you're asking for something you need.

  Please sit down.
    see-*lah*-kahn *doo*-du(k)   *Silakan duduk.*
                                   (lit: please sit)

  Please be quiet.
    to-long *sen*-yahp   *Tolong senyap.*
                             (lit: please/help quiet)

QUESTIONS

As in English, a question can be indicated simply by raising the
intonation of your voice at the end of a sentence. Other ways to
form questions include ending a sentence or a word with -*kah*.

  Where did he go?
    dee *mah*-nuh-kah(h)   *Di manakah*
    dee-uh *per*-gee?   *dia pergi?*
                              (lit: in where-*kah* he to-go?)

  Do you like spicy food?
    ah-wah(k) *soo*-kuh   *Awak suka*
    mah-kah-nan   *makanan*
    pe-*dahs*-kah(h)?   *pedaskah?*
                              (lit: you like-to food hot-*kah*?)

Another option is starting a sentence with *adakah* (lit: is it that ...?).

Is the soup hot?
   ah-duh-kah(h) soop *ee*-nee   *Adakah sup ini panas?*
   pah-nahs?   (lit: is-it-that soup this hot?)

Or you can try adding *tak*, 'no', to the end of a question:

Is it spicy or not?
   pe-*dahs* tah(k)?   *Pedas, tak?*
                      (lit: spicy, no?)

Finally, with nouns and adverbs, add *kan* (short for *bukan*, meaning 'not') to the end of the sentence.

We're going tomorrow, right?
   kee-tuh *per*-gee *eh*-so(k)   *Kita pergi esok, kan?*
   kahn?   (lit: we-(incl) to-go
                        tomorrow, not?)

YOU AND I

In the cities, you'll hear Malay conversations sprinkled with the English pronouns 'I' and 'you'.

> You *pergi mana*?   you *per*-gee *mah*-nuh?
> (lit: you go where?)   Where are you going?
>
> I *tak pergi mana-mana*. I *tah(k) per*-gee *mah*-nuh-
> (lit: I no go anywhere)   *mah*-nuh
>   I'm not going anywhere.

Speaking English carries a certain degree of status; it implies you're educated. It's possible Malaysians also use English pronouns because of the hierarchy inherent in their own language: the use of the English 'I' and 'you' lets the speaker converse on a more equal footing.

GRAMMAR

QUESTION WORDS

You can add a question word at the beginning or end of a sentence:

What?	*Apa?*

What's your name?
  Apa nama kamu?
  ah-puh *nah*-muh *kah*-moo?
  (lit: what name you?)

Who?	*Siapakah?*

Who are they?
  Siapakah mereka?
  see-*ah*-puh-kah(h) me-*reh*-kuh?
  (lit: who they?)

Where?	*Di mana?*

Where's the post office?
  Di mana pejabat pos?
  dee *mah*-nuh pe-*jah*-baht pos?
  (lit: in where post office?)

When?	*Bilakah?*

When does the bus depart for Ipoh?
  Bilakah bas akan berangkat ke Ipoh?
  bee-luh-*kah*(h) bahs *ah*-kahn be-*rang*-kaht ke *ee*-po(h)?
  (lit: when bus will depart to Ipoh?)

Why?	*Kenapa?*

Why is the food so oily?
  Kenapa makanan ini terlalu berminyak?
  ke-*nah*-puh *mah*-kah-nahn *ee*-nee ter-*lah*-loo
  ber-*min*-yah(k)?
  (lit: why food this too-much oily?)

Which?	*Yang mana?*

Which is your book?
  Yang mana buku anda?
  yahng *mah*-nuh *boo*-koo *ahn*-duh?
  (lit: which book you?)

How?	*Berapa?*

How much does a bus ticket to Melaka cost?
  Berapa harga tiket bas ke Melaka?
  be-*rah*-puh *hahr*-guh tee-*keht* bas ke me-*lah*-kuh?
  (lit: how-much price ticket bus to Melaka?)

ANSWERS

Malaysians commonly answer questions concerning availability or possession with *ada*, 'have'/'to exist', or *tidak ada*, 'don't have'/ 'no to-exist'.

Do you have Western food?	*ah*-duh *mah*-kah-nahn *bah*-raht tah(k)?	*Ada makanan Barat, tak?* (lit: have food west, no?)
Yes.	*ah*-duh	*Ada.* (lit: have)
No.	*tee*-dah(k) *ah*-duh	*Tidak ada.* (lit: no have)

NEGATIVES

Three words are used to express the negative: *tidak*, 'no', *bukan*, 'not', and *jangan*, 'don't'. *Bukan* is used with nouns.

Not me.	boo-*kahm sai*-yuh	*Bukan saya.* (lit: not me)
Not that shirt.	boo-*kahm bah*-joo ee-too	*Bukan baju itu.* (lit: not shirt that)

Both *tidak* and *jangan* are used in relation to verbs; *tidak* is also used with adjectives.

I don't want to.
   sai-yuh *tee*-dah(k) *mah*-hoo

Saya tidak mahu.
(lit: I no want)

Do not enter.
   jah-*ngahn mah*-su(k)

Jangan masuk.
(lit: don't enter)

My car is not red.
   ke-*reh*-tuh *sai*-yuh *tee*-dah(k) *meh*-rah(h)

Kereta saya tidak merah.
(lit: car my no red)

GRAMMAR

CLASSIFIERS

When you use a number with a noun in Malay you must use a
counter word (classifier) between the number and the noun. This
classifier describes the category of thing you're counting. This also
occurs in English all the time, when we talk about *slices* of toast or
pairs of pants, although we don't call them classifiers. There are
about 40 classifiers in Malay – too many to list – so here are the
most common ones.

orang   for people
    There are three women in that house.

        ah-duh *tee*-guh *o*-rahng   *Ada tiga orang*
        pe-*rem*-pwahn *dah*-lahm   *perempuan dalam*
        roo-**mah**(h) *ee*-too   *rumah itu.*
                (lit: have three *orang* woman
                    inside house that)

ekor   for other living things
    I saw six fish.

        sai-yuh *nahm*-pah(k)   *Saya nampak*
        e-*nahm* eh-kor *ee*-kahn   *enam ekor ikan.*
                (lit: I see six *ekor* fish)

batang   for stick-like objects (eg, cigarettes, trees)
    He bought two cigarettes.

        dee-uh be-*lee* doo-uh   *Dia beli dua*
        bah-tahng *ro*-ko(k)   *batang rokok.*
                (lit: he buy two *batang*
                    cigarette)

biji   for small, easily moved objects (eg, fruit, eggs)
    I ate one durian.

        sai-yuh *mah*-kahn   *Saya makan*
        sah-too *bee*-jee *doo*-ree-ahn   *satu biji durian.*
                (lit: I to-eat one *biji* durian)

buah   for bulky objects and natural features (eg, houses, rivers)
    I bought two houses.

        sai-yuh be-*lee* doo-uh   *Saya beli dua*
        boo-ah(h) *roo*-mah(h)   *buah rumah.*
                (lit: I buy two *buah* house)

PREPOSITIONS

about	*ten*-tahng/	*tentang/*
	me-*nge*-nah-ee	*mengenai*
after	se-le-*pahs*	*selepas*
at (place)	dee	*di*
at (time)	*pah*-duh;	*pada;*
	pah-duh *poo*-kool	*pada pukul;*
	wahk-too; jahm	*waktu; jam*
between	dee ahn-*tah*-ruh	*di antara*
during	se-*mah*-suh	*semasa*
for	*oon*-tu(k)	*untuk*
for (time)	se-*lah*-muh	*selama*
if	*kah*-low	*kalau*
in	dee; dee dah-*lahm*	*di; di dalam*
inside	dah-*lahm;*	*dalam;*
	dee dah-*lahm*	*di dalam*

from	*dah*-ree	*dari*
(place & time)		
to/forward	ke	*ke*
(place)		
from (people)	dah-ree-*pah*-duh	*daripada*
to (people)	ke-*pah*-duh	*kepada*
on (time/person)	*pah*-duh	*pada*
on (place)	dee	*di*
since	se-*jahk*	*sejak*
through	me-*lah*-loo-ee	*melalui*
until	*sahm*-pai/	*sampai/*
	se-*hing*-guh	*sehingga*
with	de-ngahn	*dengan*
without	*tahn*-puh	*tanpa*
by	o-*leh(h)*	*oleh*

Prepositions are used in the same way as English, eg:

I want rice with chilli sauce.
sai-yuh *mah*-hoo
nah-see de-*ngahn sahm*-bahl

*Saya mahu
nasi dengan sambal.*
(lit: I to-want rice with
chilli-sauce)

She waited for three hours.
dee-uh *toong*-goo se-*lah*-muh
tee-guh jahm

*Dia tunggu selama
tiga jam.*
(lit: she wait for three hour)

CONJUNCTIONS

and	dahn	*dan*
because	se-*bahb*/ ke-*rah*-nuh	*sebab*/ *kerana*
but	te-*tah*-pee	*tetapi*
or	ah-*tow*	*atau*
so that	soo-*pai*-yuh	*supaya*
(together) with	*ser*-tuh	*serta*
as if	se-o-lah(h)-o-lah(h)	*seolah-olah*

I want to eat because I am hungry.
sai-yuh nah(k) *mah*-kahn
se-*bahb sai*-yuh *lah*-pahr

*Saya nak makan
sebab saya lapar.*
(lit: I want-to to-eat
because I hungry)

PERKENALAN   MEETING PEOPLE

Malaysians are very interested in meeting foreigners, and they'll be happy if you even attempt to speak their language. *Lepak*, **leh**-pah(k), 'hanging out' is a national pastime and since chatting to a stranger is considered normal, you'll have plenty of opportunity to practise.

First conversations tend to include questions about family, nationality, and whether you like spicy food. People will often question what you're doing, or where you're going. The 32nd person who asks *Berasal dari mana?*, **ber**-ah-**sahl** *dah*-ree *mah*-nuh?, 'Where are you from?' may think they're the first, so go with the flow and try asking a few questions of your own.

YOU SHOULD KNOW   ANDA PATUT TAHU

Yes.	yah	*Ya.*
No.	*tee*-dah(k)	*Tidak.*
Excuse me.	mah-*ahf*	*Maaf.*
Hello.	*heh*-lo	*Helo.*

Goodbye. (if you're staying)
    se-*lah*-maht *jah*-lahn   *Selamat jalan.*
Goodbye. (if you're leaving)
    se-*lah*-maht *ting*-gahl   *Selamat tinggal.*

Please sit down.
    see-*lah*-kahn *doo*-du(k)   *Silakan duduk.*
Thank you (very much).
    te-*ree*-muh *kah*-si(h)
    (*bah*-nyah(k)-*bah*-nyah(k))   *Terima kasih (banyak-banyak).*
You're welcome.
    sah-muh-*sah*-muh   *Sama-sama.*
Excuse me; Sorry.
    mah-*ahf*; *min*-tuh mah-*ahf*   *Maaf; Minta maaf.*

May I?; Do you mind?
   bo-*leh(h)*?   *Boleh?*

That's fine; No problem.
   bo-*leh(h)*; **tah(k)** *ah*-puh   *Boleh; Tak apa.*

What did you say?
   ah-puh-*dee*-uh?   *Apadia?*

I'm (very) sorry. (apology)
   (min-tuh) mah-*ahf*   *(Minta) Maaf.*

There are two Malay words for 'please'. Use *tolong*, *to*-long, 'help', if making a request or asking someone to do something for you.

Please open the window.
   to-long *boo*-kah *ting*-kahp   *Tolong buka tingkap.*

Or, if you're offering something to somebody, use the word *silakan*, **see**-*lah*-kahn (lit: be-my-guest).

GREETINGS & GOODBYES

UCAPAN SELAMAT

Malay greetings can range from a 'Hey, you!' to a lengthy and formal exchange. Not to worry, since there are across-the-board greetings that are fine to use almost anywhere. The word *selamat*, se-*lah*-maht, comes from the Arabic word *salam*, meaning 'peace'. Putting this word together with 'morning' or 'evening' means something like 'Have a nice morning/evening'.

As in English, Malay greetings are based on the time of day – and also on routine or prayer times. While you may think the day's just begun, the person you're speaking to may have already been to market and prepared lunch.

Good morning. (sunrise – 10 am)
   se-*lah*-maht *pah*-gee   *Selamat pagi.*

Before 10 is the best time to be out and about, watching kids in starched uniforms off to school, people carrying produce to market, or drivers digging into a bowl of *bubur ayam*, **boo**-bur *ai*-yahm, 'chicken porridge.'

MEETING PEOPLE

Good day. (10 am – 4 pm)
  se-*lah*-maht te-ngah-*hah*-ree   *Selamat tengahari.*
  By this time the heat and the traffic have really kicked in.

Good afternoon. (4 – sunset)
  se-*lah*-maht pe-*tahng*   *Selamat petang.*
  The sun is beyond the danger zone and children's kites are filling the sky, or the punctual tropical downpour has begun.

Good night. (goodbye at night – a farewell)
  se-*lah*-maht *mah*-lahm   *Selamat malam.*

There's not really a term for good evening – instead you can just say hello as you would in English (also used as an informal greeting between friends):

Hello.   *heh*-lo   *Helo*

See you later.
  joom-pah *lah*-gee *nahm*-tee   *Jumpa lagi nanti.*
I'm going home now.
  sai-yuh *bah*-li(k) *doo*-loo   *Saya balik dulu.*
Bye. (pronounced as in English)   *Bye.*

FORMS OF ADDRESS   KATA SAPAAN

It's a good idea to use 'Sir' or 'Ma'am' when talking to someone older or deserving of respect.

Mrs; Ma'am	**pwahn**	*Puan*
Mr	**en-*chi(k)***	*Encik*
Sir	**twahn**	*Tuan*
Miss	**chi(k)**	*Cik*

GIVE PEACE A CHANCE

You'll often hear Muslims use the Arabic greeting *assalamualaikum* 'peace be on you' to which the response is *waalaikumsalam* 'and on you be peace'. However, it's considered offensive for non-Muslims to use this greeting, or to answer it. Just say: *Saya bukan Muslimin/Muslimah*, *sai*-yuh boo-*kahn* moos-*lee*-meen/ moos-*lee*-mah(h), 'I'm not a Muslim'. (m/f)

FIRST ENCOUNTERS

PERTEMUAN PERTAMA

What's your name?
    see-*ah*-puh *nah*-muh *ahn*-duh?   *Siapa nama anda?*
My name's ...
    nah-muh *sai*-yuh ...   *Nama saya ...*
I'd like to introduce ...
to you.
    sai-yuh nah(k)   *Saya nak*
    mem-per-ke-*nahl*-kahn ...   *memperkenalkan ...*
    ke-*pah*-duh *ahn*-duh   *kepada anda.*
I'm pleased to meet you.
    sai-yuh gem-*bi*-ruh ber-*te*-moo   *Saya gembira bertemu*
    de-*ngahn* *ahn*-duh   *dengan anda.*

MAKING CONVERSATION

PERBUALAN

Greetings aside, many people will launch straight into the guts of a conversation. Don't be surprised if you're quickly quizzed on topics 'Are you married?', 'Are your teeth real?' If you're asked 'How much money do you make?' you can just answer *cukup*, *choo*-kup, 'enough' with a smile. Common starters include:

How are you?; How's it going?
    ah-puh *khah*-bahr?   *Apa khabar?*
Fine. And you?
    khah-bahr bai(k).   *Khabar baik.*
    ah-puh *khah*-bahr?   *Apa khabar?*
Where are you going?
    nah(k) ke *mah*-nuh?   *Nak ke mana?*

Asked most often as an ice-breaker, the response *jalan-jalan*, *jah*-lahn-*jah*-lahn, 'travelling around', is perfect. Other easy answers include:

To (Petaling Jaya).
    ke (pe-*tah*-ling *jah*-yuh)   *Ke (Petaling Jaya).*
Out and about.
    mah-kahn *ah*-ngin   *Makan angin.*
                           (lit: eating the breeze)

Some of the things people will want to know about you are:

How long have you been in Malaysia?
    soo-dah(h) be-*rah*-puh *lah*-muh   *Sudah berapa lama di*
    dee mah-*lay*-see-ah?   *Malaysia?*

I've been here for two weeks.
    sai-yuh *soo*-dah(h) *doo*-uh   *Saya sudah dua minggu*
    ming-goo dee *see*-nee   *di sini.*

How long will you be in Malaysia?
    be-*rah*-puh *lah*-muh *ahn*-duh   *Berapa lama anda di*
    dee mah-*lay*-see-ah?   *Malaysia?*

I'll be in Malaysia for (one month).
    sai-yuh *ah*-kahn ber-*ah*-duh   *Saya akan berada di*
    dee mah-*lay*-see-ah se-*lah*-muh   *Malaysia selama*
    (se-*boo*-lahn)   *(sebulan).*

Where have you been so far?
    soo-dah(h) ke *mah*-nuh?   *Sudah ke mana?*

I've been to Penang and Ipoh.
    sai-yuh *soo*-dah(h) ke pee-*nahng*   *Saya sudah ke Penang*
    dan *ee*-po(h)   *dan Ipoh.*

Have you been to Mersing?
    soo-dah(h) ke *mer*-sing?   *Sudah ke Mersing?*

Not yet.
    be-*lum*   *Belum.*

Yes, I have.
    soo-dah(h)   *Sudah.*

Are you here on holiday?
    ahn-duh *choo*-tee dee *see*-nee?   *Anda cuti di sini?*

I'm here ...	*sai*-yuh ...	*Saya ...*
for a holiday	ber-*choo*-tee	*bercuti*
on business	ber-*ker*-juh	*bekerja*
to study	be-*lah*-jahr	*belajar*

How long are you here for?
    be-*rah*-puh *lah*-muh *ahn*-duh   *Berapa lama anda di sini?*
    dee *see*-nee?

I'm/We're here for ... weeks/days.
   sai-yuh/*kah*-mee dee   *Saya/Kami di*
   see-nee se-*lah*-muh   *sini selama*
   ... *ming*-goo/*hah*-ree   *... minggu/hari.*

Do you like it here?
   ah-duh-kah(h) *ahn*-duh   *Adakah anda*
   soo-kuh dee *see*-nee?   *suka di sini?*

I/We like it here very much.
   sai-yuh/*kah*-mee *sah*-ngaht *Saya/Kami sangat*
   soo-kuh dee *see*-nee   *suka di sini.*

Can you eat spicy food?
   bo-*leh*(h) *mah*-kahn   *Boleh makan*
   mah-kah-nahn pe-*dahs?*   *makanan pedas?*

I (don't) like spicy food.
   sai-yuh (tah(k)) *soo*-kuh   *Saya (tak) suka*
   mah-kah-nahn pe-*dahs*   *makanan pedas.*

USEFUL WORDS & PHRASES

Sure.	be-*tul*	*Betul.*
It's OK.	tah(k) *ah*-puh	*Tak apa.*
Are you ready?	*soo*-dah(h) see-*ahp?*	*Sudah siap?*
Just a minute.	se-*ben*-tahr/	*Sebentar/*
	se-ke-*jahp*	*Sekejap.*
Wait!	*toong*-goo!	*Tunggu!*
Look!	*lee*-haht!	*Lihat!*
Listen!	de-*ngahr*-lah(h)!	*Dengarlah!*
I'm ready.	*sai*-yuh see-*ahp*	*Saya siap.*
Slow down!	per-lah-*hahn* see-*kit!*	*Perlahan sikit!*
Hurry up!	che-*paht* see-*kit!*	*Cepat sikit!*
Go away!	per-*gee*-lah(h)!	*Pergilah!*
Watch out!	ber-*hah*-ti-*hah*-ti!	*Berhati-hati!*
It's (not) possible.	(*tee*-dah(k)/tah(k))	*(Tidak/Tak)*
	bo-*leh*(h)	*Boleh.*

I forgot.	*sai*-yuh *loo*-puh	*Saya lupa.*
It's (not)	*(tee*-dah(k)/tah(k))*	*(Tidak/Tak)*
important.	pen-*ting*	*Penting.*
It doesn't matter.	tah(k) *ah*-puh	*Tak apa.*
Let's go!	*joom*-lah(h)!	*Jumlah!*

What are you doing?
   ahm-duh *boo*-aht *ah*-puh?   *Anda buat apa?*

Are you waiting too?
   ahm-duh me-*noong*-goo   *Anda menunggu juga?*
   joo-guh?

Do you live here?
   ahm-duh *ting*-gahl dee   *Anda tinggal di sini?*
   see-nee?

What's your opinion about ...?
   ah-puh-kah(h)   *Apakah pendapat anda*
   pen-*dah*-paht   *tentang ...?*
   ahn-duh *ten*-tahng ...?

It's hot!
   pah-nahs kahn!   *Panas, kan!*

Beautiful, isn't it!
   chahn-ti(k) boo-*kahn*!   *Cantik, bukan!*

That's strange!
   pe-*li(k)*-nyuh!   *Peliknya!*

That's funny! (amusing)
   lah-*wah(k)*-nyuh!   *Lawaknya!*

LEAN ON ME

Physical contact between the same sex is considered normal in Malaysia. You'll see boys hanging out with their arms around each other's shoulders, and women holding hands with their close friends or relatives.

MEETING PEOPLE

NATIONALITIES   KEBANGSAAN

In Malay, you'll find that many names of countries are similar to the English names, but pronounced slightly differently.

Where are you from?
ahm-duh ber-*ah*-sahl *dah*-ree   *Anda berasal dari mana?*
mah-nuh?

I'm from ...   *sai*-yuh ber-*ah*-sahl   *Saya berasal*
                     dah-ree ...   *dari ...*

Australia	*	*Australia*
Canada	*	*Kanada*
England	*ing*-ge-ris	*Inggeris*
Europe	e-*ro*-pah(h)	*Eropah*
India	*	*India*
Ireland	*	*Ireland*
Japan	*jeh*-poon	*Jepun*
New Zealand	*	*New Zealand*
Scotland	*	*Scotland*
the USA	*	*Amerika*
Wales	*	*Wales*

(* as in English)

I'm ...	*sai*-yuh *o*-rahng ...	*Saya orang ...*
Australian	*	*Australia*
Dutch	be-*lahm*-duh	*Belanda*
English	*ing*-ge-ris	*Inggeris*

I live in a/the ...	*sai*-yuh *ting*-gahl dee ...	*Saya tinggal di ...*
city	*bahn*-dahr	*bandar*
countryside	loo-*ahr bahn*-dahr	*luar bandar*
seaside	*pahn*-tai	*pantai*
suburbs of ...	*ping*-geer	*pinggir*
	bahn-dahr ...	*bandar ...*
village	*kahm*-pung	*kampung*

CULTURAL DIFFERENCES

PERBEZAAN KEBUDAYAAN

How do you do this in your country?
bah-gai-*mah*-nuh ee-nee
dee-*boo*-aht dee ne-*gah*-ruh
ahm-duh?

Bagaimana ini dibuat di negara anda?

Is this a local or national custom?
ah-daht ee-nee ah-daht
dah-*eh*-rah(h) ah-*tow* ah-daht
nah-see-*o*-nahl?

Adat ini adat daerah atau adat nasional?

I don't want to offend you.
sai-yuh tah(k) nah(k)
me-*nying*-goong pe-*rah*-sah-ahn
ahm-duh

Saya tak nak menyinggung perasaan anda.

I'm sorry, it's not the custom in my country.
mah-*ahf*, ah-daht *ee*-nee tah(k)
bee-*ah*-suh dee ne-*gah*-ruh
sai-yuh

Maaf, adat ini tak biasa di negara saya.

I don't mind watching, but I'd prefer not to participate.
sai-yuh le-*bi(h)* se-nahng
me-*non*-ton dah-ree-*pah*-duh
me-*lee*-baht-kahn *di*-ree

Saya lebih senang menonton daripada melibatkan diri.

AGE

UMUR

It's not off-limits to ask someone's age in Malaysia, so expect it often. One response could be *Cuba teka*, *choo*-buh *teh*-kuh, 'Guess!'

How old are you?	be-*rah*-puh oo-moor *ahm*-duh?	*Berapa umur anda?*
I'm ... years old.	oo-moor *sai*-yuh ... tah-hoon.	*Umur saya ... tahun.*
20	*doo*-uh poo-lu(h)	*dua puluh*
35	*tee*-gah *poo*-lu(h) *lee*-muh	*tiga puluh lima*

(See Numbers & Amounts on page 199 for your age.)

OCCUPATIONS

PEKERJAAN

What's your occupation?
ah-puh pe-*ker*-jah-ahn *ahn*-duh? *Apa pekerjaan anda?*

What do you do?
ahn-duh ber-*ker*-jah se-*bah*-gai *Anda bekerja sebagai*
ah-puh? *apa?*

I'm (a/an) ...	*sai*-yuh ...	*Saya ...*
artist	*ahr*-tees	*artis*
businessperson	pe-nee-*ah*-gah	*peniaga*
chef	*too*-kahng *mah*-sah(k)	*tukang masak*
doctor	*dok*-tor	*doktor*
engineer	joo-*roo*-te-rah	*jurutera*
factory worker	pe-*ker*-jah *kee*-lahng	*pekerja kilang*
farmer	pe-*tah*-nee	*petani*
journalist	wahr-*tah*-wahn	*wartawan*
lawyer	pe-*gwahm*	*peguam*
lecturer (university)	pen-*shah*-rah(h)	*pensyarah*
mechanic	me-*kan*-ik	*mekanik*
musician	pe-*main*	*pemain*
	moo-zi(k)	*muzik*
nurse	joo-roo-*rah*-waht	*jururawat*
office worker	pe-*gah*-wai	*pegawai*
retired	pe-*sah*-ruh	*pesara*
scientist	*sain*-tees	*saintis*
secretary	joo-roo-*taip*	*jurutaip*
student (school)	*moo*-rid/pe-*lah*-jahr	*murid/pelajar*
student (uni)	pe-*lah*-jahr	*pelajar*
teacher (school)	*goo*-roo/*chi*(k)-goo	*guru/cikgu*
unemployed	pe-*ngahng*-goor	*penganggur*
waiter	pe-*lai*-ahn	*pelayan*
writer	pe-*noo*-lees	*penulis*

MEETING PEOPLE

What are you studying?	*ahn*-duh be-*lah*-jahr *ah*-puh?	*Anda belajar apa?*
I'm studying ...	*sai*-yuh be-*lah*-jahr ...	*Saya belajar ...*
art	ke-se-*nee*-ahn	*kesenian*
business	per-nee-ah-*gah*-ahn	*perniagaan*
engineering	ke-*joo*-te-rah-ahn	*kejuteraan*
languages	bah-*hah*-suh	*bahasa*
law	*oon*-dahng-*oon*-dahng	*undang-undang*
literature	sahs-*ter*-ah	*sastera*
Malay	bah-*hah*-suh me-*lah*-yoo	*Bahasa Melayu*
medicine	per-*oo*-bah-tahn	*perubatan*
science	sains	*sains*
teaching	pen-*gah*-jahr-ahn	*pengajaran*

RELIGION   AGAMA

Most Malays are Muslim; Malaysians of other backgrounds may also be Muslim, Christian, Hindu or Buddhist. Religion is considered essential in everyone's life, and you'll maintain better relations by claiming to have one, or by saying your parents belong to one.

What's your religion?	*ahn*-duh ber-ah-*gah*-muh *ah*-puh?	*Anda beragama apa?*
My religion is ...	ah-*gah*-muh *sai*-yuh ...	*Agama saya ...*
Buddhist	*boo*-duh	*Buda*
Catholic	*kah*-to-lik	*Katolik*
Christian	*kris*-ti-ahn	*Kristian*
Hindu	*hin*-doo	*Hindu*
Jewish	yah-*hoo*-dee	*Yahudi*
Muslim	*is*-lahm	*Islam*
Protestant	*pro*-tes-tahn	*Protestan*

I'm ... but not practising.
sai-yuh ber-ah-*gah*-muh ...
tah-pee jah-*rahng* ke ge-*reh*-jah

Saya beragama ...
tapi jarang ke gereja.

My parents are ...
   ee-boo *bah*-puh *sai*-yuh   *Ibu bapa saya*
   ber-ah-*gah*-muh ...   *beragama ...*
I think I believe in God.
   sai-yuh *rah*-suh *sai*-yuh   *Saya rasa saya*
   per-*chah*-yuh ke-*pah*-duh   *percaya kepada*
   too-hahn   *Tuhan.*
I'm not religious.
   sai-yuh *tee*-dah(k)   *Saya tidak*
   ber-ah-*gah*-muh   *beragama.*

TABLE MANNERS

You may offer to help prepare food or clean up, but as a guest, your host will insist you sit and do nothing:

'Don't bother yourself.'
   jah-ngahn *soo*-sah(h)-*soo*-sah(h)
   Jangan susah-susah.

If the host asks you what you'd like to eat or drink, you may reply with the same phrase. When you get to the table, you'll hear:

'Please drink/eat.'
   see-luh *mee*-num/*mah*-kahn
   Sila minum/makan.

Decline an offer when it's first made – this is good manners. Then go for it!

MEETING PEOPLE

I believe in destiny/fate.
   sai-yuh per-*chah*-yuh   *Saya percaya*
   ke-*pah*-duh *tah(k)*-dir   *kepada takdir.*
I'm interested in astrology/
philosophy.
   sai-yuh ter-*tah*-ri(k) ke-*pah*-duh   *Saya tertarik kepada*
   ahs-tro-*lo*-gee/*fahl*-sah-fah(h)   *astrologi/falsafah.*
I'm an atheist.
   sai-yuh *ay*-thee-is   *Saya atheis.*
I'm agnostic.
   sai-yuh ahg-*nos*-tik   *Saya agnostik.*

THE SISTERHOOD

Considering that the official religion of Malaysia is Islam, women in general have a great deal of freedom and rights. There's a strong female presence in the working world, both in government – several cabinet ministers are women – and the private sector.

Civil laws generally cover all Malaysians, except in the area of family law, in which Muslims must follow *Syariah* court rulings. These laws are discriminatory against women, and many are working towards addressing these inequities. For example, it is very easy for a Muslim man to divorce his wife: he simply says, "I divorce you." A woman, on the other hand, must go through the *Syariah* courts to get a divorce.

Since 1979, many Malay women have made the personal decision to wear clothing that covers their whole body, except for their face and hands. Women travelling in Malaysia will need to have a think about what is appropriate in a Muslim country. Wearing short skirts, skimpy shorts or beach gear in public will only reinforce negative stereotypes and may be seen to encourage harassment. Covering up more than you usually would, and even covering your head with a scarf in rural areas or on the east coast, will help.

BODY LANGUAGE BAHASA BADAN

A growing number of Malays feel that handshaking, or any casual physical contact between the sexes is inappropriate and against the teachings of Islam. Particularly in the more conservative northern states, or in rural areas, it's better to smile instead when meeting someone of the opposite sex. If they extend their hand, then by all means, shake it! Handshaking is otherwise widely accepted: a gentle brush of the palms rather than a knuckle-crusher is what you should aim for. It's appropriate to shake hands when being introduced, when visiting somebody in their home, or when you haven't seen someone for a while.

Touching someone's head is generally considered rude. If someone is sitting on the floor in a home, stepping over their legs is not the thing to do either. Walk around their legs, no matter how inconvenient it is. It's also considered polite to bow your body slightly and extend your right arm straight downwards towards the floor when crossing the path of someone who's seated, or when interrupting people. At the same time you can say *maaf*, **mah-***ahf*, 'excuse me'.

TAKE IT EASY

The general pace of life in Malaysia may seem slower than in some other countries. Indeed, most Malaysians seem to take things at an easier pace, and considering the climate and the effort needed to get around, slowing down and chilling out is probably a wise decision — as if you need any encouragement!

FEELINGS

I'm ...	*sai*-yuh ...	*Saya ...*
Are you ...?	*ah*-duh-kah(h) *ahm*-duh ... ?	*Adakah anda ...?*
afraid	tah-*kut*	*takut*
angry	*mah*-rah(h)	*marah*
bored	*bo*-sahn	*bosan*
cold	se-*joo(k)*	*sejuk*
disgusted	men-*yahm*-pah(h)	*menyampah*
full	ken-*yahng*	*kenyang*
grateful	ber-*shoo*-koor	*bersyukur*
happy	gem-*bee*-ruh	*gembira*
hot	*pah*-nahs	*panas*
hungry	*lah*-pahr	*lapar*
in a hurry	ter-*ge*-suh-*ge*-suh	*tergesa-gesa*
keen	ber-*soong*-guh *soong*-guh	*bersungguh-sungguh*
alright (content)	pwahs	*puas*
sad	se-*di(h)*	*sedih*
sick	*sah*-kit	*sakit*
sleepy	meng-*ahn*-to(k)	*mengantuk*
snobbish	som-*bong*	*sombong*
sorry (condolence)	*ta(k)*-zee-ah(h)	*takziah*
sorry (regret)	me-nye-*sahl*	*menyesal*
thirsty	hows	*haus*
tired	le-*ti(h)*	*letih*
well	bai(k)	*baik*
worried	*bim*-bahng	*bimbang*

PERASAAN

HEART-WARMING

You'll find that many people, especially the Malays, follow the handshake with a touch of the heart, a habit worth forming. In cases where respect is called for, such as when a young child greets an elder, the child will kiss the elder's hand and then sometimes touch it to their own forehead.

BREAKING THE LANGUAGE BARRIER

MENGATASI KESUKARAN BAHASA

Do you speak English?
  ah-duh-kah(h) *ahn*-duh
  ber-bah-*hah*-suh *ing*-ge-ris?

*Adakah anda
berbahasa Inggeris?*

Yes./No.
  yah/tah(k) bo-*leh(h)*

Ya./Tak boleh.

I can only speak a little Malay.
  sai-yuh *hahm*-yuh
  ber-bah-*hah*-suh me-*lah*-yoo
  se-*dee*-kit *sah*-juh

*Saya hanya
berbahasa Melayu
sedikit saja.*

Does any one here speak English?
  ah-*duh* o-rahng yahng
  ber-bah-*hah*-suh *ing*-ge-ris
  dee *see*-nee?

*Ada orang yang
berbahasa Inggeris
di sini?*

Do you understand?
  ah-duh-kah(h) *ahn*-duh
  fah-hahm?

*Adakah anda
faham?*

I (don't) understand.
  sai-yuh (tah(k)) *fah*-hahm

Saya (tak) faham.

How do you say ... in Malay?
  mah-chahm *mah*-nuh
  chah-kahp ... dah-*lahm*
  bah-*hah*-suh me-*lah*-yoo?

*Macam mana
cakap ... dalam
Bahasa Melayu?*

What's this called?
  ah-puh nee?

Apa ni?

What does this mean?
  ah-puh *mah(k)*-sud-nyuh?

Apa maksudnya?

Please speak slowly.
  to-long *chah*-kahp
  per-*lah*-hahn *see*-kit

*Tolong cacap
perlahan sikit.*

Please write that word
down for me.
  to-long *too*-lis-kahn
  per-kah-*tah*-ahn *ee*-too
  oon-tu(k) *sai*-yuh

*Tolong tuliskan
perkataan itu
untuk saya.*

Please repeat that.
    to-long oo-*lah*-ngee   *Tolong ulangi.*

Please translate for me.
    to-long ter-je-*mah(h)*-kahn   *Tolong terjemahkan*
    oon-tu(k) *sai*-yuh   *untuk saya.*

STAYING IN TOUCH   MEMBUAT JANJI

Where are you staying?
    ahn-duh *doo*-du(k) dee   *Anda duduk di mana?*
    mah-nuh?

What's your address?
    ah-puh-kah(h) *ah*-lah-maht   *Apakah alamat anda?*
    ahn-duh?

I'm staying at ...
    sai-yuh *doo*-du(k) dee ...   *Saya duduk di ...*

Can we meet again?
    bo-*leh(h)*-kah(h) *kee*-tuh   *Bolehkah kita*
    ber-*joom*-puh *lah*-gee?   *berjumpa lagi?*

Let's meet at (6 o'clock) at ...
    kee-tuh ber-*te*-moo *pah*-duh   *Kita bertemu*
    (*poo*-kool e-*nahm*) dee ...   *(pukul enam) di ...*

Come to my house any time.
    dah-tahng ke *roo*-mah(h)   *Datang ke rumah*
    sai-yuh *bee*-luh-*bee*-luh   *saya bila-bila*
    sah-juh   *saja.*

NO MEANS NO

Malaysians have a variety of ways of avoiding a direct answer, especially when it's a negative one. If you feel uncomfortable answering a particular question try some of the following (a smile works too!):

I don't know.	*sai*-yuh tah(k) *tah*-hoo	*Saya tak tahu.*
I'm busy.	*sai*-yuh *see*-bu(k)	*Saya sibuk.*
It's not appropriate.	*ee*-nee tah(k) se-*swai*	*Ini tak sesuai.*

HOMESTAYS

Hospitality on a formal level is the norm when you're invited into a Malaysian home. If you stay in a rural or small town setting, you'll probably be treated like a star! Don't be surprised to see the neighbourhood children peering in a door or window to gawk at the *orang asing*, o-**rahng** ah-**sing**, 'foreigner'.

It's good to bring a small gift *buah tangan*, **boo**-ah(h) *tah*-**ngahn**, (lit: fruit hand): a bag of fruit such as oranges or apples, or a small souvenir from your country. It's considered polite to greet and shake hands with every adult present – remember to wait for the hand extended from the opposite sex – and sometimes the children, too. Bringing photos of your home or family, or a map of your country, is a good idea.

Savoury and sweet cakes and tidbits are common fare in Malaysian homes. If they're not to your liking, just take a few bites. It's considered rude to refuse to eat or drink what is served. If you're unable to eat certain things, it's best to tell your host or hostess early.

I'm sorry, I can't eat wheat flour;
I have an allergy.
    mah-*ahf*, *sai*-yuh tah(k) bo-*leh(h)*   *Maaf, saya tak boleh*
    mah-kahn te-*pong gahm*-doom   *makan tepong gandum,*
    se-*bahb sai*-yuh *ah*-duh *ah*-ler-jee   *sebab saya ada alergi.*

(the English word 'allergy' is also widely understood)

I have diabetes so I can't have sugar.
    sai-yuh *ah*-duh dai-ah-*bee*-tees   *Saya ada diabetes,*
    jah-dee tah(k) bo-*leh(h)*   *jadi tak boleh*
    mah-kahn *goo*-luh   *makan gula.*
Sorry, I've just eaten.
    mah-*ahf sai*-yuh bah-*roo*   *Maaf, saya baru*
    mah-kahn   *makan.*

When you feel it's time to go, say *Saya nak balik dulu, sai-*yuh nah(k) bah-*li(k) doo-*loo, 'I'm going home first'. The family will undoubtedly urge you to stay, but take your leave with *Terima kasih banyak-banyak!*, te-*ree-*muh *kah-*si(h) *bah-*nyah(k)-*bah-*nyah(k), 'thanks very, very much'.

JALAN-JALAN

GETTING AROUND

Kuala Lumpur's public transport system has undergone massive changes in the last 10 years, with the introduction of the LRT (light rapid transit), improved roadways and commuter trains. Travelling in other parts of the country requires a little more patience, and even in Kuala Lumpur a heavy downpour can bring things to a stop! Buses, trains and taxis are available throughout most of the country. Road maps of the cities can be found at hotels, bookstores and newsagents.

FINDING YOUR WAY

CARI JALAN

Excuse me.	mah-*ahf*	*Maaf.*
I'm lost.	*sai*-yuh ter-se-saht	*Saya tersesat.*
Where's the ...?	dee *mah*-nuh ...?	*Di mana ...?*
airport	lah-*pahng*-ahn ter-bahng	*lapangan terbang*
intercity	*steh*-sehn bahs	*stesen bas*
bus station	*bahn*-dahr	*bandar*
road to (Raub)	*jah*-lahn ke (rowb)	*jalan ke (Raub)*
train station	*steh*-sehn ke-reh-tuh-*ah*-pee	*stesen keretapi*

What time does the ... leave/arrive?	... ber-*to*-lah(k)/*tee*-buh *poo*-kool be-*rah*-puh?	... *bertolak/tiba pukul berapa?*
(inter) city bus	bahs *bahn*-dahr	*Bas bandar*
plane	*kah*-pahl *ter*-bahng	*Kapal terbang*
ship	*kah*-pahl	*Kapal*
train	ke-reh-tuh-*ah*-pee	*Keretapi*

How can I get to ...?	
mah-chahm *mah*-nuh *sai*-yuh bo-*leh*(h) per-gee ke ...?	*Macam mana saya boleh pergi ke ...?*
Is it near/far?	
de-*kaht*-kah(h)/*jow*(h)-kah(h)?	*Dekatkah/Jauhkah?*

GETTING AROUND

Can we walk there?
   bo-*leh*(h) *jah*-lahn *kah*-kee
   tah(k) ke *sah*-nuh?

*Boleh jalan kaki
tak ke sana?*

Can you show me (on the map)?
   to-long *toon*-joo(k)-kahn
   (dee *peh*-tuh)?

*Tolong tunjukkan
(di peta)?*

Are there other means of
getting there?
   ah-duh *chah*-ruh
   lain ke *sah*-nuh?

*Ada cara
lain ke sana?*

What street is this?
   jah-lahn *ee*-nee
   jah-lahn *ah*-puh?

*Jalan ini
jalan apa?*

What ... is this?	*ee*-nee ... *ah*-puh?	*Ini ... apa?*
city	*bahn*-dahr	*bandar*
village	*kahm*-pong	*kampung*

DIRECTIONS   ARAHAN

(Go) Straight ahead!	(*jah*-lahn) *te*-roos!	*(Jalan) Terus!*
To the left/right.	ke *ki*-ree/*kah*-nahn	*Ke kiri/kanan.*

Turn left/right	*beh*-lo(k) *ki*-ree/	*Belok kiri/*
at the ...	*kah*-nahn dee ...	*kanan di ...*
corner	*sim*-pahng	*simpang*
intersection	*sim*-pahng	*simpang*
next corner	*sim*-pahng yang	*simpang yang*
	ber-ee-*koot*-nyuh	*berikutnya*
T-junction	*sim*-pahng tee	*simpang T*
traffic lights	*lahm*-poo	*lampu*
	ee-*shah*-raht	*isyarat*

behind	dee be-lah-*kahng*	*di belakang*
far	jow(h)	*jauh*
in front of	dee de-*pahn*	*di depan*
next to	se-be-*lah*(h)	*sebelah*
opposite	ber-lah-*wah*-nahn	*berlawanan*
near	de-*kaht*	*dekat*

north	oo-*tah*-ruh	*utara*
south	se-*lah*-tahn	*selatan*
east	*tee*-mur	*timur*
west	*bah*-raht	*barat*

ADDRESSES   ALAMAT

Common words that make up Malaysian addresses include:

jalan raya	a bigger road, like a dual carriageway
jalan	road
lorong	smaller road
pesiaran	even smaller road
lebuh raya	a highway
taman	garden, as in 'Serenity Gardens' housing estate
kampong	village

Malaysian city and town addresses look similar to this:

> Ali Abubakar
> 204, Jalan Air Hitam
> Taman Mewah
> 44300 Serdang, Selangor

This means Ali Abubakar lives at number 204, Air Hitam Street (*Jalan*), Mewah Gardens (*Taman*), a housing area, in the town/city of Serdang in the state of Selangor, postcode 44300.

Addresses in rural areas may look something like this:

> Aishah Mohamed
> Lt 1445, Kampung Mangga
> Kubang Kerian, Kota Baru
> Kelantan

Lt means lot number, *kampung* means village. *Kubang Kerian* in this case is the name of a larger village area and *Kota Baru* is the name of the *daerah*, 'county', and *Kelantan* is the state.

BUYING TICKETS

MEMBELI TIKET

Ticket prices are usually posted on noticeboards for ferry, LRT, bus and train travel. Commuter and LRT tickets can be bought from ticket machines or from employees at the stations. Fares on public transport are not negotiable.

How much does it cost to go to ...?
    be-*rah*-puh *hahr*-guh-nyuh
    oon-tu(k) ke ...?
                             Berapa harganya
                             untuk ke ...?

How much is it from Johor to Ipoh?
    be-*rah*-puh *hahr*-guh tee-*keht*
    dah-ree *jo*-hor ke *ee*-po(h)?
                             Berapa harga tiket
                             dari Johor ke Ipoh?

Where can I buy a ticket?
    tee-*keht* dee-*joo*-ahl
    dee *mah*-nuh?
                             Tiket dijual
                             di mana?

We want to go to ...
    kah-mee nah(k) ke ...
                             Kami nak ke ...

Do I need to book?
    ah-duh-kah(h) *hah*-roos peh-*sahn*?   *Adakah harus pesan?*

I'd like to book a seat to ...
    sai-yuh nah(k) me-*me*-sahn
    tem-*paht doo*-du(k) ke ...
                             Saya nak memesan
                             tempat duduk ke ...

I'd like (a) ...	*sai*-yuh nah(k) ...	*Saya nak ...*
one-way ticket	tee-*keht* se-*hah*-luh	*tiket sehala*
return ticket	tee-*keht* per-gee-*bah*-li(k)	*tiket pergi-balik*
two tickets	*doo*-ah tee-*keht*	*dua tiket*
student's fare	*hahr*-guh pe-*lah*-jahr	*harga pelajar*
1st class	ke-*lahs* per-*tah*-muh	*kelas pertama*
2nd class	ke-*lahs* ke-*doo*-ah/	*kelas kedua/*
	bis-nis	*bisnis*
economy class	ke-*lahs* ee-ko-*no*-mee	*kelas ekonomi*
child's/pensioner's	*hahr*-guh *ah*-nah(k)/	*harga anak/pesara*
fare	pe-*sah*-ruh	

What about my change?
    doo-it *bah*-li(k) *mah*-nuh?   *Duit balik mana?*

confirmation	kon-fir-*mah*-see	*konfirmasi*
destination	de-sti-*nah*-see	*destinasi*
seat	tem-*paht doo*-du(k)	*tempat duduk*
ticket	tee-*keht*	*tiket*
ticket counter	*kown*-ter tee-*keht*	*kaunter tiket*
timetable	ja-*doo*-al	*jadual*

AIR   PENERBANGAN

Malaysian Airlines (MAS) and Pelangi Air offer services within the
country to most locations. Both airlines have a good safety record.

Is there a flight to Penang on (Monday)?
    ah-duh-kah(h)   *Adakah*
    pe-ner-*bah*-ngahn ke   *penerbangan ke*
    pe-*nahng pah*-duh   *Penang pada*
    (*hah*-ree *ees*-nin)?   (*hari Isnin*)?
What time is the flight to
Penang on (Monday)?
    poo-kool be-*rah*-puh   *Pukul berapa*
    pe-ner-*bahng*-ahn   *penerbangan*
    ber-*to*-lah(k) ke pe-*nahng*   *bertolak ke Penang*
    pah-duh (*hah*-ree *ees*-nin)?   *pada (hari Isnin)*?
What time do I have to be at
the airport?
    poo-kool be-*rah*-puh   *Pukul berapa*
    sai-yuh *hah*-roos *ah*-duh dee   *saya harus ada di*
    lah-*pahng*-ahn *ter*-bahng?   *lapangan terbang*?
When's the next flight to ...?
    bee-luh pe-ner-*bahng*-ahn   *Bila penerbangan*
    ke ... yahng se-te-*roos*-nyuh?   *ke ... yang seterusnya*?
I'd like to reconfirm my ticket to Perlis.
    sai-yuh nah(k) me-mas-*tee*-kahn   *Saya nak memastikan*
    tee-*keht sai*-yuh ke *per*-lees   *tiket saya ke Perlis.*
How long does the flight take?
    per-jah-lah-*nahn*-nya   *Perjalanannya*
    be-*rah*-puh *lah*-muh?   *berapa lama*?
Where's the baggage claim?
    bah-*gah*-see dee *mah*-nuh?   *Bagasi di mana*?

Customs   **Kastam**

Customs officers are generally friendly (unless you're a smuggler)
and are impressed if you greet them in Malay and make an
attempt to speak the language.

I have nothing to declare.
 bah-*rahng sai*-yuh *tee*-dah(k)   *Barang saya tidak*
 per-*loo* dee-lah-*por*-kahn   *perlu dilaporkan.*
I have something to declare.
 sai-yuh *ah*-duh bah-*rahng*   *Saya ada barang*
 yahng per-*loo* dee-lah-*por*-kahn   *yang perlu dilaporkan.*
Do I have to declare this?
 ah-duh-kah(h) *sai*-yuh per-*loo*   *Adakah saya perlu*
 me-lah-*por*-kahn *ee*-nee?   *melaporkan ini?*
This is all my luggage.
 ee-nee se-*moo*-uh   *Ini semua barang saya.*
 bah-*rahng sai*-yuh
I didn't know I had to declare it.
 sai-yuh *tee*-dah(k) *tah*-hoo   *Saya tidak tahu*
 bah-*rahng ee*-nee *hah*-roos   *barang ini harus*
 dee-lah-*por*-kahn.   *dilaporkan.*

aeroplane   *kah*-pahl *ter*-bahng   *kapal terbang*
airport   lah-*pahng*-ahn *ter*-bahng   *lapangan terbang*

SIGNS

BARANG HILANG	LOST PROPERTY
PERTOLAKAN	DEPARTURES
KETIBAAN	ARRIVALS
PENDAFTARAN	CHECK-IN
IMIGRASI	PASSPORT CONTROL

BUS   BAS

Malaysia's buses are usually fast, economical and comfortable. Local and city buses can be hailed at bus stops, which usually are well signposted. You may need to make reservations for long distance buses, especially around festive times. In rural areas buses tend to be older and without air-con. For sightseeing and really experiencing local life, these are ideal. Just pay your fare to the conductor or driver.

Most city buses have complete air-con. Check when you purchase your tickets by asking: *Bas ini ada air-con tak?*, **bahs ee-nee ah-duh air-con tah(k)?**, 'Does this bus have air-con or not?'. Long distance buses have toilets and usually stop to let passengers off for meals; some will also combine a meal-stop with a prayer-stop for the Muslim passengers.

Which bus goes to ...?
  bahs yahng *mah*-nuh   *Bas yang mana*
  nahk ke ...?   *nak ke ...?*
Does this bus go to ...?
  bahs ee-nee *per*-gee ke ...?   *Bas ini pergi ke ...?*
Do buses come often?
  bahs ee-nee *dah*-tahng   *Bas ini datang*
  se-*lah*-loo kahn?   *selalu, kan?*
Often./Rarely.
  se-*lah*-loo/*jah*-rahng   *Selalu./Jarang.*
Where do I get the bus for ...?
  bahs ke ... dee *mah*-nuh?   *Bas ke ... di mana?*

What time's   **poo-kool be-*rah*-puh**   *Pukul berapa*
the ... bus (to ...)?   **bahs ... (ke ...)?**   *bas ... (ke ...)?*
  first   **per-*tah*-muh**   *pertama*
  last   **ter-*ah*-khir**   *terakhir*
  next   **ber-ee-*koot*-nyuh**   *berikutnya*

Will the bus stop at a restaurant?
  bahs ee-nee ber-*hen*-tee   *Bas ini berhenti*
  dee *res*-to-rahn?   *di restoran?*

Could you let me know when
we arrive at ...?
    to-long ber-ee-*tah*-hoo
    sai-yuh *bee*-luh *kee*-tuh
    soo-dah(h) *sahm*-pai dee ...?

Tolong beritahu
saya bila kita
sudah sampai di ...?

Where are we now?
    kee-tuh *mah*-nuh
    se-*kah*-rahng?

Kita mana
sekarang?

I want to get off.
    sai-yah nah(k) *too*-roon

Saya nak turun.

TRAIN   KERETAPI

Train travel in Malaysia is fun, cheap, easy and trains are generally
on time. Express trains only stop at the main stations, but some
of the local services, especially on the east coast, offer a colourful
experience, stopping in small towns and even in the jungle to let
passengers off.

I want to go by express train to ...
    sai-yuh nah(k) nai(k)
    ke-reh-tuh-*ah*-pee
    ehk-sprehs ke ...

Saya nak naik
keretapi
ekspres ke ...

Which platform does the train
leave from?
    dah-ree *lahn*-dah-sahn
    mah-nuh ke-reh-tuh-*ah*-pee
    ber-*ahng*-kaht?

Dari landasan
mana keretapi
berangkat?

Where do I need to change trains?
    sai-yuh ber-*too*-kahr
    ke-reh-tuh-*ah*-pee dee *mah*-nuh?

Saya bertukar
keretapi di mana?

Does this train stop at Kuala Pilah?
    ah-duh-kah(h) ke-reh-tuh-*ah*-pee
    ee-nee ber-*hen*-tee dee
    kwah-luh *pee*-lah(h)?

Adakah keretapi
ini berhenti di
Kuala Pilah?

Can I get off at Kuala Pilah?
    bo-*leh*(h) *sai*-yuh *too*-roon
    dee *kwah*-luh *pee*-lah(h)?

Boleh saya turun
di Kuala Pilah?

Is this seat free?
   ke-*roo*-see *ee*-nee   *Kerusi ini kosongkah?*
   ko-song-kah(h)?
This seat's taken.
   soo-dah(h) *ah*-duh *o*-rahng   *Sudah ada orang.*
Would you mind if I open
the window?
   bo-*leh(h) sai*-yuh   *Boleh saya*
   boo-kuh *ting*-kahp?   *buka tingkap?*

What's ... station?	*ah*-puh *nah*-muh-nyuh *steh*-sehn ...?	*Apa namanya stesen ...?*
this	*ee*-nee	*ini*
the next	yahng ber-ee-*koot*-nyuh	*yang berikutnya*

Do I need to change trains?
   ah-duh-kah(h) *sai*-yuh   *Adakah saya*
   hah-*roos* ber-*too*-kahr   *harus bertukar*
   ke-reh-tuh-*ah*-pee?   *keretapi?*
You must change at ...
   ahn-dah *hah*-roos   *Anda harus bertukar di ...*
   ber-*too*-kahr dee ...
I want to get off at ...
   sai-yuh nah(k) *too*-roon dee ...   *Saya nak turun di ...*
How long will it be delayed?
   be-*rah*-puh *lahm*-baht-nyuh?   *Berapa lambatnya?*

THEY MAY SAY ...

ke-reh-tuh-*ah*-pee   This/That train is ...
ee-nee/*ee*-too ...

   dee-bah-*tahl*-kahn   cancelled
   lahm-baht   delayed/late
   te-*paht*   on time

TAXI   TEKSI

Taxis in most big cities now operate with meters – if not, it's best to sort out the fare before getting in! Long distance taxis are a convenient way to get around, and still cheap. These taxis take up to four passengers, and will often wait around to find the full number bound for the same destination. You can pay a little more and have the whole vehicle to yourself.

Is this taxi available?
　　tehk-see *ee*-nee *ko*-song-kah(h)?　　*Teksi ini kosongkah?*
Please use the meter.
　　to-long *pah*-kai *mee*-ter　　*Tolong pakai meter.*
How much is the fare?
　　be-*rah*-puh *hahr*-guh
　　per-jah-*lah*-nahn?　　*Berapa harga perjalanan?*

Please take me　　*to*-long *hahn*-tahr　　*Tolong hantar*
to ...　　*sai*-yuh ke ...　　*saya ke ...*
　　this address　　*ah*-lah-maht *ee*-nee　　*alamat ini*
　　the airport　　lah-*pahng*-ahn *ter*-bahng　　*lapangan terbang*

Instructions   Arahan

Here's fine, thanks.
　　ber-*hen*-tee dee
　　see-nee *sah*-juh　　*Berhenti di sini saja.*
The next street, please.
　　jah-lahn ber-ee-*koot*-nyuh　　*Jalan berikutnya.*

FINDING YOUR RELIGION

Be forewarned, the drivers of long distance taxis often drive at high speeds. Malaysian drivers will overtake almost anywhere, and the motto in the cities seems to be 'if there's a space, fill it'. There aren't as many accidents as you might imagine, so just close your eyes and hang on.

The next street (to the left/right).
    jah-lahn (dee se-be-*lah(h)*   *Jalan (di sebelah*
    ki-ree/*kah*-nahn)   *kiri/ kanan)*
    yahng ber-ee-*koot*-nyuh   *yang berikutnya.*

Continue/Straight on!	te-*roos*-kahn!	*Teruskan!*
Please slow down.	per-lah-*hahn*-kahn	*Perlahankan*
	se-*dee*-kit	*sedikit.*
Please hurry.	*to*-long che-*paht*	*Tolong cepat*
	se-*dee*-kit	*sedikit.*
Stop here!	ber-*hen*-tee dee	*Berhenti di sini!*
	see-nee!	
Stop at the corner.	ber-*hen*-tee dee	*Berhenti di*
	soo-dut ee-*too*	*sudut itu.*
Please wait here.	*to*-long *toong*-goo	*Tolong tunggu*
	dee *see*-nee	*di sini.*

I'll be right back.
    sai-yuh *ah*-kahn kem-*bah*-lee   *Saya akan kembali*
    se-ke-*jahp lah*-gee   *sekejap lagi.*

BOAT   BOT/KAPAL

Some isolated areas in Sabah and Sarawak can only be reached by
small river boats. Ferries are commonly used to reach islands off
the coast. Some local operators are lax about observing safety rules;
if you think a boat is overloaded or otherwise unsafe, don't board
it. Speedboat ferries are faster but the journey can be rough.

THEY MAY SAY ...

soo-dah(h) pe-*nu(h)*
It's full.

tah(k) *ah*-duh ke-*roo*-see *lah*-gee
There aren't any seats.

eh-so(k) *ah*-duh *ko*-song/tem-*paht* doo-du(k)
There are seats for tomorrow.

GETTING AROUND

boat	bot/ *kah*-pahl/ *sahm*-pahn	bot/kapal/ sampan
cabin	*bee*-li(k)	bilik
dock	*jeh*-tee	jeti
harbour/port	pe-lah-*boo*-hahn	pelabuhan
river	*soo*-ngai	sungai
sail	*lai*-yahr	layar
sea	lowt	laut

Where does the boat leave from?
    kah-pahl *ee*-too
    ber-*ahng*-kaht dee *mah*-nuh?
    Kapal itu
    berangkat di mana?

What time does the boat arrive at ...?
    poo-kool be-*rah*-puh
    kah-pahl *ee*-too *tee*-buh dee ...?
    Pukul berapa
    kapal itu tiba di ...?

CAR   KERETA

Car hire is possible throughout Malaysia; you can also hire a driver, although this is much more expensive. Most petrol stations are self-service. Look for a *layanan-penuh*, lai-*yah*-nahn-pe-*nu(h)*, sign if you want your car filled for you.

Where can I hire a car?
    dee *mah*-nuh *sai*-yuh
    bo-*leh(h)* men-*yeh*-wuh
    ke-*reh*-tuh?
    Di mana saya
    boleh menyewa
    kereta?

How much is it daily/weekly?
    be-rah-*puh*-kah(h) *hahr*-guh
    seh-*wah*-nyuh *oon*-tu(k)
    se-*hah*-ree/se-*ming*-goo?
    Berapakah harga
    sewanya untuk
    sehari/seminggu?

Does that include insurance?
    ah-duh-kah(h) *hahr*-guh-nyuh
    ter-*mah*-su(k) in-soo-*rahns*-kah(h)?
    Adakah harganya
    termasuk insuranskah?

Can we get a driver?
    bo-*leh(h)*-kah(h) *kah*-mee
    men-*dah*-paht pe-*mahn*-doo?
    Bolehkah kami
    mendapat pemandu?

Where's the next petrol station?
steh-sehn *min*-yah(k)
ber-ee-*koot*-nyuh dee *mah*-nuh? | *Stesen minyak berikutnya di mana?*

I want ... litres of petrol.
sai-yuh nah(k) ...
lee-ter *min*-yah(k) | *Saya nak ... liter minyak.*

Please fill up the tank.
to-long pe-*nu(h)*-kahn
tahng-kee | *Tolong penuhkan tangki.*

Please check the ...	*to*-long pe-*rik*-suh ...	*Tolong periksa ...*
oil	*min*-yahk *hee*-tahm	*minyak hitam*
tyre pressure	te-*kah*-an *tai*-yahr	*tekanan tayar*
water	air	*air*

Is this the road to ...?
ee-*nee*-kah(h) *jah*-lahn ke ...? | *Inikah jalan ke ...?*

Can I park here?
bo-*leh(h)* *leh*-tah(k)
ke-*reh*-tuh dee *see*-nee? | *Boleh letak kereta di sini?*

How much does it cost to park here?
be-*rah*-puh *hahr*-guh
me-*leh*-tah(k) ke-*reh*-tuh
dee *see*-nee? | *Berapa harga meletak kereta di sini?*

ROAD SIGNS

BERI JALAN	GIVE WAY
DILARANG ...	NO ...
MASUK	ENTRY
LETAK KERETA	PARKING
JALAN TOL	TOLLWAY
KERJA RAYA	ROADWORKS
SEHALA	ONE WAY
TEMPAT	CAR PARK

air	oo-*dah*-ruh	*udara*
automatic	oh-toh-*mah*-tik	*otomatik*
battery	bah-*te*-ree	*bateri*
brakes	brehk	*brek*
car	ke-*reh*-tuh	*kereta*
clutch	klahch	*klac*
driver	pe-*mahn*-doo	*pemandu*
drivers licence	*leh*-sen me-*mahn*-doo	*lesen memandu*
engine	*ehn*-jin	*enjin*
garage	*gah*-rahj	*garaj*
horn	hon	*hon*
indicator	pe-*noon*-joo(k)	*penunjuk*
lights	*lahm*-poo	*lampu*
main road	*jah*-lahn *rai*-yuh/ oo-*tah*-muh	*jalan raya/utama*
oil	*min*-yah(k) *hee*-tahm	*minyak hitam*
petrol (gas)	*min*-yah(k)/*peh*-trol	*minyak/petrol*
diesel	*dee*-sel	*disel*
premium	pre-*mee*-um *tahm*-puh	*premium tanpa*
unleaded	*ploom*-boom	*plumbum*
unleaded	*tahm*-puh	*tanpa*
	ploom-boom	*plumbum*
puncture	ke-bo-*cho*-rahn	*kebocoran*
radiator	rah-dee-*ah*-tor	*radiator*
roadmap	*peh*-tuh *jah*-lahn	*peta jalan*
seatbelt	*tah*-lee *ping*-gahng	*tali pinggang*
	ke-*reh*-dahr	*keledar*
self-service	*lai*-yahn *dir*-ree	*layan diri*
speed limit	hahd *lah*-joo	*had laju*
tyres	*tai*-yahr	*tayar*
windscreen	*kah*-chuh de-*pahm*	*kaca depan*
distance	*jah*-rah(k)	*jarak*
length of time	*lah*-muh	*lama*

Car Problems

We need a mechanic.
**kah-mee me-mer-loo-kahn
me-ka-nik**

What make is it?
**ke-reh-tuh je-nis
ah-puh ee-nee?**

Our car broke down at ...
**ke-reh-tuh kah-mee
ro-sah(k) dee ...**

The car isn't working.
ke-reh-tuh ee-nee ro-sah(k)

The engine's dead.
ehn-jin mah-tee

The engine is overheating.
ehn-jin ter-lah-loo pah-nahs

I've run out of petrol
min-yah(k) soo-dah(h) hah-bees

Masalah Kereta

*Kami memerlukan
mekanik.*

*Kereta jenis
apa ini?*

*Kereta kami
rosak di ...*

Kereta ini rosak.

Enjin mati.

Enjin terlalu panas.

Minyak sudah habis.

A COUNTRY MILE ...

With traffic jams in bigger cities, confusing signs in smaller towns, and some poor maintenance on out-of-the-way roads, you might be better off asking 'how long' rather than 'how far' your destination is!

How long (time/distance)
is the journey?
**be-rah-puh (lah-muh/jow(h))
ber-jah-lah-nahn ee-nee?**
*Berapa (lama/jauh)
perjalanan ini?*

It's 50km away.
**jah-rah(k)-nyah lee-mah
poo-lu(h) ki-lo-mee-ter**
*Jaraknya lima
puluh kilometer.*

The trip takes two hours.
**per-jah-lah-nahn ee-nee
me-ngahm-bil doo-uh jahm**
*Perjalanan ini
mengambil dua jam.*

The battery's flat.
    bah-*ter*-ee *ee*-nee *mah*-tee

Bateri ini mati.

The radiator's leaking.
    rah-dee-*ah*-tor *bo*-chor

Radiator bocor.

I have a flat tyre.
    tai-yahr-nyuh *kem*-pis

Tayarnya kempis.

I've lost my car keys.
    koon-chee ke-*reh*-tuh
    sai-yuh *hee*-lahng

*Kunci kereta
saya hilang.*

BICYCLE   BASIKAL

Bike hire is becoming popular throughout the region and is a great way to get around resort areas. Serious cyclists will need to buy or bring their own bikes.

Where can I hire a bicycle?
    dee *mah*-nuh *sai*-yuh bo-*leh*(h)
    me-*nyeh*-wuh bah-*see*-kahl?

*Di mana saya boleh
menyewa basikal?*

I have a flat tyre.
    tai-yahr *sai*-yuh *kem*-pis

Tayar saya kempis.

How much is it ...?	be-*rah*-puh *hahr*-guh-nyuh ...?	*Berapa harganya ...?*
per hour	*oon*-tu(k) se-*jahm*	*untuk sejam*
until (3 o'clock)	*sahm*-pai (*poo*-kool *tee*-guh)	*sampai (pukul tiga)*
the day	*oon*-tu(k) se-*hah*-ree	*untuk sehari*

bike	bah-*see*-kahl	*basikal*
brakes	brayk	*brek*
to cycle	ber-bah-*see*-kahl	*berbasikal*
gears	*gee*-gee	*gigi*
handlebars	*gah*-gahng bah-*see*-kahl	*gagang basikal*
helmet	*to*-pee ke-*leh*-dahr	*topi keledar*
inner tube	*tee*-oob dah-*lah*-mahn	tiub dalaman
lights	*lahm*-poo	*lampu*
lock	*koon*-chee	*kunci*
pump	pahm	*pam*
puncture	ke-bo-*cho*-rahn	*kebocoran*
saddle	ke-*roo*-see	*kerusi*
wheel	*ro*-duh	*roda*

LOCAL TRANSPORT   KENDARAAN TEMPATAN

Beca, *beh*-chuh, bicycle-rickshaws, used to be found in many towns and cities across the nation, but these days they are only common in some northern towns.

Wait!	toong-*goo*!	*Tunggu!*
I want to get off!	*sai*-yuh nah(k) *too*-roon!	*Saya nak turun!*
Careful!	ber-*hah*-ti-*hah*-ti see-kit!	*Berhati-hati sikit!*
Danger!	bah-*hai*-yuh!	*Bahaya!*
Stop!	ber-*hen*-tee!	*Berhenti!*

BABY YOU CAN GUARD MY CAR

When you park on the streets in larger towns and cities, you may be helped into your parking space by a smiling character, madly waving his arms. He is a *jaga kereta* boy, *jah*-guh ke-*reh*-tuh (lit: guard car). Although some cities have tried to eradicate this freelance job, it is best to give him a small amount of money, one or two *ringgit*, for helping you. You can pay up before leaving the car, or say 'Guard my car well', *Jaga kereta saya baik-baik*, *jah*-guh ke-*reh*-tuh *sai*-yuh bai(k)-bai(k), and pay when you come back.

ACCOMMODATION
PENGINAPAN

Accommodation choices in Malaysia run from cheap as chips to very expensive, from no-frills *rumah tumpangan*, roo-mah(h) toom-*pahng*-ahn, to government-run 'rest houses', *rumah rihat*, roo-mah(h) ree-haht, to 5-star hotels. Guest houses, which can be little huts or dorm-like accommodation, are available at beach centres and in major tourist cities. Homestays are still possible in some towns.

FINDING ACCOMMODATION
MENCARI PENGINAPAN

I'm looking for a ...	*sai*-yuh men-*chah*-ree ...	*Saya mencari ...*
camping ground	tem-*paht*	*tempat*
	per-kheh-*mah*-hahn	*perkhemahan*
guesthouse	*roo*-mah(h) te-*tah*-moo	*rumah tetamu*
upmarket hotel	ho-tehl *meh*-wah(h)	*hotel mewah*
Where's a ... hotel?	ho-tehl yahng ...	*Hotel yang ...*
	dee *mah*-nuh?	*di mana?*
cheap	ter-moo-*rah*	*termurah*
clean	*ber*-si(h)	*bersih*
good	bah-*gus*	*bagus*
nearby	de-*kaht*	*dekat*

I've already found a hotel.
   sai-yuh *soo*-dah(h) *joom*-puh
   se-*boo*-ah(h) ho-tehl

Saya sudah jumpa
sebuah hotel.

Please take me to the ... hotel.
   to-long *hahn*-tahr
   sai-yuh ke ho-tehl ...

Tolong hantar
saya ke hotel ...

ACCOMMODATION

What's the address?
ah-puh-kah(h) *ah*-lah-maht-nyuh? *Apakah alamatnya?*

Could you write down the
address, please?
to-long too-*lis*-kahn *Tolong tuliskan*
ah-lah-*maht* ee-too *alamat itu?*

The hotel is near	*ho*-tehl-nyuh	*Hotelnya dekat ...*
the ...	de-*kaht* ...	
alley	lo-*rong*	*lorong*
beach	*pahn*-tai	*pantai*
shop	ke-*dai*	*kedai*
street	*jah*-lahn	*jalan*
town square	*dah*-tah-rahn	*dataran*

BOOKING AHEAD MEMBUAT TEMPAHAN

Can I book a room?		
bo-*leh(h)* mem-*boo*-aht		*Boleh membuat*
tem-*pah*-hahn *bee*-li(k)?		*tempahan bilik?*

My name's ...
nah-muh *sai*-yuh ... *Nama saya ...*

For (three) nights.
se-*lah*-muh *(tee*-guh) mah-lahm *Selama (tiga) malam.*

How much for ...?	be-*rah*-puh	*Berapa*
	hahr-gah-nyuh ...?	*harganya ...?*
one night	*oon*-tu(k) *sah*-too	*untuk satu*
	mah-lahm	*malam*
a week	*oon*-tu(k)	*untuk*
	se-*ming*-goo	*seminggu*
two people	*oon*-tu(k) *doo*-uh	*untuk dua*
	o-rahng	*orang*

I'll/We'll be	*sai*-yuh/ *kah*-mee	*Saya/Kami*
arriving ...	ah-*kahm* tee-buh ...	*akan tiba ...*
on the (3rd)	*pah*-duh (*tee*-guh	*pada (tiga*
	hah-ree-*bu*-lahn)	*haribulan)*
later tonight	*mah*-lahm ee-nee	*malam ini*
	nahm-tee	*nanti*

CHECKING IN   MENDAFTARKAN DIRI

No matter how long you're staying, you may be able to arrange a *diskaun*, dis-**kown**, 'discount'. An easy way to get cheaper room rates is to exclaim *Mahalnya!*, mah-*hal*-nyuh!, 'So expensive!' in mock horror, and act like you're going elsewhere. See what offer comes up then, but be sure you look at the room before you decide to take it.

I'd like a room for ...	*sai*-yuh men-*chah*-ree *bee*-li(k) *oon*-tu(k) ...	*Saya mencari bilik untuk ...*
one person	se-*o*-rahng	*seorang*
two people	*doo*-uh *o*-rahng	*dua orang*
I'd like a room with a ...	*sai*-yuh men-*chah*-ree *bee*-li(k) yahng mem-*poon*-yah-ee ...	*Saya mencari bilik yang mempunyai ...*
bathroom	*bee*-li(k) air	*bilik air*
fan	*kee*-pahs	*kipas*
shower	tem-*paht mahn*-dee	*tempat mandi*
TV	tee vee	*TV*
window	*ting*-kahp	*tingkap*
I'm going to stay for (one) ...	*sai*-yuh ah-*kahn* ber-*mah*-lahm se-*lah*-muh (*sah*-too) ...	*Saya akan bermalam selama (satu) ...*
day	*hah*-ree	*hari*
week	*ming*-goo	*minggu*

I'd like to share a dorm.

    sai-yuh nah(k) ber-*kong*-see   *Saya nak berkongsi*
    bee-li(k) *hos*-tehl   *bilik hostel.*

Is there a room available?

    ah-duh *bee*-li(k) yahng *ko*-song?   *Ada bilik yang kosong?*

Can I see the room?

    bo-*leh*(h) *sai*-yuh me-*lee*-haht   *Boleh saya melihat*
    bee-li(k) *ee*-too?   *bilik itu?*

ACCOMMODATION

Is there a discount for ...?
*ah-**duh** **dis**-kown **oon**-tu(k) ...?*
Ada diskaun untuk ...?

    children
    *ah-**nah**(k)*
    anak

    students
    *pe-**lah**-jahr*
    pelajar

I'm not sure how long I'm staying.
*sai-yuh be-**lum** tah-hoo be-rah-puh la-muh sai-yuh ah-kahn ber-**mah**-lahm dee **see**-nee*
Saya belum tahu berapa lama saya akan bermalam di sini.

I (don't) like this room.
*sai-yuh (tah(k)) **soo**-kuh **bee**-li(k) **ee**-nee*
Saya (tak) suka bilik ini.

Do you have a better room?
*ah-**duh** **bee**-li(k) yahng le-**bi**(h) bai(k)?*
Ada bilik yang lebih baik?

Do you have a room with ..?
*ah-**duh** tah(k) **bee**-li(k) yahng ah-**duh** ...?*
Ada tak bilik yang ada ...?

    two beds
    *doo-uh **kah**-til*
    dua katil

    a double bed
    ***kah**-til be-sahr*
    katil besar

Where's the bathroom?
***bee**-li(k) **mahn**-dee dee **mah**-nuh?*
Bilik mandi di mana?

Is there hot water all day?
*ah-**duh**-kah(h) air **pah**-nahs se-**pah**-jahng **hah**-ree?*
Adakah air panas sepanjang hari?

Is breakfast included?
***mah**-kahn **pah**-gee ter-**mah**-su(k)-kah(h)?*
Makan pagi termasukkah?

This room's fine.
***bee**-li(k) **ee**-nee se-swai*
Bilik ini sesuai.

Paying

Pembayaran

How much does it cost per day?
  be-*rah*-puh *hahr*-guh-nyuh
  oon-tu(k) se-*hah*-ree?

*Berapa harganya
untuk sehari?*

What's the daily rate?
  be-*rah*-puh *hahr*-guh
  hah-ree-*ahm*-nyuh?

*Berapa harga
hariannya?*

Does the price include breakfast/tax?
  hahr-guh-nyuh ter-*mah*-su(k)
  sah-rah-pahn-kah(h)/
  choo-kai-kah(h)?

*Harganya termasuk
sarapankah/
cukaikah?*

Do you allow children?
  bo-*leh(h) sai*-yuh
  bah-wah *ah*-nah(k)?

*Boleh saya
bawa anak?*

Is there an extra charge for children?
  ah-duh *hahr*-guh tahm-*bah*-hahn
  oon-tu(k) *ah*-nah(k)?

*Ada harga tambahan
untuk anak?*

Can I pay by ...?   bo-*leh(h) bai*-yahr
              de-*ngahn* ...?

*Boleh bayar
dengan ...?*

credit card	kahd *kreh*-dit	*kad kredit*
travellers cheque	chehk	*cek pelancong*
	pe-*lahn*-chong	

ACCOMMODATION

THEY MAY SAY ...

soo-dah(h) pe-*nu(h)*	We're full.
be-*rah*-puh *lah*-muh?	For how long?
be-*rah*-puh
mah-lahm/o-rahng?	How many
nights/people?
ter-*mah*-su(k)
teh(h)/*ko*-pee	It includes
tea/coffee.
bai-*yahr doo*-loo	Please pay now.
bai-*yahr* ke-*moo*-dee-ahn	Pay later.

REQUESTS & COMPLAINTS

PERMINTAAN & ADUAN

Do you have a safe where I can leave my valuables?
ah-duh pe-*tee* keh-bahl
oon-tu(k) men-*yim*-pahn
bah-rahng ber-*hahr*-guh?

Ada peti kebal
untuk menyimpan
barang berharga?

Could I have a receipt for them?
ah-duh *reh*-seet
oon-tu(k) me-*reh*-kuh?

Ada resit untuk mereka?

Where can I wash my clothes?
dee *mah*-nuh *sai*-yuh
bo-*leh*(h) men-*choo*-chee
pah-kai-ahn?

Di mana saya
boleh mencuci
pakaian?

Do you have a laundry service?
ah-duh *ser*-vis *choo*-chee
pah-kai-ahn?

Ada servis cuci
pakaian?

When will they be ready?
bee-luh *see*-ahp?

Bila siap?

Can I use the telephone?
bo-*leh*(h) *pah*-kai
teh-*leh*-fon tah(k)?

Boleh pakai telefon tak?

There are mosquitoes.
ah-duh *nyah*-mu(k)-lah(h)

Ada nyamuklah.

Do you have (a) ...?	*ah*-duh ...?	*Ada ...?*
insect repellant	*oo*-baht *nyah*-mu(k)	*ubat nyamuk*
mosquito net	ke-*lahm*-boo	*kelambu*

I need another ...	*sai*-yuh me-mer-*loo*-kahn *lah*-gee sah-too ...	*Saya memerlukan lagi satu ...*
blanket	se-*lee*-moot	*selimut*
pillow	*bahn*-tahl	*bantal*
pillowcase	sah-*rong bahn*-tahl	*sarung bantal*
sheet	*chah*-dahr	*cadar*
towel	too-*ah*-lah	*tuala*

Please change it/them.
to-long *too*-kahr-kahn *ee*-nee   *Tolong tukarkan ini.*

Please clean my room.
to-long *ber*-si(h)-kahn   *Tolong bersihkan*
bee-li(k) *sai*-yuh   *bilik saya.*

Excuse me, I have a problem.
mah-*ahf, ah*-duh mah-*sah*-lah(h)   *Maaf, ada masalah.*

The (window) is broken.
(ting-kahp) *ee*-too ro-*sah(k)*   *(Tingkap) itu rosak.*

I can't open/	*sai*-yuh tah(k) bo-*leh(h)*	*Saya tak boleh*
close the ...	*boo*-kuh/too-*tup* ...	*buka/tutup* ...
door	*peen*-too	*pintu*
window	ting-*kahp*	*tingkap*

I can't lock the door.
sai-yuh *tee*-dah(k)   *Saya tidak*
bo-*leh(h)* koon-chee *pin*-too   *boleh kunci pintu.*

I've locked myself out.
koon-chee *sai*-yuh   *Kunci saya*
ter-*ting*-gahl *dah*-lahm *bee*-li(k)   *tertinggal dalam bilik.*

Can you get it fixed?
bo-*leh(h) bai*-kee tah(k)?   *Boleh baiki tak?*

The room is	*bee*-li(k) *ee*-nee	*Bilik ini*
too ...	ter-*lah*-loo ...	*terlalu* ...
cold	se-*joo(k)*	*sejuk*
dark	ge-*lahp*	*gelap*
hot	*pah*-nahs	*panas*
noisy	bee-*sing*	*bising*
smelly	boo-*soo(k)*	*busuk*

ACCOMMODATION

candle	*li*-leen	*lilin*
chair	ke-*roo*-see	*kerusi*
door	*pin*-too	*pintu*
electricity	eh-*lehk*-trik	*elektrik*
key	*koon*-chee	*kunci*
lamp	*lahm*-poo	*lampu*
lock	*koon*-chee	*kunci*
mattress	tee-*lahm*	*tilam*
mosquito coil	*oo*-baht *nyah*-mu(k)	*ubat nyamuk*
quiet	sen-*yahp*	*senyap*
roof	*ah*-tahp; *boom*-boong	*atap; bumbung*
soap	*sah*-bon	*sabun*
toilet paper	*ti*-soo; *ti*-soo *tahn*-dahs	*tisu; tisu tandas*
towel	*twah*-lah	*tuala*
to wake	*bah*-ngoon	*bangun*
wardrobe	ahl-*mah*-ree	*almari*
... water	air ...	*air ...*
drinking	*mee*-num	*minum*
hot	*pah*-nahs	*panas*

TIME AFTER TIME

Malaysians divide up their day this way:

> morning (from dawn until noon)
> *pah*-gee   *pagi*

> midday (from noon until about three o'clock)
> te-ngah-*hah*-ree   *tengahari*

> afternoon/evening (from about three o'clock until sunset)
> pe-*tahng*   *petang*

> night (from sunset until dawn)
> *mah*-lahm   *malam*

CHECKING OUT   MENINGGALKAN HOTEL

I'm leaving today.
   sai-yuh ber-*ahng*-kaht
   hah-ree *ee*-nee   *Saya berangkat hari ini.*

Please prepare my/our bill.
   to-long se-*dee*-ah-kahn   *Tolong sediakan*
   bil *sai*-yuh/*kah*-mee   *bil saya/kami.*

There's a mistake in the bill.
   bil *ee*-nee *sah*-lah(h)   *Bil ini salah.*

Please call me a taxi.
   to-long *pahng*-gil-kahn tehk-see   *Tolong panggilkan teksi.*

Can I leave my	bo-*leh(h)* tah(k)	*Boleh tak*
things here	*sai*-yuh sim-pahn	*saya simpan*
until ...?	*bah*-rahng dee	*barang di*
	see-nee *sahm*-pai ...?	*sini sampai ...?*
this afternoon	te-ngah-*hah*-ree/	*tengahari/*
	pe-*tahng ee*-nee	*petang ini*
this evening	pe-*tahng ee*-nee	*petang ini*
tonight	*mah*-lahm	*malam*

LONGER STAYS   PENGINAPAN JANGKA PANJANG

Some guesthouses offer cheaper rates for longer stays. Also look into homestays, available in Kota Baru, Kuala Lumpur and Johor Baru.

to rent   me-*nyeh*-wuh   *menyewa*

Is there a room available?
   ah-duh *bee*-li(k) *ko*-song?   *Ada bilik kosong?*

I'm looking for a room near the beach/city-centre.
   sai-yuh *chah*-ree *bee*-li(k)   *Saya cari bilik*
   de-*kaht pan*-tai/   *dekat pantai/*
   poo-saht *bahn*-dahr   *pusat bandar.*

I want to rent a room/house for
(three) months.

    sai-yuh nah(k) me-*nyeh*-wuh   *Saya nak menyewa*
    bee-li(k)/*roo*-mah(h)   *bilik/rumah*
    se-*lah*-muh *(tee*-guh) *bu*-lahn *selama (tiga) bulan.*

How much per month?

    be-*rah*-puh *hahr*-guh-nyuh   *Berapa harganya*
    oon-tu(k) se-*bu*-lahn?   *untuk sebulan?*

DI BANDAR   AROUND TOWN

The atmosphere on the streets of Malaysia is action-packed. People are out and about from early morning long into the night. Shops are usually open until 9 or 10pm, restaurants much later, and roadside stalls later still. Night markets, *pasar malam*, **pah**-**sahr** *mah*-**lahm**, are a must for the visitor who wants a taste of the Malaysian way of life.

LOOKING FOR ...   MENCARI ...

How far is a/an/ the ...?	be-*rah*-puh jow(h) ...?	*Berapa jauh ...?*
I'm going to a/an/ the ...	*sai*-yuh *per*-gee ke ...	*Saya pergi ke ...*
I'm looking for a/an/the ...	*sai*-yuh men-*chah*-ree ...	*Saya mencari ...*

bank	bank	*bank*
barber shop	ke-*dai goon*-ting *rahm*-boot	*kedai gunting rambut*
consulate	*kon*-soo-laht	*konsulat*
crossroad	*sim*-pahng em-*paht*	*simpang empat*
embassy	ke-*doo*-tah-ahn be-*sahr*	*kedutaan besar*
hairdresser; hair salon	sa-*lon*; ke-*dai goon*-ting *rahm*-boot	*salon; kedai gunting rambut*
hospital	*hos*-pee-tahl	*hospital*
hotel	ho-*tehl*	*hotel*
money changer	tem-*paht* pe-*noo*-kahr-ahn wahng	*tempat penukaran wang*
museum	moo-*zee*-um	*muzium*
police station	*bah*-lai *po*-lis	*balai polis*
post office	pe-*jah*-baht pos	*pejabat pos*
public telephone	teh-*leh*-fon *ah*-wahm	*telefon awam*
public toilet	*tahm*-duhs *ah*-wahm	*tandas awam*
restaurant	*res*-to-rahn	*restoran*
school	se-*ko*-lah(h)	*sekolah*
temple	*chan*-dee/*poo*-rah	*candi/pura*
town square	dah-*tah*-rahn	*dataran*
traditional market	*pah*-sahr	*pasar*
village	*kahm*-pong	*kampong*
zoo	zoo	*zoo*

What time does it open/close?

poo-kool be-*rah*-puh *boo*-kuh/too-*tup*	*Pukul berapa buka/tutup?*

Is it still open?

boo-kuh *lah*-gee tah(k)?	*Buka lagi tak?*

AT THE BANK

DI BANK

All tourist areas and large towns have money changers as well as banks. Money changers, *tempat penukaran wang*, **tem-*paht* pe-*noo*-kahr-ahn wahng**, usually have longer opening hours and exchange rates are generally better than banks. Hotels and some department stores will also change money for you, but the rates aren't as good.

Can I exchange money here?
   bo-*leh(h)* *too*-kahr wahng
   dee *see*-nee?

Boleh tukar wang di sini?

Can I use my credit card to withdraw money?
   bo-*leh(h)* *sai*-yuh
   meng-*goo*-nah-kahn kahd
   kreh-dit *oon*-tu(k)
   me-nge-*loo*-ahr-kahn *doo*-it?

Boleh saya menggunakan kad kredit untuk mengeluarkan duit?

Please write it down.
   to-long *too*-lis-kahn

Tolong tuliskan.

Can I have smaller notes?
   ah-duh *doo*-it ke-*chil* tah(k)?

Ada duit kecil tak?

The ATM swallowed my card.
   kahd *sai*-yuh dee-*teh*-lahn
   ay tee em

Kad saya ditelan ATM.

Where can I cash a travellers cheque?
   dee *mah*-nuh *sai*-yuh bo-*leh(h)*
   me-*noo*-kahr-kahn chehk
   kem-*bah*-ruh *ee*-nee ke-*pah*-duh
   wahng *too*-nai?

Di mana saya boleh menukarkan cek kembara ini kepada wang tunai?

I want to change ...	*sai*-yuh nah(k) me-*noo*-kahr-kahn ...	*Saya nak menukarkan ...*
Australian dollars	*do*-lahr os-*trah*-lee-ah	*dolar Australia*
cash	wahng *too*-nai	*wang tunai*
Pounds Sterling	paun stuh-*ling*	*Pounds Stirling*
travellers cheques	chehk kem-*bah*-ruh	*cek kembara*
US dollars	*do*-lahr ah-*mehr*-ree-kah	*dolar Amerika*

What's the exchange rate?
ah-puh-kah(h) *kah*-dahr
pe-*noo*-kahr-ahn?

Apakah kadar penukaran?

Has any money arrived for me?
ah-duh-kah(h) *hahn*-tahr-ahn
wahng *oon*-tu(k) *sai*-yuh?

Adakah hantaran wang untuk saya?

Can I transfer money
from my bank to here?
bo-*leh*(h)-kah(h) bank
sai-yuh meng-*hahn*-tahr
doo-it ke bank *ee*-nee?

Bolehkah bank saya menghantar duit ke bank ini?

How long will it take?
be-*rah*-puh *lah*-muh?

Berapa lama?

Do I have to pay commission?
ah-duh-kah(h) ko-*mi*-shen
per-*loo* dee-*bai*-yahr?

Adakah komisyen perlu dibayar?

branch	chah-*wah*-gahn	*cawangan*
cash	wahng *too*-nai	*wang tunai*
cashier	joo-roo-wahng	*juruwang*
cashier's window	*ting*-kahp	*tingkap*
	joo-roo-wahng	*juruwang*
cheque	chehk	*cek*
coins	*doo*-it *shi*-ling	*duit syiling*
commission	ko-*mi*-shen	*komisyen*
credit card	kahd *kreh*-dit	*kad kredit*
ID card	kahd pe-nge-*nah*-lahn	*kad pengenalan*
main office	*ee*-boo pe-*jah*-baht	*ibu pejabat*
letter of credit	soo-*raht kreh*-dit	*surat kredit*
manager	pe-*ngoo*-rus	*pengurus*
money	wahng/*doo*-it	*wang/duit*
money order	wahng *ki*-ree-mahn	*wang kiriman*
note (bill)	*doo*-it *ker*-tahs	*duit kertas*
signature	*tahn*-duh *tah*-ngahn	*tanda tangan*
teller	*teh*-ler	*teler*

AT THE POST OFFICE   DI PEJABAT POS

Post offices, *pejabat pos*, pe-*jah*-baht pos, with their bright red facades, can be found in all towns.

I want to buy ...	*sai*-yuh nah(k) mem-be-*lee* ...	*Saya nak membeli ...*
envelopes	*sahm*-pul soo-*raht*	*sampul surat*
postcards	*pos*-kahd	*poskad*
stamps	se-*tehm*	*setem*

I want to send a/an ...	*sai*-yuh nah(k) meng-*hahn*-tahr ...	*Saya nak menghantar ...*
aerogram	*ehr*-o-gram	*aerogram*
letter	soo-*raht*	*surat*
parcel	*boong*-koo-sahn	*bungkusan*
telegram	*teh*-le-gram	*telegram*

Please send it (by) ... mail.	to-long *hahn*-tahr de-*ngahn* ...	*Tolong hantar dengan ...*
air	mehl oo-*dah*-ruh	*mel udara*
express	pos *lah*-joo	*pos laju*
registered	soo-*raht* ber-*dahf*-tahr	*surat berdaftar*
surface	pos bee-*ah*-suh	*pos biasa*

AROUND TOWN

How much does it cost
to send this to ...?
   be-*rah*-puh *hahr*-guh
   peng-hahn-*tah*-rahn *ee*-nee ke ...?

*Berapa harga
penghantaran ini ke ...?*

How much is an airmail letter
to (the US)?
   be-*rah*-puh ki-*ree*-mahn
   soo-*raht* pos oo-*dah*-ruh ke
   (ah-*mehr*-ee-kah)?

*Berapa kiriman
surat pos udara ke
(Amerika)?*

Please send this parcel to ...
by surface mail.

    to-long *ki*-reem-kahn
    boong-koo-sahn *ee*-nee ke ...
    de-*ngahn* pos bee-*ah*-suh

*Tolong kirimkan
bungkusan ini ke ...
dengan pos biasa.*

Please weigh this letter.

    to-long *tim*-bahng
    soo-*raht* *ee*-nee

*Tolong timbang
surat ini.*

glue	gahm	*gam*
mailbox	pe-*tee* soo-*raht*	*peti surat*
pen	pen	*pen*
postcode	*pos*-kod	*poskod*
receiver	pe-ner-*ree*-muh	*penerima*
sender	pen-*gee*-rim	*pengirim*
string	*tah*-lee	*tali*

AROUND TOWN

SIGNS

AWAS	CAUTION
BAHAYA	DANGER
BERHENTI	STOP
BUKA	OPEN
DILARANG ...	NO ...
MASUK	ENTRY
MEROKOK	SMOKING
DINGIN	COLD
HALAL	ALLOWED FOR MUSLIM CONSUMPTION
KELUAR	EXIT
LELAKI	MEN
MASUK	ENTRANCE
PANAS	HOT
TANDAS	TOILETS
TARIK	PULL
TOLAK	PUSH
TUTUP	CLOSED

TELECOMMUNICATIONS   TELEKOMUNIKASI

Making domestic telephone calls in Malaysia is easy. You can
direct-dial local and long-distance calls using coins and there are
card telephones operated by Telecom Malaysia and Uniphone.
The cards are widely available at small shops, 7-Eleven stores, post
offices and newsagents. Calling Singapore is not considered an
international call. All operators speak English, although you may
need to speak slowly.

Could I please use the telephone?
   bo-*leh*(h) *pah*-kai teh-*leh*-fon?   *Boleh pakai telefon?*
What's the area code for ...?
   kod kah-*wah*-sahn teh-*leh*-fon   *Kod kawasan telefon*
   ... be-*rah*-puh?   *... berapa?*
I want to call ...
   sai-yuh nah(k) me-neh-*leh*-fon ...   *Saya nak menelefon ...*
The number is ...
   nom-bor-nyuh ee-*ah*-lah(h) ...   *Nombornya ialah ...*
I want to speak for (three) minutes.
   sai-yuh nah(k) ber-*chah*-kahp   *Saya nak bercakap selama*
   se-*lah*-muh *(tee*-guh) *mi*-nit   *(tiga) minit.*
How much is a
(three)-minute call to ...?
   be-*rah*-puh *ring*-git   *Berapa ringgit panggilan*
   pang-*gil*-ahn *(tee*-guh)   *(tiga) minit ke ...?*
   mi-nit ke ...?
I want to make a
reverse-charge phone call.
   sai-yuh nah(k) me-neh-*leh*-fon   *Saya nak menelefon*
   poong-*oo*-tahn   *pungutan.*
When's a cheap time to call?
   poo-kool be-*rah*-puh *mah*-suh   *Pukul berapa masa*
   moo-rah(h) *oon*-tu(k)   *murah untuk*
   meng-*goo*-nuh-kahn   *menggunakan telefon?*
   teh-*leh*-fon?

AROUND TOWN

Operator, I've been cut off.
  o-pe-*ray*-tor, pang-*gil*-ahn
  sai-yuh ter-*poo*-toos

Operator, panggilan saya terputus.

The line is busy.
  tah-lee-ahn *ee*-too *see*-bu(k)/ehn-*gehj*

Talian itu sibuk/engage.

Sorry, you've got the wrong number.
  mah-*ahf* sah-*lah(h)* *nom*-bor

Maaf, salah nombor.

Hello, do you speak English?
  heh-lo bo-*leh(h)* *chah*-kahp
  bah-*hah*-suh *ing*-ge-ris?

Helo, boleh cakap bahasa Inggeris?

Making a Call

Membuat Panggilan

Hello.
  heh-lo

Helo.

May I speak to ...?
  bo-*leh(h)* *sai*-yuh
  ber-*chah*-kahp de-*ngahn* ...?

Boleh saya bercakap dengan ...?

Who's calling?
  see-*ah*-puh nee?

Siapa ni?

This is ... speaking.
  ee-nee ...

Ini ...

Yes, she's/he's here.
  yah *dee*-uh *ah*-duh dee *see*-nee

Ya, dia ada di sini.

One moment, please.
  toong-goo se-ke-*jahp*

Tunggu sekejap.

I'm sorry, they're not here.
  mah-*ahf* me-*reh*-kah tah(k)
  ah-duh dee *see*-nee

Maaf, mereka tak ada di sini.

What time will she/he be back?
   poo-kool be-*rah*-puh *dee*-uh
   poo-*lahng*?   *Pukul berapa dia pulang?*

Can I leave a message?
   bo-*leh(h)* *ting*-gahl-kahn
   pe-*sah*-nahn?   *Boleh tinggalkan*
                                pesanan?

Please tell him/her I called.
   to-long be-ree-*ta*-hoo *dee*-uh
   sai-yuh teh-*leh*-fon   *Tolong beritahu dia saya*
                                telefon.

I'll call back later.
   sai-yuh teh-*leh*-fon
   ke-*moo*-dee-ahn   *Saya telefon kemudian.*

operator	o-pe-*ray*-tor	*operator*
phone book	*boo*-koo teh-*leh*-fon	*buku telefon*
phone box	teh-*leh*-fon *ah*-wahm	*telefon awam*
phone call	pahng-*gil*-ahn teh-*leh*-fon	*panggilan telefon*
phonecard	kad teh-*leh*-fon	*kad telefon*
reverse charges	*poong*-oo-tahn	*pungutan*
telephone	teh-*leh*-fon	*telefon*
to telephone	me-neh-*leh*-fon	*menelefon*
urgent call	pahng-*gil*-ahn *pen*-ting	*panggilan penting*

Internet   **Internet**

Internet cafes have sprung up all over Malaysia in the past few years, offering cheap – yet sometimes slow – email access.

Is there a local Internet cafe?
   ah-duh *sai*-ber ka-*fay* tah(k)
   dee kah-*wah*-sahn *ee*-nee?   *Ada cyber cafe tak di*
                                  kawasan ini?

Where can I get access
to the Internet?
   dee *mah*-nuh *sai*-yuh bo-*leh(h)*
   pah-kai *in*-ter-neht?   *Di mana saya boleh*
                                pakai internet?

What's the rate per hour?
   kah-dahr se-*jahm* be-*rah*-puh?   *Kadar sejam berapa?*

AROUND TOWN

SIGHTSEEING   **BERSIAR-SIAR**

Malaysians love to go sightseeing, *makan angin*, **mah-kahn
ah-ngin** (lit: to-eat air). You don't have to visit the big sights to
enjoy Malaysia – the local markets and shopping areas are just as
interesting. Notice the differences in multilingual signs, smells
and sounds of the predominantly Chinese, Indian or Malay
neighbourhoods.

Where's the tourist office?
    pe-*jah*-baht pe-*lahn*-chong-ahn   *Pejabat pelancongan*
    dee *mah*-nuh?   *di mana?*
What's that building?
    bahn-*goo*-nahn *ah*-puh ee-too?   *Bangunan apa itu?*
What's this monument?
    too-goo *ah*-puh ee-too?   *Tugu apa itu?*
Who lived there?
    see-*ah*-puh *per*-nah(h)   *Siapa pernah*
    ting-gahl dee *sah*-nuh?   *tinggal di sana?*

Do you have a local map?
    ah-duh pe-*tuh*   *Ada peta*
    tem-*pah*-tahn tah(k)?   *tempatan tak?*
Can I take (your) photo(s)?
    bo-*leh*(h) *sai*-yuh *ahm*-bil   *Boleh saya ambil*
    fo-to/*gahm*-bahr (*ahn*-dah)?   *foto/gambar (anda)?*
I'll send you the photograph.
    nahn-tee *sai*-yuh *hahn*-tahr   *Nanti saya hantar*
    fo-to/*gahm*-bahr ee-nee   *foto/gambar ini kepada*
    ke-*pah*-duh *ahn*-dah   *anda.*
Could you take a photo of (me)?
    to-long *ahm*-bil *fo*-to/   *Tolong ambil foto/*
    gahm-bahr (*sai*-yuh)?   *gambar (saya)?*

I want to see a/the ...	*sai*-yuh nah(k) me-*lee*-haht ...	*Saya nak melihat ...*
I'd like to go to a/the ...	*sai*-yuh nah(k) *per*-gee ke ...	*Saya nak pergi ke ...*
church	ge-*reh*-juh	*gereja*
garden (botanical)	*tah*-mahn bo-*tahn*-i-kahl	*taman botanikal*
mosque	*mahs*-jid	*masjid*
museum	moo-*zee*-um	*muzium*
nightclub	ke-*lahb mah*-lahm	*kelab malam*
palace	ees-*tah*-nuh	*istana*
park	*tah*-mahn	*taman*
performance	per-*toon*-joo(k)-kahn	*pertunjukan*
public square	dah-*tah*-rahn	*dataran*
royal palace	ees-*tah*-nuh dee-*rah*-juh	*istana diraja*
statue	*pah*-tung	*patung*
university	yoo-ni-*ver*-si-tee	*universiti*

PAPERWORK   MENGISI BORANG

AROUND TOWN

If you need to deal with the Malaysian government for any reason, you'll get further if you dress neatly and do your best to be polite and soft-spoken. Most government officials are Malays, who can be easily offended by obvious displays of impatience or anger, or what they define as loud voices or any form of arrogance. Many printed forms in Malaysia are in Malay and English, so you shouldn't have a lot of trouble.

Forms   Borang

name	*nah*-muh	*nama*
address	*ah*-lah-maht	*alamat*
date/place of birth	*tah*-rikh/tem-*paht* lah-*hir*	*tarikh/tempat lahir*
age	*oo*-moor	*umur*
sex	jahn-*tee*-nuh	*jantina*
nationality	*bahng*-suh	*bangsa*
religion	ah-*gah*-muh	*agama*
profession	pe-*ker*-jah-ahn	*pekerjaan*

marital status	*tah*-rahf	*taraf*
	per-*kah(h)*-wi-nahn	*perkahwinan*
single	be-*lum kah(h)*-win	*belum kahwin*
married	ber-*kah(h)*-win	*berkahwin*
divorced	ber-*che*-rai	*bercerai*
widow	*jahm*-duh	*janda*
widower	*doo*-duh	*duda*
identification	pe-*nge*-nahl-ahn	*pengenalan*
passport number	*nom*-bor *pahs*-port	*nombor pasport*
visa	*vee*-suh	*visa*
birth certificate	soo-*raht* ber-*ah*-nah(k)	*surat beranak*
drivers licence	*leh*-sehn me-*mahn*-doo	*lesen memandu*
purpose of visit	se-*bahb* lah-*wah*-tahn	*sebab lawatan*
business	pe-*ker*-jah-ahn	*pekerjaan*
holiday	per-*choo*-tee-ahn	*percutian*
visiting	me-*lah*-waht	*melawat*
relatives	ke-loo-*ahr*-guh	*keluarga*

BERJALAN-JALAN   GOING OUT

When the hot sun goes down over Malaysia, the air cools and activity picks up! Bustling night markets open just before sunset, offering a myriad of food, goods and people-watching opportunities. Shopping malls are packed and the big cities have plenty of coffee shops, clubs, pubs and bars. Sampling the variety of Malaysian cuisine at some of the outdoor food stalls is a must.

Where's a ...?	... dee *mah*-nuh?	... *di mana?*
I'd like to go	*sai*-yuh nah(k)	*Saya nak*
to a ...	*per*-gee ke ...	*pergi ke ...*
bar	bahr	*bar*
cafe	ka-*fay*	*cafe*
food stalls	ge-*rai*	*gerai*
nightclub	ke-*lahb mah*-lahm	*kelab malam*
night market	*pah*-sahr *mah*-lahm	*pasar malam*

I feel like ...	*sai*-yuh nah(k) ...	*Saya nak ...*
dancing	me-*nah*-ree	*menari*
eating	*mah*-kahn	*makan*
watching a film	me-*non*-ton *fee*-lem	*menonton filem*

I feel like going	*sai*-yuh nah(k) ke ...	*Saya nak ke ...*
to a/the ...		
cinema	*pahng*-gung	*panggung*
	wai-yahng	*wayang*
concert	*kon*-sert	*konsert*
shadow	per-*toon*-joo(k)-ahn	*pertunjukan*
puppet show	*wai*-yahng *koo*-lit	*wayang kulit*
theatre	*tee*-ah-ter; *chan*-dee	*teater; candi*
	wah-rah	*wara*

INVITATIONS

Would you like to go to a
cinema with me?

JEMPUTAN

nah(k) *per*-gee te-*ngo*(k)
wai-yahng ber-*sah*-muh *sai*-yuh?

*Nak pergi tengok wayang
bersama saya?*

Do you know a good club?

ahn-duh *tah*-hoo tah(k)
ke-*lahb* yahng bah-*gus*?

*Anda tahu tak
kelab yang bagus?*

I'll pay.

sai-yuh nah(k) *bai*-yahr-lah(h)

Saya nak bayarlah.

Come along.

joom/*mah*-ree!

Jum/Mari!

The night's young!

mah-lahm *mah*-si(h) *moo*-duh!

Malam masih muda!

Responding to Invitations

I'd like to.   yah/bo-*leh*(h)

I can't.   tah(k) bo-*leh*(h)

Jemputan Membalas

Ya/Boleh.

Tak boleh.

STAND BY ME

Apart from shaking hands, physical contact in public
between the sexes is very minimal in Malaysian society,
except perhaps in discos. Malaysians take a dim view
of canoodling couples, even if they're married.

Nightclubs & Bars

How should we get there?

nai(k) *ah*-puh ke *sah*-nuh?

Kelab Malam & Bar

Naik apa ke sana?

Are these clothes OK?

pah-*kai*-yahn *ee*-nee
se-*swai* tah(k)?

Pakaian ini sesuai tak?

Is there an admission charge?

ah-duh bai-*yahr*-ahn *mah*-su(k)
tah(k)?

Ada bayaran masuk tak?

What sort of music do you like?

ahn-duh *soo*-kuh *moo*-zik *ah*-puh?

Anda suka muzik apa?

I like techno.
   sai-yuh *soo*-kuh *tek*-no   *Saya suka tekno.*
Let's dance.
   joom *kee*-tuh me-*nah*-ree   *Jum kita menari.*

This place is ...	tem-*paht* ee-nee ...	*Tempat ini ...*
That person's ...	*dee*-uh ...	*Dia ...*
cool	behst	*best*
sleazy	*ko*-tor	*kotor*
strange	pe-*li(k)*	*pelik*

Let's go somewhere else.
   joom *per*-gee tem-*paht* lain   *Jum pergi tempat lain.*

DATING & ROMANCE
KELUAR BERDUA & PERCINTAAN
Looking for a Date
Mencari Pasangan

Remember the different pronouns in Malay. Usually the more casual, intimate and egalitarian pronouns (*aku* or *ku* for 'I' and *engkau* or *kau*, *kamu* or *mu* for 'you') are used in dating situations, especially after the first date or two (see the box on page 18).

Would you like to get together ...?	nah(k) ber-*joom*-puh ... tah(k)?	*Nak berjumpa ... tak?*
again	*lah*-gee	*lagi*
later tonight	*mah*-lahm *nahn*-tee	*malam nanti*
tomorrow	eh-*so(k)*	*esok*

I'd like to.	yah/bo-*leh(h)*	*Ya/Boleh.*
No thanks.	tah(k) nah(k)-*lah(h)*	*Tak naklah.*
Go away!	*per*-gee/be-*lah(h)*!	*Pergi/Belah!*
Don't hassle me.	jah-ngahn *kah*-chow ah-koo	*Jangan kacau aku.*

I have a ...	*sai*-yuh ah-duh ...	*Saya ada ...*
boyfriend	*pah(k)*-we	*pakwe*
girlfriend	*mah(k)*-we	*makwe*
husband	swah-mee	*suami*
wife	ees-te-ree	*isteri*

GOING OUT

Love
Cinta

You're beautiful.	*kah*-moo *chahn*-ti(k)	*Kamu cantik.*
Let's kiss.	joom ber-*chee*-oom	*Jum bercium.*
(Don't) Stop!	*(jah*-ngahn) ber-*hen*-tee!	*(Jangan) Berhenti!*
Delicious!	se-*dahp*-nyuh!	*Sedapnya!*
Great!	heh-*baht*!	*Hebat!*

Do you have a condom?
   ah-duh kon-dom? — *Ada kondom?*

No condom, no sex.
   tah(k) bo-*leh(h) tahn*-puh — *Tak boleh tanpa*
   kon-dom — *kondom.*

Do you want to smoke?
   kah-moo nah(k) *ro*-ko(k)? — *Kamu nak rokok?*

Can I stay?
   bo-*leh(h) sai*-yuh — *Boleh saya*
   ber-*mah*-lahm dee *see*-nee? — *bermalam di sini?*

Can I see you again?
   bo-*leh(h) kee*-tuh ber-*te*-moo — *Boleh kita bertemu lagi?*
   lah-gee?

FORBIDDEN LOVE

Muslims can be arrested by Department of Religion officials for drinking alcohol and for eating or smoking in public during the fasting month, *Ramadhan*, *rah*-mah-dhahn. But there's another activity that's really not on. *Khalwat*, *khahl*-waht, is translated as 'close proximity' – when two people of the opposite sex are alone in a situation where sex might be a possibility. *Khalwat* is *haram*, hah-*rahm*, 'forbidden' in Islam.

Be aware that going alone to a secluded place, or entering a hotel room alone with a Muslim, might result in an embarrassing intrusion by the Department of Religion officials – and a fine (although usually the non-Muslim partner does not have to pay). Hope this box hasn't killed the mood!

I'll call you.
nahm-tee *sai*-yuh teh-*leh*-fon   *Nanti saya telefon.*

Do you want to be my
girlfriend/boyfriend?
kah-moo nah(k) *jah*-dee   *Kamu nak jadi pakwe/*
pah(k)-we/*mah(k)*-we *sai*-yuh   *makwe saya tak?*
tah(k)?

I like you.   *ah*-koo *soo*-kuh kow   *Aku suka kau.*
I love you.   *ah*-koo *chin*-tuh   *Aku cinta*
        pah-duh moo   *pada mu.*

HOT IN THE CITY

Malaysians are a fascinating combination of traditional
and modern, Asian and Western. You'll see Muslim
women and some Indian women completely covered
up, and others (of all backgrounds) in mini-skirts.

Although Islam prohibits drinking alcohol and the
'close proximity' of people of the opposite sex, a lot of
both still goes on, particularly in the big cities. Chinese
Malaysians are probably the most accepting of dating,
the various Indian-Malaysian groups are not as happy
about it and the Malays are the most conservative.

Leaving & Breaking Up

Memutuskan Hubungan Percintaan

I leave tomorrow.
eh-so(k) *sai*-yuh ber-*ahng*-kaht   *Esok saya berangkat.*

I'll miss you.
ah-koo ah-*kahm* me-*rin*-doo-ee   *Aku akan merindui*
kah-moo   *kamu.*

Let's keep in touch.
ah-koo *hah*-rahp *kee*-tuh   *Aku harap kita akan*
ah-*kahm* te-*tahp*   *tetap berkomunikasi.*
ber-ko-moon-i-*kah*-see

This relationship isn't appropriate.
hoo-*boong*-ahn *ee*-nee tah(k)   *Hubungan ini tak*
se-*swai bah*-gee *kee*-tuh ber-*doo*-uh   *sesuai bagi kita berdua.*

'GOING TO THE CHAPEL'

- You will see mosques, large and small, everywhere in Malaysia, distinguished by their minarets and beautiful domes of different shapes. You'll certainly hear the call to prayer, *azan*, which blasts out five times a day and will notice the arrow on almost every hotel room ceiling, pointing to Mecca. Most Malays are not comfortable seeing travellers who appear to be non-Muslim entering their places of worship. Women should dress in loose-fitting clothes covering everything but their faces and hands; men should cover up too, in a long-sleeved shirt and pants. Ensure you don't walk in front of anyone who's praying.

- Hindu temples are usually ornate and colourful. The roofs are often a riot of vividly painted Hindu gods. Again, conservative dress is a good idea.

- Chinese temples have elaborate roofs, some with a multi-storey pagoda design. Inside the temples, incense spices the air and the hall is filled with carved and gilded wood and ornaments.

- Sikh temples, often modest buildings, can be recognised by the triangular flag flying outside. Any one is welcome within the temple, and as with all the other religions, you must take off your shoes before entering.

KELUARGA   FAMILY

QUESTIONS   PERTANYAAAN

Family is all-important to Malaysians. Family ties are expressed
in everyday conversations through the use of words like *abang*,
ah-**bahng**, 'big brother' and *makcik*, **mah**(k)-**chi**(k), 'auntie'.
Whether at the market or in someone's home, you'll almost
certainly be asked questions about yourself and the members of
your family.

Are you married?   *soo*-**dah**(h) **kah**(h)-**win**?   *Sudah kahwin?*

Unless you have tied the knot, in which case you reply *soo*-**dah**(h)
'already', the best answer is:

Not yet.   be-*lum* **lah**-gee   *Belum lagi.*

Saying *tidak*, **tee**-**dah**(k), 'no', would be grammatically fine, but
many Malaysians might think it's weird if you're not married, or
at least thinking about it. Also, the word for 'friend', *kawan*,
kah-**wahn**, often implies a romantic relationship. *Ada kawan?*,
ah-**duh** *kah*-**wahn**?, may actually mean:

Do you have a boyfriend/girlfriend?
    ah-**duh** *pah*(k)-we/*mah*(k)-**we**?   *Ada pakwe/makwe?*
Is your husband/wife here?
    swah-**mee**/*ees*-te-ree *ahn*-**duh**   *Suami/Isteri anda di sini?*
    dee *see*-**nee**?
Do you have any brothers and sisters?
    ah-**duh** *ah*-**di**(k)-be-*rah*-**di**(k)?   *Ada adik-beradik?*
Do you have any children?
    soo-**dah**(h) *ah*-**duh** *ah*-**nah**(k)?   *Sudah ada anak?*
How many children do you have?
    be-*rah*-**puh** *o*-**rahng** *ah*-**nah**(k)?   *Berapa orang anak?*

FAMILY

REPLIES   ## JAWAPAN

I'm not married yet.
  sai-yuh be-*lum*
  kah(h)-win/*nee*-kah(h)   *Saya belum
                                     kahwin/nikah.*

I'm still single.
  sai-yuh *mah*-si(h) *boo*-jahng   *Saya masih bujang.*

I'm married.
  sai-yuh *soo*-dah(h) *kah(h)*-win *Saya sudah kahwin.*

I don't have any children (yet).
  sai-yuh *tee*-dah(k) (be-*lum*)   *Saya tidak (belum)
  ah-duh *ah*-nah(k)   *ada anak.*

This is my ...   *ee*-nee ... *sai*-yuh   *Ini ... saya.*

I have ...   *sai*-yuh *ah*-duh ...   *Saya ada ...*
  one son   se-*o*-rahng *ah*-nah(k)   *seorang anak
                    le-*lah*-kee   lelaki*
  three sons   *tee*-guh *o*-rahng   *tiga orang
                    ah-nah(k) le-*lah*-kee   anak lelaki*
  one daughter   se-*o*-rahng *ah*-nah(k)   *seorang anak
                    pe-*rem*-pwahn   perempuan*
  three daughters   *tee*-guh *o*-rahng   *tiga orang
                    pe-*rem*-pwahn   perempuan*

I have two younger brothers.
  sai-yuh *ah*-duh *doo*-uh *o*-rahng   *Saya ada dua orang
  ah-*di(k)* le-*lah*-kee   adik lelaki.*

| **DID YOU KNOW ...** | One word for a second wife for Muslims is *madu*, *mah*-doo, which literally means honey, as in honey to the bee. |

FAMILY MEMBERS   ANGGOTA KELUARGA

Brothers and sisters are always referred to as older or younger.

aunt	*mah(k)*-chi(k)	*makcik*
boyfriend	*pah(k)*-we/te-*mahn*	*pakwe/teman*
	le-*lah*-kee	*lelaki*
child(ren)	*ah*-nah(k)(-*ah*-nah(k))	*anak(-anak)*
cousin	se-*poo*-poo	*sepupu*
daughter	*ah*-nah(k)	*anak*
(unmarried)	pe-*rem*-pwahn	*perempuan*
	ah-nah(k) *dah*-ruh	*anak dara*
eldest	*soo*-long	*sulong*
family	ke-loo-*ahr*-guh	*keluarga*
father	*bah*-pah(k)/*ai*-yah(h)	*bapak/ayah*
friend	*kah*-wahn	*kawan*
girlfriend	*mah(k)*-we/te-*mahn*	*makwe/teman*
	wah-*nee*-tuh	*wanita*
grandchild	*choo*-choo	*cucu*
grandfather	*dah*-tu(k)	*datuk*
grandmother	neh-*neh(k)*	*nenek*
husband	*swah*-mee	*suami*
mother	mah(k)/*ee*-boo	*mak/ibu*
older brother	ah-*bahng* le-*lah*-kee	*abang lelaki*
older sister	*kah*-kah(k)	*kakak*
	pe-*rem*-pwahn	*perempuan*
partner	*pah*-sahng-ahn	*pasangan*
son	*ah*-nah(k) le-*lah*-kee	*anak lelaki*
uncle	*pah(k)*-chi(k)	*pakcik*
wife	*ees*-te-ree	*isteri*
younger brother	ah-*di(k)* le-*lah*-kee	*adik lelaki*
younger sister	ah-*di(k)* pe-*rem*-pwahn	*adik perempuan*
youngest	*bong*-soo	*bongsu*

FAMILY

FAMILY

IT'S A FAMILY AFFAIR

Malaysians of all backgrounds are very specific in relating to others in terms of how old people are and their placement in the family hierarchy. With larger families this can become a bit complicated. Introductions are often made simply by identifying relationships. If you meet the extended family, including the many aunts and uncles, you may be introduced to 'youngest uncle' *paksu*, **pah(k)-soo**. The wife of *paksu* will probably be called *maksu*, **mah(k)-soo**, except in her own family, where, if she were the middle auntie, she might be called *makngah*, **mah(k)-ngah(h)**. Of course there's always the eldest of the uncles in the family, *paklong*, **pah(k)-long**. Got it?

Malay women keep their own names when they marry, so it's not possible to keep track of family relations through surnames. Instead, each person has their own first name, followed by the words *bin*, **bin**, 'son of' or *binti*, **bin-tee**, 'daughter of', followed by their father's first name. So a family may actually have three different 'last' names.

When addressing male and female adults in a family respectively, you'd call them *Encik*, **en-chi(k)**, (plus his first name) and *Puan*, **poo-ahn**, (plus her first name). People may also use this custom on you, and address you as 'Mr Mick' instead of 'Mr Jagger'.

COMMON INTERESTS   MINAT BERSAMA

Malaysians undertake leisure time with gusto. The worst feeling for many is *boringlah*, *boh*-reeng-lah(h), an adaption of the English word boring. The opposite feeling is *shiok*, *shee*-oh(k) 'delicious and wonderful'.

Do you like ...?	*ahn*-duh *soo*-kuh ...?	*Anda suka ...?*
I (don't) like ...	*sai*-yuh (tah(k))	*Saya (tak)*
	soo-kuh ...	*suka ...*
art	ke-se-*nee*-ahn	*kesenian*
cooking	me-*mah*-sah(k)	*memasak*
dancing	me-*nah*-ree	*menari*
(traditional)	trah-di-see-*o*-nahl	*tradisional*
discos	*dis*-ko	*disko*
film	*fee*-lem;	*filem;*
	wai-yahng	*wayang*
	gahm-bahr	*gambar*
going out	ber-*jah*-lahn-*jah*-lahn	*berjalan-jalan*
going shopping	mem-be-*lee*-be-*lah(h)*	*membeli-belah*
music	*moo*-zi(k)	*muzik*
photography	fo-to-*grah*-fee	*fotografi*
playing sport	ber-*soo*-kahn	*bersukan*
reading books	mem-*bah*-chuh	*membaca*
	boo-koo	*buku*
the theatre	*tee*-ah-ter;	*teater;*
	sahn-dee-*wah*-rah	*sandiwara*
travelling	men-gem-*bah*-ruh	*mengembara*
travel	kem-*bah*-ruh	*kembara*
watching TV	me-*non*-ton tee vee	*menonton TV*
writing	me-*noo*-lis	*menulis*

What do you do in your
spare time?
> *ahm*-duh *soo*-kuh *boo*-aht
> *ah*-puh *dah*-lahm *mah*-suh
> *lah*-pahng?

*Anda suka buat
apa dalam masa
lapang?*

What hobby do you have?
> *ah*-puh *ho*-bee *ahm*-duh?

Apa hobi anda?

HOW TO WINTER YOUR SHEEP

Malaysia's TV and radio improved drastically in the '90s. Long gone are the days of only two government TV channels, with incredibly boring and sometimes inappropriate programming – such as a documentary imported from England on 'How to Winter Your Sheep'.

The government sponsors two channels, TV1 and TV2, and there are three commercial stations. TV1 is almost all in Malay; TV2 has much more English as well as the other languages of Malaysia in its programming. Various satellite and cable companies bring an even wider array of foreign programming.

The modern Malaysian film industry has a lot of competition overseas, as Chinese, Indian, American and European films all crowd out local production. Modern Malay movies tend to be melodramatic and have simplistic story lines, maybe due to censorship or the view that morals are powerfully conveyed through film. Try to catch some of the older black and white films, especially those starring the famous and hilarious P Ramlee. They all have English subtitles.

SPORT   SUKAN

Malaysians are into sport, especially *badminton*, *bahd*-min-ton, 'badminton' and *bola sepak*, *bo*-luh *seh*-pah(k), 'soccer'. Malaysian badminton players rank among the best in the world, and are in hot competition with the nearby Indonesians. The national soccer league *Liga Malaysia* also has a passionate following throughout the country. *Sepak takraw*, *seh*-pah(k) *tah*-kraw, is an impressive game, common in Malaysia, Indonesia and Thailand. Balls made of *rotan*, *ro*-tahn, 'rattan' are used like volleyballs. Players can only use their heads and feet to get the ball back and forth over the net, without letting it touch the ground.

INTERESTS

Do you like sport?
ahn-duh *soo*-kuh
ber-*soo*-kahn?

*Anda suka
bersukan?*

I like playing sport.
sai-yuh *soo*-kuh
ber-*soo*-kahn.

*Saya suka
bersukan.*

I prefer to watch rather
than play sport.
sai-yuh le-*bi(h) soo*-kuh
me-*non*-ton dah-ree-*pah*-duh
ber-*main soo*-kahn

*Saya lebih suka
menonton daripada
bermain sukan.*

Do you play ...?	*ahn*-duh main ... tah(k)?	*Anda main ... tak?*
Would you like to play/go/do ...?	*ahn*-duh nah(k) main ...?	*Anda nak main ...?*
badminton	*bahd*-min-ton	*badminton*
basketball	*bo*-luh ke-*rahm*-jahng	*bola keranjang*
boxing	*teen*-joo	*tinju*
diving	me-nye-*lahm*	*menyelam*
soccer	*bo*-luh seh-*pah*(k)	*bola sepak*
gymnastics	jim-*nahs*-tik	*gimnastik*
hockey	*ho*-kee	*hoki*
martial arts	se-*nee* mem-per-tah-*hahn*-kahn *di*-ree	*seni memperta-hankan diri*
rugby	*rahg*-bee	*ragbi*
water skiing	main skee air	*main ski air*
soccer	*bo*-luh seh-*pah*(k)	*bola sepak*
surfing	ber-se-*lahm*-chahr	*berselancar*
swimming	be-re-*nahng*	*berenang*
table tennis	*ping*-pong	*ping-pong*
tennis	*teh*-nis	*tenis*
takraw	seh-*pah*(k) *tah*-kraw	*sepak takraw*
top (spinning)	*gah*-sing	*gasing*

WRITING LETTERS   MENULIS SURAT

Once you get back home, you may want to drop a line to people.
Letter writing in Malay tends to be formal, so the sentences and
phrases below are a little more serious than conversational Malay.

Dear ...,
  ke-*pah*-duh ...   *Kepada ...*
  yahng dee-kah-*si(h)*-ee   *yang dikasihi,*
I'm sorry it's taken me so
long to write.
  min-tuh mah-*ahf* se-*bahb*   *Minta maaf sebab*
  dah(h) *lah*-muh *sai*-yuh   *dah lama saya*
  tee-dah(k) men-*gi*-reem soo-raht   *tidak mengirim surat.*
It was great to meet you.
  sai-yuh gem-*bee*-ruh *kee*-tuh   *Saya gembira kita dapat*
  dah-*paht* ber-*te*-moo dah-*hoo*-loo   *bertemu dahulu.*
Thanks so much for
your hospitality.
  te-*ree*-muh *kah*-si(h) ah-*tahs*   *Terima kasih atas*
  ke-re-moo-tah-*mah*-hahn   *keremutamahan*
  ahn-duh   *anda.*
I miss you.
  sai-yuh me-*rin*-doo-ee   *Saya merindui*
  ahn-duh/*kah*-lee-ahn (sg/pl)   *anda/kalian.*
I had a fantastic time in ...
  pe-ngah-*lah*-mahn *sai*-yuh   *Pengalaman saya*
  dee ... be-*gee*-too   *di ... begitu*
  me-nye-ro-*no(k)*-kahn   *menyeronokkan.*
My favourite place was ...
  ... ee-*ah*-la(h) tem-*paht*   *... ialah tempat*
  yahng *pah*-ling *sai*-yuh   *yang paling saya*
  soo-kai   *sukai.*
I hope to visit ... again.
  se-*mo*-guh *sai*-yuh *dah*-paht   *Semoga saya dapat*
  me-ngoon-*joo*-ngee ... *lah*-gee   *mengunjungi ... lagi.*
Send my regards to ...
  to-long sahm-*pai*-kahn   *Tolong sampaikan*
  sah-lahm *sai*-yuh ke-*pah*-duh ...   *salam saya kepada ...*

I'd love to see you again.
    sai-yuh *ee*-ngin se-*kah*-lee   *Saya ingin sekali*
    ber-*te*-moo de-*ngahn*   *bertemu dengan*
    ahn-duh *lah*-gee   *anda lagi.*
Write soon!
    to-long *bah*-lahs   *Tolong balas!*
With love/regards,
    de-*ngahn* kah-si(h)   *Dengan kasih,*

SOCIAL ISSUES   ISU SOSIAL

Malaysians often enjoy talking about social issues, perhaps because
so much that comes out in local papers and TV broadcasts is
censored. Coffee shops are a great place to catch up on national
gossip. Malaysians, however, do not appreciate criticism from
foreigners, so be sensitive to 'what side' they are on. Politics in
recent years have been very sensitive and fractured.

I (don't) agree.   *sai*-yuh (tah(k))   *Saya (tak)*
                        se-*too*-joo   *setuju.*
Do you like ...?   *ahn*-duh *soo*-kuh ...? *Anda suka ...?*
I (don't) like ...   *sai*-yuh (tah(k))   *Saya (tak)*
                        soo-kuh ...   *suka ...*
Really?; Is that so?   be-*tul*-kah(h)?   *Betullkah?*
Really!   be-*tul!*   *Betul!*

What do people/you think about ...?
    ah-puh pen-*dah*-paht   *Apa pendapat*
    rah(k)-yaht/ *ahn*-duh   *rakyat/anda*
    ten-tahng ... ?   *tentang ...?*
I support the ... party.
    sai-yuh me-*nyo*-kong *pahr*-tee ... *Saya menyokong parti ...*
What party do you support?
    pahr-tee yahng *mah*-nuh   *Parti yang mana*
    ahn-duh me-*nyo*-kong?   *anda menyokong?*
In my country, we have a
conservative/liberal government.
    ke-*rah*-jah-ahn dee ne-*gah*-ruh   *Kerajaan di negara*
    sai-yuh kon-*ser*-vah-tif/   *saya konservatif/*
    li-be-rahl   *liberal.*

POLITICS

		POLITIK
cronism	kro-*nis*-me	*kronisme*
demonstration	*toon*-ju(k) pe-*rah*-sah-ahn	*tunjuk perasaan*
democracy	deh-*mo*-krah-see	*demokrasi*
general election	pi-lee-hahn-*rai*-yuh	*pilihanraya*
government	ke-*rah*-jah-ahn	*kerajaan*
monetary crisis	*kri*-sis ke-*wahng*-ahn	*krisis kewangan*
Malaysian Armed Forces	*ahng*-kah-tahn *ten*-te-ruh mah-*lay*-see-ah	*Angkatan Tentera Malaysia (ATM)*
Parliament	*pahr*-li-mehn	*Parlimen*
policy	*po*-li-see	*polisi*
politician	*ah*-lee *po*-li-tik	*ahli politik*
President	*preh*-si-dehn	*Presiden*
Prime Minister	per-*dah*-nuh *men*-te-ree	*Perdana Menteri*
reformation	reh-for-*mah*-see	*reformasi*
peaceful	*dah*-mai	*damai*
revolution	reh-vo-*loo*-see	*revolusi*
socialism	so-see-ahl-*is*-me	*sosialisme*
economy	eh-*ko*-no-mee	*ekonomi*
exploitation	ehks-ploy-*tah*-see	*eksploitasi*
history	se-*jah*-rah(h)	*sejarah*
justice	ke-*ah*-di-lahn	*keadilan*
the people	*rah*-kyaht	*rakyat*
poverty	ke-mis-*ki*-nahn	*kemiskinan*
riot	roo-*su*-hahn	*rusuhan*
unemployment	pe-*ngahng*-goo-rahn	*pengangguran*
welfare	ke-*bah*-jee-kahn	*kebajikan*
worker	pe-*ker*-juh	*pekerja*

INTERESTS

PRAISE YOU

Malaysians love to hear praise of their own country, but may perceive too many positive comments about the traveller's home country as 'boasting' or 'arrogance'. So, be humble about your own country's advantages.

INTERESTS

MUSIC   MUZIK

A variety of music abounds in Malaysia. You'll find well-known musicians and pop singers from many countries performing in the big cities or on TV. Around sunset, you might tune in to troops of *nasyid*, *nah*-**sheed**, singers, all-male or female groups who sing religious songs in Malay or Arabic, with a Middle-Eastern flavour. Featuring plenty of percussion instruments, traditional types of music include:

Dikir barat, *dee*-**kir** *bah*-**raht**
From Kelantan, men wearing traditional dress sit in a group and chant a story, accompanied by drums.

Dondang sayang, *don*-**dahng** *sai*-**yahng**
Mainly from Melaka, these are Chinese-influenced romantic songs with orchestral instrumentation .

Ghazal, *ghah*-**zahl**
Mainly found in Johor, these female singers are accompanied by an orchestra of Middle-Eastern instruments.

Zikir, *zee*-**kir**
A type of religious singing.

CRAFTS   KRAFTANGAN

The traditional arts and crafts of Malaysia are now mainly found on the east coast, and to a certain extent in East Malaysia. If you are looking for modern art, there are galleries and roadside artists in the bigger cities.

Batik, *bah*-**teek**, is the beautifully patterned material, usually cotton or silk, which is coloured with a wax and dye system that creates intricate and beautifully designed fabrics.

Kain songket, **kain song-keht**, is also a specialty of Kelantan and Terengganu. It is a hand-woven fabric with gold and silver threads through the material. This is the material traditionally worn in wedding ceremonies, coronations and other official functions.

Perak, *peh*-**rah(k)**, is the fine silver filigree jewellery of the east coast.

FIGHTING KITES & BIG TOPS

These two traditional games are not child's play. The tops, *gasing*, *gah*-sing, made of polished hardwood and metal can weigh up to 7kg. The cords used to spin them are about 5m long, and it takes real strength to hurl the tops onto a polished mud slab. The player must then scoop up the spinning top with a thin wooden paddle and place it on a small, metal-tipped wooden post. Players compete to see whose top will spin the longest. Teams of players have traditionally played this game when the rice is ripening and there is less work to do.

Kite flying contests include events for the highest flyer and competitions between fighting kites. Both top spinning and kite, *wau*, wow, flying contests are held in the north-eastern states of Kelantan and Terengannu. There are bird kites, cat kites and the ever-popular moon kite *wau bulan*, wow *bu*-lahn. They are superb works of art as well as flying instruments, and can be up to 2.5m wide. Kites and tops are popular souvenirs, and a traditional kite is the symbol of Malaysia Airlines.

INTERESTS

PERFORMING & MARTIAL ARTS

SENI PERSEMBAHAN DAN PERTAHANAN DIRI

Many of the traditional performing arts are finally dying out. Kelantan banned *wayang kulit*, **wai**-**yahng** *koo*-**lit**, and *mak yong*, **mah(k) yong**, for having 'unislamic influences'. They are only performed for tourists in that state. Tourism has saved these troops of performers from total extinction.

Wayang kulit, **wai**-**yahng** *koo*-**lit**
These shadow play puppets are found in many countries in South-East Asia. Performances, generally at night, can last for hours and are based on characters from the Hindu epic, the *Ramayana*.

Mak yong, **mah(k) yong**
A dance drama of Thai origin, with an all-female cast, associated with magical forces.

Menora, **me**-*no*-**ruh**
Similar to *mak yong*, with an all-male cast, wearing grotesque masks.

MEMBELI BELAH SHOPPING

LOOKING FOR ...   MENCARI ...

Malaysians are big on shopping, and you can join the frenzy in a
variety of shops, malls, traditional markets and stalls throughout
the country. Whether you're shopping for electronic goods,
handicrafts, antiques, brand name clothes or something that's
excitingly near the real thing, everything's a bargain, so get going!

Where's a/the ...?	... dee *mah*-nuh?	... *di mana*?
bakery	ke-*dai ro*-tee	*Kedai roti*
barber	ke-*dai goon*-ting *rahm*-but	*Kedai gunting rambut*
bookshop	ke-*dai boo*-koo	*Kedai buku*
camera shop	ke-*dai ka*-me-ruh	*Kedai kamera*
chemist	*fahr*-mah-see; ke-*dai oo*-baht	*Farmasi; Kedai ubat*
clothing store	ke-*dai* pah-*kai*-ahn	*Kedai pakaian*
general store	ke-*dai roon*-chit	*Kedai runcit*
market	*pah*-sahr	*Pasar*
music store	ke-*dai moo*-zi(k)	*Kedia muzik*
night market	*pah*-sahr *mah*-lahm	*Pasar malam*
shopping centre	*poo*-saht mem-be-*lee*-be-*lah*(h)	*Pusat membeli-belah*
souvenir shop	ke-*dai* chehn-de-rah-*mah*-tuh	*Kedai cenderamata*
supermarket	pah-sah-*rai*-yuh	*Pasaraya*
tailor	*too*-kahng *jah*-hit	*Tukang jahit*

MAKING A PURCHASE MEMBELI SESUATU

Shopkeepers might assume that you'll want a foreign product –
set them straight if you're looking for locally made things *barang
tempatan*, *bah*-rahng tem-*pah*-tahn

Where can I buy ...?
    *... dee-joo-ahl dee mah-*nuh?   *... dijual di mana?*
Do you have any ...?
    *... ah-*duh tah(k)?   *... ada tak?*
I'm looking for (a) ...
    *sai-*yuh nah(k) *chah-*ree ...   *Saya nak cari ...*
I'm just looking.
    *sai-*yuh nah(k) te-*ngo(k) sah-*juh   *Saya nak tengok saja.*
How much is it?
    be-*rah-*puh *hahr-*guh-nyuh?   *Berapa harganya?*
Can you write down the price?
    *to-*long *too-*lis-kahn   *Tolong tuliskan*
    *hahr-*guh-nyuh   *harganya.*
Can I try this on?
    bo-*leh(h) sai-*yuh *choo-*buh?   *Boleh saya cuba?*
Can I pay by credit card?
    bo-*leh(h) bai-*yahr   *Boleh bayar*
    de-*ngahn* kahd *kreh-*dit?   *dengan kad kredit?*
Do you have others?
    *ah-*duh yahng lain?   *Ada yang lain?*
Where are these made?
    *bah-*rahng-*bah-*rahng *ee-*nee   *Barang-barang ini*
    dee-*boo-*aht dee *mah-*nuh?   *dibuat di mana?*
Can I see it?
    bo-*leh(h) sai-*yuh te-*ngo(k)?   *Boleh saya tengok?*
I don't like it.
    *sai-*yuh tah(k) *soo-*kuh *ee-*nee   *Saya tak suka ini.*
It's beautiful!
    in-*dah*(h)/*chahn-*ti(k) se-*kah-*lee!   *Indah/Cantik sekali!*
I'll take it.
    *sai-*yuh nah(k) be-*lee ee-*nee   *Saya nak beli ini.*

BARGAINING   TAWAR-MENAWAR

Bargaining is something of a game to Malaysians. Be good-humoured in your bargaining: steady, but not aggressive pressure is the best. If you don't like the price, or think you can do better, there are usually other places to try.

It's too expensive.
    mah-*hahl*-nyuh!   *Mahalnya!*
Can you lower the price?
    bo-*leh(h) koo*-rahng-kahn
    hahr-guh tah(k)?   *Boleh kurangkan*
                         harga tak?

THEY MAY SAY ...

bo-*leh(h) sai*-yuh *to*-long *ahn*-duh?	Can I help you?
chah-ree *ah*-puh?	What are you looking for?
ah-duh, se-*ke*-jahp	We've got that, just a moment.
wahr-nuh *ah*-puh?	What colour?
ee-nee-kah(h) *bah*-rahng yahng *ah*-wah(k) *chah*-ree?	Is this what you're looking for?
hahr-guh-nyuh *lee*-muh *poo*-lu(h) *ring*-git	The price is RM50.
tee-dah(k)/tah(k) *ah*-duh	We don't have any.

SHOPPING

How much discount?
　　be-*rah*-puh-kah *dis*-kown?　　　*Berapakah diskaun?*
I'll give you ...
　　sai-yuh *bah*-gee *ahn*-duh ...　　*Saya bagi anda ...*
No more/less than ...
　　tah(k) le-*bi(h)*/　　　　　　　　*Tak lebih/*
　　koo-rahng dah-ree-*pah*-duh ...　*kurang daripada ...*
This is my final offer.
　　ee-nee *tah*-wahr-ahn　　　　　*Ini tawaran*
　　te-*rah*-khi(r) *sai*-yuh　　　　　*terakhir saya.*

cheap	*moo*-rah(h)	*murah*
discount	*dis*-kown	*diskaun*
expensive	mah-*hahl*	*mahal*

ESSENTIAL ITEMS   BARANGAN YANG PERLU

I'm looking for (a) ...　*sai*-yuh *chah*-ree ...　*Saya cari ...*

batteries	*bah*-te-ree	*bateri*
bread	*ro*-tee	*roti*
butter	men-*teh*-guh	*mentega*
cheese	*keh*-joo	*keju*
chocolate	*chok*-laht	*coklat*
eggs	te-*lur*	*telur*
flour	te-*pung*	*tepung*
ham	*dah*-ging *bah*-bee	*daging babi*
honey	*mah*-doo	*madu*
margarine	men-*teh*-guh	*mentega*
matches	*mahm*-chis	*mancis*
milk	*soo*-soo	*susu*
toilet paper	*tee*-soo	*tisu*
toothpaste	*oo*-baht *gee*-gee	*ubat gigi*
torch (flashlight)	*lahm*-poo *soo*-lu(h)	*lampu suluh*
towel	*twah*-luh	*tuala*
washing powder	*ser*-bu(k) *choo*-chee	*serbuk cuci*
yogurt	*yo*-gurt	*yogurt*

SOUVENIRS   CENDERA HATI

Traditional handicraft production has declined due to changes in
national lifestyle, so arty items you see may often be from Indonesia. The east coast, Sabah and Sarawak still have some excellent
crafts; Melaka is a centre for antiques, as is Penang.

basket	*bah*-kool	*bakul*
... batik	*bah*-ti(k) ...	*batik* ...
hand painted	*loo*-kis *tah*-ngahn	*lukis tangan*
printed	chahp	*cap*
bracelet	ge-*lahng*	*gelang*
cane ware	*bah*-rahng-ahn *ro*-tahn	*barangan rotan*
... carving	*oo*-ki-rahn	*ukiran* ...
stone	*bah*-too	*batu*
wood	*kai*-yoo	*kayu*
earrings	*soo*-bahng	*subang*
handcrafts	krahf-*tah*-ngahn	*kraftangan*
jewellery	*bah*-rahng ke-*mahs*	*barang kemas*
machete	*pah*-rahng	*parang*
carved masks	*to*-peng yahng	*topeng*
	dee-*oo*-kir	*yang diukir*
material (fabric)	kain	*kain*
necklace	*rahn*-tai *leh*-hehr	*rantai leher*
Malay knives	ke-*ris*	*keris*
paintings	loo-*kee*-sahn	*lukisan*
pottery	tem-*bee*-kahr	*tembikar*
shadow puppets	*wai*-yahng *koo*-lit	*wayang kulit*
ring	*chin*-chin	*cincin*
sarong	*sah*-rung	*sarung*
statue	*pah*-tung	*patung*

CLOTHING

PAKAIAN

bra	*cho*-lee	*coli*
cardigan	*bah*-joo se-*joo(k)* yahng	*baju sejuk yang*
	ber-*boo*-tahng de-*pahn*	*berbutang depan*
dress	*bah*-joo gown	*baju gaun*
gloves	*sah*-rung tah-*ngahn*	*sarung tangan*
hat	*to*-pee	*topi*
jacket	jah-*keht*	*jaket*
jeans	jeens	*jeans*
jumper	*bah*-joo se-*ju(k)*	*baju sejuk*
pants	se-*loo*-ahr *pahn*-jahng	*seluar panjang*
raincoat	*bah*-joo *hoo*-jahn	*baju hujan*
sandals	se-*lee*-pahr	*selipar*
shirt	*bah*-joo/ke-*meh*-juh	*bajul kemeja*
shoelaces	*tah*-lee *kah*-sut	*tali kasut*
shoes	*kah*-sut	*kasut*
shorts	se-*loo*-ahr *pehn*-deh(k)	*seluar pendek*
skirt	sket	*skirt*
socks	*sto*-king	*stoking*
swimsuit	pah-*kai*-ahn/	*pakaian/*
	bah-joo *reh*-nahng	*baju renang*
tie	*tah*-lee *leh*-hehr	*tali leher*
trousers	se-*loo*-ahr *pahn*-jahng	*seluar panjang*
Tshirt	*bah*-joo tee	*baju T*
underwear	se-*loo*-ahr *dah*-lahm	*seluar dalam*

HOT AND COLD

Think hot, hot, hot. It simply never cools down, except during the rainy season on the east coast. You'll need cotton clothes that breathe, and protect you from the sun (and any eager eyes checking you out). If you head into the highlands you may need to rug up, so take waterproof gear or a light jumper.

MATERIALS   BAHAN

The *Jalan Masjid India* and *Jalan Tuanku Abdul Rahman* areas of
Kuala Lumpur have a huge variety of shops selling material.

bone	*too*-lahng	*tulang*
cotton	*kah*-pahs	*kapas*
gold	e-*mahs*	*emas*
jackfruit wood	*kai*-yoo *nahng*-kuh	*kayu nangka*
leather	*koo*-lit	*kulit*
rattan/cane	*ro*-tahn	*rotan*
sandalwood	chehn-*dah*-nuh	*cendana*
shell	*koo*-lit *see*-put	*kulit siput*
silk	*soo*-te-ruh	*sutera*
silver	*peh*-rah(k)	*perak*
wood	*kai*-yoo	*kayu*
wool	*boo*-loo *bi*-ree-*bi*-ree	*bulu biri-biri*

THE REAL McCOY

When looking for souvenirs or items made in Malaysia, ask:

'Is this made in Malaysia?'
ee-nee *bah*-rahng	*Ini barang*
boo-ah-tahn mah-*lay*-see-ah?	*buatan Malaysia?*

COLOURS   WARNA

black	*hee*-tahm	*hitam*
blonde/tan	*peh*-rahng	*perang*
blue	*bee*-roo	*biru*
brown	*chok*-laht	*coklat*
dark ...	... *too*-uh	... *tua*
green	*hee*-jow	*hijau*
grey	ke-*lah*-boo/*ah*-sahp	*kelabu/asap*
light ...	... *moo*-duh	... *muda*
multicoloured	ber-*wahr*-nah-*wahr*-nee	*berwarna-warni*
orange	*o*-rehn/*jing*-guh	*oren/jingga*
pink	*meh*-rah(h) *jahm*-boo	*merah jambu*
purple	*oon*-goo	*ungu*
red	*meh*-rah(h)	*merah*
white	*poo*-ti(h)	*putih*
yellow	*koo*-ning	*kuning*

TOILETRIES   BARANGAN BILIK AIR

In smaller towns you may find some of these items in traditional Chinese medicine shops.

comb	*see*-kaht	sikat
condoms	*kon*-dom	kondom
contraceptive ...	*oo*-baht/	ubat/
device/	*ah*-laht pe-*rahn*-chang	alat perancang
medicine	ke-loo-*ahr*-guh	keluarga
deodorant	dee-*o*-do-rahn	deodoran
laxative	*joo*-lahp	julap
lip balm	bahm *bee*-bir	bam bibir
lipstick	*gin*-choo/chaht *bee*-bir	gincu/cat bibir
moisturising	kreem	krim
cream	pe-*lehm*-bahb *koo*-lit	pelembab kulit
mosquito repellent	*oo*-baht *nyah*-mu(k)	ubat nyamuk
razor	pen-*choo*-kur	pencukur
razor blade	*pee*-sow *choo*-kur	pisau cukur
sanitary napkins	*twah*-luh wah-*nee*-tuh	tuala wanita
shampoo	*shahm*-poo	syampu
shaver	pen-*choo*-kur	pencukur
shaving cream	kreem *choo*-kur	krim cukur
soap	*sah*-bun	sabun
sunblock cream	kreem pe-*lin*-dung	krim pelindung
	chah-*hai*-yuh	cahaya
	mah-tuh-*hah*-ree	matahari
tampons	*tahm*-pohn	tampon
tissues	*ti*-soo	tisu
toothbrush	be-*roos gee*-gee	berus gigi

SHOPPING

FRESH IS BEST

Malaysians have at least two showers a day to combat the extreme heat and humidity. Take the hint. As well as ensuring you're sweet-smelling, more frequent showers and using talcum powder will help to avoid fungal infections.

FOR THE BABY

baby's bottle	*bo*-tol *bah*-yee	*botol bayi*
baby clothes (children's)	pah-*kai*-ahn *bah*-yee (*kah*-nah(k)-*kah*-nah(k))	*pakaian bayi* (*kanak-kanak*)
baby food	*mah*-kah-nahn *bah*-yee	*makanan bayi*
baby powder	be-*dahk bah*-yee	*bedak bayi*
bib	bib	*bib*
boiled water	air *mah*-sah(k)	*air masak*
lukewarm	swahm	*suam*
disposable nappies (diapers)	kain *lahm*-pin yahng bo-*leh(h)* dee-*boo*-ahng	*kain lampin yang boleh dibuang*
dummy (pacifier)	*poo*-ting	*puting*
nappy rash cream	kreem *roo*-ahm *bah*-yee	*krim ruam bayi*
powdered milk	*soo*-soo *ser*-bu(k)	*susu serbuk*

UNTUK BAYI

MUSIC

I'm looking for a ... CD.
sai-yuh nah(k) men-*chah*-ree CD ...

Saya nak mencari CD ...

Do you have ...?
ah-duh ...?

Ada ...?

I heard a band/singer called ...
sai-yuh *per*-nah(h) men-*deh*-ngahr koom-poo-lahn/ pe-*nyah*-nyee ber-*nah*-muh ...

Saya pernah mendengar kumpulan/ penyanyi bernama ...

Can I listen to this CD here?
bo-*leh(h)* tah(k) *sai*-yuh men-*deh*-ngahr CD *ee*-nee dee *see*-nee?

Boleh tak saya mendengar CD ini di sini?

I want a blank tape.
sai-yuh nah(k) ka-seht *ko*-song

Saya nak kaset kosong.

MUZIK

STATIONERY & PUBLICATIONS

ALAT TULIS-MENULIS & PENERBITAN

There are many bookstores and newsagents in the larger cities that carry English titles. Stock up before you head out.

Is there an English-language
bookshop here?

ah-duh ke-*dai* boo-koo
bah-*hah*-suh *ing*-ge-ris tah(k)
dee *see*-nee?

*Ada kedai buku
bahasa Inggeris
tak di sini?*

Is there an English-language section?

ah-duh bah-*hah*-gee-ahn
bah-*hah*-suh *ing*-ge-ris tah(k)?

*Ada bahagian
bahasa Inggeris tak?*

Do you sell ...?	*ah*-duh-kah(h) ... dee-*joo*-ahl?	*Adakah ... dijual?*
envelopes	*sahm*-pool *soo*-raht	*sampul surat*
magazines	mah-*jah*-luh(h)	*majalah*
newspapers (English-language)	soo-*raht khah*-bahr (bah-*hah*-suh *ing*-ge-ris)	*surat khabar (bahasa Inggeris)*
novels	*no*-vel/*boo*-koo che-*ree*-tuh	*novel/buku cerita*
pens	pehn	*pen*
postcards	*pos*-kahd	*poskad*
stamps	se-*tehm*	*setem*
writing paper	*ker*-tahs *too*-lis	*kertas tulis*
... dictionaries	*kah*-moos ...	*kamus ...*
bilingual	*dwee*-bah-hah-suh	*dwibahasa*
pocket	*po*-keht	*poket*
... maps	*peh*-tuh ...	*peta ...*
city	bahn-duh-*rai*-yuh	*bandaraya*
regional	dah-*eh*-rah(h)/ *rahm*-tow	*daerah/ rantau*
road	*jah*-lahn	*jalan*

SHOPPING

PHOTOGRAPHY   **FOTOGRAFI**

There are film and processing shops all over Malaysia, which also take passport photos. Photo processing is good quality and it's much cheaper than many places overseas. You can bargain for cameras and other equipment, unless you're buying them in a department store.

I'd like a film for this camera.
   sai-yuh nah(k) *fee*-lem   *Saya nak filem*
   oon-tu(k) ka-*me*-ruh *ee*-nee   *untuk kamera ini.*
How much is it for
processing and developing?
   be-*rah*-puh *hahr*-guh   *Berapa harga*
   pen-*choo*-chee-ahn   *pencucian filem ini?*
   fee-lem *ee*-nee?
When will it be ready?
   bee-luh see-*ahp*?   *Bila siap?*
Do you repair cameras here?
   bo-*leh*(h) *bai*-kee   *Boleh baiki*
   ka-me-ruh tah(k) dee *see*-nee?   *kamera tak di sini?*

battery	*ba*-te-ree	*bateri*
B&W (film)	(*fee*-lem) *hee*-tahm *poo*-ti(h)	*(filem) hitam putih*
camera	*ka*-me-ruh	*kamera*
colour (film)	(*fee*-lem) ber-*wahr*-nuh	*(filem) berwarna*
to develop	men-*choo*-cee	*cuci*
film	(*fee*-lem)	*filem*
flash(bulb)	pahn-*chah*-rahn (*mehm*-tul)	*pancaran (mentul)*
lens	*lehn*-suh	*lensa*
light meter	*mee*-ter chah-*hai*-yuh	*meter cahaya*
photograph	fo-to/*gahm*-bahr	*foto/gambar*
to print	men-*choo*-chee	*mencuci*
(make) reprints	(*boo*-aht) *sah*-lee-nahn	*(buat) salinan*
slides	slaid	*slaid*
videotape	*pee*-tuh *vi*-dee-o	*pita video*

SMOKING   MEROKOK

Some cigarettes in Malaysia have a higher tar/nicotine content
than they do in other countries. If you're smoking 'lights' they
may not be as 'light' as you think! The intense spicy aroma of the
imported Indonesian 'clove cigarettes', *kretek*, *kreh*-teh(k), will
be the smell of your Malaysian memories. Smuggling *kretek* into
Malaysia is a big but illegal business.

A packet of cigarettes, please.
   to-long *bah*-gee   *Tolong bagi*
   se-*ko*-tah(k) *ro*-ko(k)   *sekotak rokok.*
Do you have a light?
   ah-duh *mahm*-chis?   *Ada mancis?*
Are these cigarettes strong or mild?
   ah-duh-kah(h) *ro*-ko(k)   *Adakah rokok*
   ee-nee ke-*rahs* ah-*tow* ri-*ngahn*? *ini keras atau ringan?*
Can I smoke here?
   bo-*leh(h)* tah(k)   *Boleh tak*
   me-*ro*-ko(k) dee *see*-nee?   *merokok di sini?*
Do you have an ashtray?
   ah-duh-kah(h) be-*kahs*   *Adakah bekas*
   ah-boo *ro*-ko(k)?   *abu rokok?*
Please don't smoke.
   to-long jah-*ngahn* me-*ro*-ko(k)   *Tolong jangan merokok.*
I'm trying to give up smoking.
   sai-yuh se-*dahng* men-*choo*-buh   *Saya sedang mencuba*
   ber-*hen*-tee me-*ro*-ko(k)   *berhenti merokok.*

cigarette papers	*ker*-tahs *ro*-ko(k)	kertas rokok
cigarettes	*ro*-ko(k)	rokok
clove cigarette	*kreh*-teh(k)	kretek
filter	*fil*-ter	filter
lighter	*mahn*-chis *ah*-pee	mancis api
matches	*mahn*-chis	mancis
menthol	*mehn*-tol	mentol
pipe	paip	paip
smoke	*ah*-sahp	asap
to smoke	me-*ro*-ko(k)	merokok
tobacco	tehm-*bah*-kow	tembakau

SIZES & COMPARISONS

UKURAN & PERBANDINAGAN

a little bit	se-*dee*-kit	sedikit
big	be-*sahr*	besar
bigger	le-*bi(h)* be-*sahr*	lebih besar
biggest	*pah*-ling be-*sahr*	paling besar
enough	*choo*-kup	cukup
heavy	be-*raht*	berat
too much/many	ter-*lah*-loo *bah*-nyah(k)	terlalu banyak
less	koo-*rahng*	kurang
light	ri-*ngahn*	ringan
long	pahn-*jahng*	panjang
many	*bah*-nyah(k)	banyak
more	le-*bi(h)* *bah*-nyah(k)	lebih banyak
narrow	sem-*pit*	sempit
short	*pehm*-deh(k)	pendek
small	ke-*chil*	kecil
smaller	le-*bi(h)* ke-*chil*	lebih kecil
smallest	*pah*-ling ke-*chil*	paling kecil
spacious	loo-*ahs*	luas
tall	*ting*-gee	tinggi
too big	ter-*lah*-loo be-*sahr*	terlalu besar
very big	*sah*-ngaht be-*sahr*	sangat besar
wide	le-*bahr*	lebar

SHOPPING

WEIGHTS & MEASURES

millimetre	*mi*-li-*mee*-ter	*milimeter*
centimetre	*sen*-ti-*mee*-ter	*sentimeter*
metre	*mee*-ter	*meter*
kilometre	*ki*-lo-*mee*-ter	*kilometer*
litre	*lee*-ter	*liter*
gram	gram	*gram*
kilogram	*ki*-lo-gram	*kilogram*

BERAT & UKURAN

STREET LIFE

You are unlikely to be harassed by people on the streets, even in the rougher parts of town.

Come here!
  see-nee-lah(h)/*mah*-ree   *Sinilah/Mari*
  see-nee-lah(h)   *sinilah.*
Go away!
  per-gee!/be-*lah(h)*!   *Pergi!/Belah!*
I don't have any money.
  tah(k) *ah*-duh *doo*-it   *Tak ada duit.*

alley	lo-rong	*lorong*
footpath	*ping*-gir *jah*-lahn	*pinggir jalan*
hawker	pen-*joo*-ahl	*penjual*
homeless person	o-rahng *gee*-luh	*orang gila*
thief	pen-*choo*-ree	*pencuri*
street	*jah*-lahn	*jalan*
street stall (food)	ge-*rai/wah*-rung	*gerai/warung*
traffic lights	*lahm*-poo	*lampu*
	ee-*shah*-raht	*isyarat*

SHOPPING

USEFUL WORDS

PERKATAAN YANG BERGUNA

to buy	mem-be-*lee*	*membeli*
cheap	*moo*-rah(h)	*murah*
to export	meng-*ehk*-sport	*mengeksport*
to import	meng-*im*-port	*mengimport*
made in	dee-per-*boo*-aht dee	*diperbuat di*
old	*too*-uh/*lah*-muh	*tua/lama*
to order	me-*nehm*-pah(h)	*menempah*
quality	*moo*-too/*kwah*-li-tee	*mutu/kualiti*
quantity	*joom*-lah(h)	*jumlah*
to sell	men-*joo*-ahl	*menjual*
type (of product)	je-*nis*/*mah*-chahm	*jenis/macam*

MAKANAN   FOOD

The fabulous array of Malaysian food will impress you from the moment you arrive. You'll probably eat a lot of your meals in *kedai kopi*, ke-*dai ko*-pee, coffee shops or *gerai*, ge-*rai*, hawker stalls that serve tasty dishes, snacks and cooling drinks. Cooked up on the spot or served buffet-style, these are clean and delicious. Of course there are also restaurants in bigger cities, and fast food outlets are spreading around the country like fat on a hot grill. But for authentic tastes, try the hawkers' stalls and smaller restaurants, teeming with people from early in the morning till late at night.

During fasting month in the Malay areas, only Chinese or non-Muslim Indian shops will be open during daylight hours. Fast food chains usually remain open for non-Muslim clientele. However, in northern states and some rural areas, you should keep a low profile while eating and drinking in public out of respect for those who are fasting.

breakfast	*mah*-kahn *pah*-gee; *sah*-rah-pahn	*makan pagi; sarapan*
lunch	*mah*-kahn te-ngah-*hah*-ree	*makan tengahari*
dinner	*mah*-kahn *mah*-lahm	*makan malam*

BREAKFAST   MAKAN PAGI

Having breakfast out is a national pastime. Some roadside stalls and *mamak*, *mah*-mah(k), (Muslim Indian) restaurants open before sunrise. A mid-morning snack or meal is also called breakfast, and many of these foods are available all day. Sweet *teh tarik*, teh *tah*-rik, is a must for a true Malaysian-style breakfast. Of course, for the unadventurous, hotels and fast food chains serve Western style breakfasts, and the big cities have patisseries and bakeries.

COMMON MALAYSIAN BREAKFASTS:

nasi lemak   *nah*-see le-*mah(k)*
  rice cooked with coconut milk and pandan leaves, served with a very spicy anchovy sauce, peanuts, a hardboiled egg, tomato and cucumber, and sometimes chicken. Utterly, utterly delicious. Don't leave Malaysia without trying it.

roti canai   *ro*-tee *chah*-nai
  flat bread fried in ghee and served with curried lentils or some other spicy sauce. A little milder than nasi lemak.

tosai   *to*-sai
  similar to *roti canai*, but lighter and roasted rather than fried

kueh   *koo*-eh(h)
  include the savoury curry puff, as well as small sweet cakes. Bite-sized, to add to your breakfast.

nasi dagang   *nah*-see *dah*-gahng
  an east coast specialty, this super-rich coconut rice – served with some form of curry or meat dish – will fill you up immediately

VEGETARIAN & SPECIAL MEALS
MAKANAN SAYURAN & MAKANAN KHAS

If you're a vegetarian, you can specify *tanpa daging*, *tahn*-pah *dah*-ging, 'without meat', or *sayur saja*, *sai*-yur *sah*-juh, 'vegetables only'. To some Malays *daging*, 'meat', means beef only, so you may need to elaborate: *tanpa daging, ayam dan lain-lain*, *tahn*-pah *dah*-ging, *ai*-yahm dahn lain-lain, 'without meat/beef, chicken and other things.'

I'm vegetarian.
  sai-yuh *mah*-kahn *sai*-yur   *Saya makan sayur*
  sah-juh/*sai*-yuh tah(k)   *saja/saya tak*
  mah-kahn *dah*-ging   *makan daging.*

FOOD

I don't/	*sai*-yuh tah(k) *soo*-kuh/	*Saya tak suka/*
can't eat ...	bo-*leh(h) mah*-kahn ...	*boleh makan ...*
chicken	*ai*-yahm	*ayam*
beef	*dah*-ging *lehm*-boo	*daging lembu*
eggs	te-*lur*	*telur*
fish	*ee*-kahn	*ikan*
ham	*dah*-ging *bah*-bee;	*daging babi;*
	hahm	*ham*
meat	*dah*-ging	*daging*
milk and cheese	*soo*-soo dahn *keh*-joo	*susu dan keju*
prawns	*oo*-dahng	*udang*

I'm allergic to ...	*sai*-yuh ah-*ler*-jik	*Saya alergik*
	kah-low *mah*-kahn ...	*kalau makan ...*
dairy products	*soo*-soo	*susu*
peanuts	*kah*-chahng	*kacang*

Do you have any vegetarian dishes?
    ah-duh *mah*-kah-nahn   *Ada makanan*
    sai-yu-rahn *sah*-juh?   *sayuran saja?*
Does this dish have meat/chicken?
    ah-duh *dah*-ging/   *Ada daging/*
    ai-yahm tah(k) dah-*lahm*   *ayam tak dalam*
    mah-sah-kahn *ee*-nee?   *masakan ini?*
Can I get this without meat/chicken?
    bo-*leh(h)* tah(k) *mah*-sah(k)   *Boleh tak masak*
    tahm-puh *dah*-ging/*ai*-yahm?   *tanpa daging/ayam?*
Does it contain eggs?
    mah-kah-nahn *ee*-nee   *Makanan ini*
    ah-duh te-*lur* tah(k)?   *ada telur tak?*

Kosher restaurants are unknown in Malaysia, however *halal*, *hah*-lahl, restaurants do not use pork products.

Is there a halal restaurant here?
    ah-duh *reh*-sto-rahn   *Ada restoran*
    hah-lahl dee *see*-nee?   *halal di sini?*
Is this halal?
    ee-nee *hah*-lahl-kah(h)?   *Ini halalkah?*

FOOD

EATING OUT   MAKAN DI LUAR

Where can   ... dee *mah*-nuh?   ... *di mana?*
 I find a ... ?
   food stall   ge-*rai*   *Gerai*
   night market   *pah*-sahr *mah*-lahm   *Pasar malam*
   restaurant   *reh*-sto-rahn   *Restoran*

Where's a ...   *reh*-sto-rahn ...   *Restoran ...*
restaurant?   dee *mah*-nuh?   *di mana?*
   cheap   moo-*rah*(h)   *murah*
   fish head curry   *kah*-ree ke-*pah*-luh   *kari kepala*
                       ee-kahn   *ikan*

We'd like a table for (five), please.
   to-long *bah*-gee *meh*-juh   *Tolong bagi meja*
   oon-tu(k) (*lee*-muh) o-rahng   *untuk (lima) orang.*
I want to eat ...
   sai-yuh nah(k) *mah*-kahn ...   *Saya nak makan ...*
What dish is that?
   mah-sah-kahn *ah*-puh ee-*too*? *Masakan apa itu?*
What's in that dish?
   ah-duh *ah*-puh dah-*lahm*   *Ada apa dalam*
   mah-sah-kahn ee-*too*?   *masakan itu?*
Is it spicy?
   pe-*dahs* tah(k)?   *Pedas tak?*
How much does one portion cost?
   ber-*rah*-puh *hahr*-guh *oon*-tu(k) *Berapa harga untuk*
   sah-too bah-*hah*-gee-ahn?   *satu bahagian?*

THEY MAY SAY ...

mah-kahn *ah*-puh?   What would you like to eat?

mee-num *ah*-puh?   What would you like to drink?

We're in a hurry. Please
bring our food quickly.

    kah-mee nah(k) che-*paht* nee.   *Kami nak cepat ni.*
    to-long *bah*-wuh *mah*-kah-nahn   *Tolong bawa makanan*
    che-*paht* see-*kit*   *cepat sikit.*

Do I get it myself or
do they bring it to us?

    lai-yahn *di*-ree ah-*tow*   *Layan diri atau*
    me-*reh*-kuh yahng *bah*-wuh?   *mereka yang bawa?*

UP TO YOUR ELBOWS

There's a certain finesse that needs to be developed
when eating food with your hands. Always use your right
hand only. Hold a piece of *roti canai*, *ro-tee chah-nai*,
or meat between your thumb and two smallest fingers
and then use your pointer and index fingers to
separate a bite-sized chunk. If you're eating rice, use
your fingers like a scoop and shovel the food into your
mouth with your thumb. Tastes even better!

Please bring a/an/the ...	*to*-long *bah*-wuh ...	*Tolong bawa ...*
ashtray	be-*kahs* ah-boo *ro*-ko(k)	*bekas abu rokok*
bill	bil	*bil*
cup	*chah*-wahn	*cawan*
fork	*gahr*-foo	*garfu*
glass	ge-*lahs*	*gelas*
glass of water (with/ without ice)	se-ge-*lahs* air *ko*-song (de-*ngahn*/ *tahm*-puh ais)	*segelas air kosong (dengan/ tanpa ais)*
knife	*pee*-sow	*pisau*
menu	*meh*-noo	*menu*
plate	*ping*-gahn	*pinggan*
spoon	*soo*-doo	*sudu*
toothpick	pen-*choo*-li(k) *gee*-gee	*penculik gigi*

FOOD

This isn't cooked properly.

    tah(k) *choo*-kup *mah*-sah(k) nee   *Tak cukup masak ni.*

Not too spicy please.

    jah-*ngahn* ter-*lah*-loo pe-*dahs*   *Jangan terlalu pedas.*

No MSG please.

    to-long jah-*ngahn*   *Tolong jangan*
    pah-kai *ah*-jee-no-*mo*-to   *pakai ajinomoto.*

No ice, please.

    tahn-puh ais   *Tanpa ais.*

Less oily please.

    koo-*rahng* min-yah(k)   *Kurang minyak.*

FOOD FOR THOUGHT

Bear hugs or a peck on the cheek as a way of greeting are totally foreign to the vast majority of Malaysians, and are best avoided. Keep in mind that there are simply some things you shouldn't do with your left hand, because Malays use their left hand for cleaning themselves. It's a good idea to get into the habit of using your right hand for passing items – and definitely for eating. It's shocking and filthy to touch food with your left hand. So don't do it. Ever!

This is (too) ...	*mah*-kah-nahn	*Makanan*
	ee-nee (ter-*lah*-loo) ...	*ini (terlalu) ...*
bitter	pah-*hit*	*pahit*
cold	se-*joo*(k)	*sejuk*
delicious	se-*dahp*/eh-*nah*(k)	*sedap/enak*
fresh	se-*gahr*	*segar*
hot	*pah*-nahs	*panas*
salty	*mah*-sin	*masin*
sour	*mah*-sahm	*masam*
spicy	pe-*dahs*	*pedas*
spoiled	*bah*-see	*basi*
stale	*mah*-su(k) *ah*-ngin	*masuk angin*
sweet	*mah*-nis	*manis*
unripe	be-*lum mah*-sah(k)	*belum masak*
uncooked	*men*-tah(h)	*mentah*

TYPICAL DISHES   MAKANAN BIASA

Many small restaurants, stalls and coffee shops don't have menus –
what's available is usually advertised on the wall, the stall tarpaulin
or the side of the *kaki-lima*, **kah-kee lee-muh**, 'footpath'.

The names of many dishes specify how they're prepared, such
as *ayam bakar*, **ai-yahm bah-kahr**, 'grilled chicken'.

MENU DECODER

Main Course		Makanan Utama
arnab	**ahr**-nahb	rabbit
ayam ...	**ai-yahm** ...	... chicken
bakar	**bah**-kahr	grilled
goreng	**go**-rehng	fried
babi	**bah**-bee	pig
bakso/ba'so	**bah(k)**-so/**bah**-so	meatball soup
bubur nasi	**boo**-bur **nah**-see	rice porridge with anchovies, vegetables, and chicken
bubur kacang	**boo**-bur	mung bean
hijau	**kah**-chahng **hee**-jow	porridge (sweet)
capati	chah-**pah**-tee	Indian flat flour pancake
daging lembu	**dah**-ging **lehm**-boo	beef
daging biri-biri	**dah**-ging **bi**-ree-**bi**-ree	lamb/mutton
gado-gado	**gah**-do-**gah**-do	boiled vegetables and peanut sauce
hati	**hah**-tee	(chicken) liver
ikan	**ee**-kahn	fish
air tawar	air **tah**-wahr	freshwater
air masin	air **mah**-sin	saltwater
ikan bilis	**ee**-kahn **bi**-lis	dried anchovies, usually made into a spicy sauce
ikan keli	**ee**-kahn ke-**lee**	catfish
itik	**ee**-tik	duck
jagung bakar	**jah**-gung **bah**-kahr	roasted corn
kambing	**kahm**-bing	goat
kangkung	**kahng**-kung	water spinach

FOOD

kari	*kah*-ree	curry
kentang	ken-*tahng*	potatoes
kepah	ke-*pah(h)*	mussels
ketam	ke-*tahm*	crab
ketupat	ke-*too*-paht	boiled pressed rice
kicap	*kee*-chahp	soy sauce
kuay teow	koo-*ay tee*-ow	flat, wide rice noodles
laksa Kelantan	*lah(k)*-suh ke-lahn-*tahn*	spicy rice noodle soup with coconut milk
laksa Penang	*lah(k)*-suh pe-*nahng*	rice noodle soup in fish sauce
mee	mee	wheat noodles
mee ...	mee ...	
goreng	*go*-rehng	fried noodles with meat and vegetables
kuah/sup	koo-*ah(h)*/ soop	noodle soup with meat and vegetables
rebus	*ree*-bus	noodle soup with starchy, spicy sauce, fried tofu and vegetables
murtabak	moor-*tah*-bah(k)	pancakes stuffed with beef or chicken filling with onions and spices

THAT'S NOT A KNIFE!

When you eat in stalls or small restaurants, you'll usually receive a large spoon and a fork (in Chinese restaurants, of course, you'll get chopsticks). No knife is provided. Malaysians, if they're eating with their hands, have a technique of pinning down the meat with their thumb and tearing it with the other fingers (the left hand is not involved at all, since it is considered dirty). If you want a knife, you'll have to ask for one!

nan	nahn	Indian grilled bread
nasi	nah-see	cooked rice
nasi ...	nah-see ...	
campur	chahm-pur	cooked rice with a selection of meat and vegetable dishes on one plate
goreng	go-rehng	fried rice
goreng istimewa	go-rehng is-tee-meh-wuh	special fried rice
ayam	ai-yahm	chicken rice
beriyani	be-ree-yah-nee	Indian rice with spicy chicken, beef, or lamb curry
dagang	dah-gahng	special rice cooked with coconut milk eaten with fish shrimp, or eggs (Peninsular East Coast specialty)
impit	im-pit	cubes of pressed rice, often served with peanut sauce
kerabu	ke-rah-boo	rice with cut up vegetables and a roasted grated coconut (Peninsular East Coast specialty)
lemak	le-mah(k)	rice cooked in coconut milk with spicy sauce and anchovies, with or without meat
minyak	min-yah(k)	ghee rice with curries
patprik	paht-pri(k)	rice with beef in a special Thai sauce
otak	o-tah(k)	brains

FOOD

perut	pe-*rut*	tripe
petai	pe-*tai*	large, tasty bean
pulut	pu-*lut*	glutinous rice
rendang	rehn-dahng	meat cooked slowly in spices and coconut
rojak	ro-jah(k)	fruit and vegetables cut up with a sweet and spicy peanut sauce
roti	ro-tee	bread
roti ...	ro-tee ...	
bakar	*bah*-kahr	toast with jam
canai	*chah*-nai	Indian breakfast bread, shaped like a pancake, served with curry or lentils
jala	*jah*-luh	thin, yellow netted bread eaten with curry
sambal	sahm-bahl	spicy sauce to eat with rice
sate ...	sah-teh ...	... satay
ayam	*ai*-yahm	chicken
daging	*dah*-ging	beef
kambing	*kahm*-bing	goat
soto	so-to	chicken soup with rice cubes
sotong	so-tong	squid
tahu	*tah*-hoo	tofu
telur ...	te-*lur* ...	... egg
goreng	*go*-rehng	fried
rebus	*ree*-bus	boiled
masak	*mah*-sah(k)	soft-boiled
separuh	se-*pahr*-u(h)	
telur dadar	te-*lur* dah-*dahr*	omelette

tempeh	*tehm*-peh(h)	tempeh (fermented soybean cakes)
tempeh goreng	*tehm*-peh(h) go-rehng	fried tempeh
tiram	*ti*-rahm	oysters
ubi	*oo*-bee	potatoes
udang	*oo*-dahng	shrimp
udang karang	*oo*-dahng kah-rahng	lobster

Snacks & Sweets

Makanan Ringan & Makanan Manis

agar-agar	ah-*gahr*-ah-*gahr*	gelatine (made with seaweed)
ais krim	ais krim	ice cream
dodol	*do*-dol	chewy, toffee-like sweet pudding, also in durian flavour
karipap	*kah*-ree-pahp	curry puff
keropok	ke-*ro*-po(k)	prawn or rice crackers
kueh	*koo*-eh(h)	sweet or savoury snacks (various kinds)
kueh (lapis)	*koo*-eh(h) *lah*-pis	(layer) cake
manisan	*mah*-nee-sahn	sweets
onde-onde; buah melaka	on-*deh*-on-*deh*; *boo*-uh(h) me-*lah*-kuh	glutinous rice ball stuffed with palm sugar
pau	pow	steamed rice flour buns with a variety of fillings
pisang goreng	*pee*-sahng go-rehng	fried banana
rojak	*ro*-jah(k)	fruit salad in a sweet, spicy peanut sauce
tahu	*tah*-hoo	tofu

FOOD

SELF-CATERING   MASAKAN SENDIRI

Can I please have ...?	*to*-long *bah*-gee ... ?	*Tolong bagi ...?*
an orange	*o*-rehn se-*bee*-jee	*oren sebiji*
a kilo of oranges	*o*-rehn se-*kee*-lo	*oren sekilo*
two kilos of oranges	*doo*-uh *kee*-lo *o*-rehn	*dua kilo oren*
half a kilo of oranges	se-te-*ngah(h)* *kee*-lo *o*-rehn	*setengah kilo oren*
seven mangoes	too-*juh bee*-jee *mahng*-guh	*tujuh biji mangga*

AT THE MARKET   DI PASAR

Delicious fresh fruit, exotic vegetables and spices, fresh fish and meats abound in the Malaysian *pasar*, **pah-sahr**. Whether you want to cook a meal yourself or try to find a taste of home, this should be your first stop – the nucleus of any Malaysian town. A multitude of other goods are on offer: rice and grains, packaged goods, kitchenware, tobacco and so on. Your nose will tell you when you've hit the meat section.

How much is this?
    be-*rah*-puh   *Berapa*
    hahr-guh-nyuh *ee*-nee?   *harganya ini?*
How much is a kilogram of ...?
    be-*rah*-puh   *Berapa*
    hahr-guh se-*kee*-lo ... ?   *harga sekilo ...?*
Can I taste it?
    bo-*leh(h) choo*-buh?   *Boleh cuba?*
I don't want that one.
    tah(k) nah(k) yahng *ee*-too   *Tak nak yang itu.*
Please give me another one.
    to-long *bah*-gee yahng lain   *Tolong bagi yang lain.*

bread	*ro*-tee	*roti*
noodles	mee	*mee*
rice (cooked)	*nah*-see	*nasi*
rice (uncooked)	be-*rahs*	*beras*

WORLD FOOD

In Malaysia you'll find a variety of Chinese cuisines, including Cantonese, Hokkien, Szechuan, Teochew, Hakka, Shanghai, and Beijing styles of cooking.

Among the Indian restaurants, stalls and *kedai kopi*, ke-*dai ko*-pee, you'll get to try South Indian, Muslim Indian, *mamat*, *mah*-maht, and North Indian and Pakistani dishes. Of course Malay food is widely available, as is Indonesian – the two are very similar. *Nyonya* is a unique blend of Chinese and Malay styles of cooking, and *Baba-Nyonya* or *Peranakan* is the style of early Chinese immigrants who adopted some of the cooking of the Malays. Thai cuisine is also widely available in Malaysia.

Meat / Daging

English	Pronunciation	Malay
beef	*dah*-ging *lehm*-boo	*daging lembu*
brains	*o*-tahk	*otak*
chicken	*ai*-yahm	*ayam*
duck	*ee*-tik	*itik*
goat	*kahm*-bing	*kambing*
lamb	*ah*-nah(k) *bi*-ree-*bi*-ree	*anak biri-biri*
liver	*hah*-tee	*hati*
mutton	*bi*-ree-*bi*-ree	*biri-biri*
pig	*bah*-bee	*babi*
rabbit	*ahr*-nahb	*arnab*

Seafood / Makanan Laut

English	Pronunciation	Malay
catfish	*ee*-kahn ke-*lee*	*ikan keli*
cockles	ke-*rahng*	*kerang*
crab	ke-*tahm*	*ketam*
freshwater fish	*ee*-kahn air *tah*-wahr	*ikan air tawar*
lobster	*oo*-dahng *kah*-rahng	*udang karang*
mussels	ke-*pah(h)*	*kepah*
oysters	*ti*-rahm	*tiram*
saltwater fish	*ee*-kahn air *mah*-sin	*ikan air masin*
salted dried fish	*ee*-kahn ke-*ring*	*ikan kering*
shrimp	*oo*-dahng	*udang*
squid	*so*-tong	*sotong*

Vegetables / Sayur-Sayuran

English	Pronunciation	Malay
beans	*kah*-chahng	*kacang*
cabbage	*ku*-bis	*kubis*
carrot	*lo*-ba(k)	*lobak*
cauliflower	*ku*-bis *boo*-nguh	*kubis bunga*
corn	*jah*-gung	*jagung*
cucumber	*tee*-mun	*timun*
eggplant	te-*rung*	*terung*
mushrooms	*chen*-dah-wahn/*koo*-laht	*cendawan/kulat*
onion	*bah*-wahng	*bawang*
potato	*ken*-tahng	*kentang*
pumpkin	*lah*-boo	*labu*
tomato	to-*mah*-to	*tomato*

FOOD

Fruit   Buah-Buahan

Malaysia is the land of heavenly fruit. Whether you shop at road-side stalls, in the markets or in supermarkets, you'll find a devastatingly delicious variety of tropical and temperate fruits. Some fruits are only found here, like the *ciku*, **chee**-**koo**, which resembles a fuzzy potato with a hint of vanilla flavour.

FEAST ON FRUIT

guava   *jahm*-boo   *jambu*
    a hard, pear-shaped fruit. The small black seeds should not be eaten. *Jambu air*, *jahm*-**boo air**, is a small, pink, smooth, strawberry shaped variety with a fragrant taste.

jackfruit   *nahng*-kah   *nangka*
    sellers often break the fruit up into segments, which are then packed, ready to eat. The flesh is rubbery, sweet and strongly flavoured. Jackfruit trees are everywhere and can be recognised by their huge pendulous fruit, often wrapped in plastic bags for protection while they ripen on the tree.

mangosteen *mang*-gis   *manggis*
    easily recognised by its thick, purple-brown, fibrous skin, which protects mouth-watering, sweet-sour, white flesh

rambutan   *rahm*-boo-tahn   *rambutan*
    bright red fruit covered in soft, hairy spines, and containing a delicious, lychee-like, sweet white flesh

salak   *sah*-lah(k)   *salak*
    brown snake-skin fruit of the Zalacca palm, the flesh of which is crunchy and nutty. An Indonesian fruit, occasionally sold in Malaysian markets.

starfruit   **be**-*lim*-bing   *belimbing*
    A watery, thirst-quenching fruit shaped like a star, end on. It's one of the few fruits eaten without being peeled.

FOOD

apple	*eh*-pahl	*epal*
avocado	ah-vo-*kah*-do	*avokado*
banana	*pee*-sahng	*pisang*
cempedak	*chem*-pe-dah(k)	*cempedak*
coconut	ke-*lah*-puh	*kelapa*

Look for *kelapa muda*, (ke-*lah*-puh *moo*-duh), 'young coconut', which makes a refreshing drink.

lemon	*leh*-mon	*lemon*
lime	*lee*-mow	*limau*
mango	*mang*-guh	*mangga*
orange	*o*-rehn	*oren*
papaya	*beh*-ti(k)	*betik*
peanuts	*kah*-chang	*kacang*
pineapple	*neh*-nahs	*nenas*
strawberry	*strah*-beh-ree	*strawberi*
soursop	doo-*ree*-ahn be-*lahn*-duh	*durian belanda*
watermelon	tem-*bee*-kai	*tembikai*

ROYAL STINK

An encounter with *durian*, *doo*-ree-ahn, the 'king of fruits', is a memorable experience for the fruit lover. *Durians* announce themselves in any market by exuding an incredibly pungent stench. If you can hold your breath long enough to approach, and swallow the rich, creamy flesh, you may get to crave the unique flavour.

Spices & Condiments   Rempah-Rempahan

chilli	chi-lee	cili
chilli shrimp paste	sam-bahl be-lah-chahn	sambal belacan
chilli sauce	sam-bahl; sos chi-lee	sambal; sos cili
cinnamon	kai-yoo mah-nis	kayu manis
cloves	cheng-ki(h)	cengkih
curry	kah-ree	kari
garlic	bah-wahng poo-ti(h)	bawang putih
ginger	hah-lee-uh	halia
mortar and pestle	bah-too toom-bu(k)	batu tumbuk
MSG	ah-jee-no-mo-to	ajinomoto
oil	min-ya(k)	minyak
black pepper	lah-duh hee-tahm	lada hitam
salt	gah-rahm	garam
soy sauce (salty)	kee-chahp (mah-sin)	kicap (masin)
sugar	goo-luh	gula
sweet soy sauce	kee-chahp mah-nis	kicap manis
tomato sauce	sos to-mah-to	sos tomato
turmeric	koon-yit	kunyit
vinegar	choo-kuh	cuka

FEELING HOT HOT HOT

cili (the smaller, the hotter)	chi-lee	chilli
pedas	pe-dahs	spicy
sambal	sahm-bahl	chilli sauce/paste

Cooking Methods   Cara Masakan

baked	bah-kahr dah-lahm o-vehn/ke-too-hahr	bakar dalam oven/ketuhar
boiled	ree-bus	rebus
cooked in coconut milk	mah-sah(k) le-mah(k); goo-lai	masak lemak; gulai
fried	go-rehng	goreng
grilled	bah-kahr	bakar
smoked	ah-sahp	asap
spit-roasted	pahng-gang	panggang
steamed	koo-koos	kukus

FOOD

DRINKS   MINUMAN

I want to drink ...
sai-yuh nah(k) *mee*-num ...   *Saya nak minum ...*
Do you have ...?
ah-duh ...?   *Ada ...?*

Hot/Warm Drinks   Minuman Panas/Suam

Except in upmarket restaurants and hotels, tea and coffee are nearly
always served sweet and milky. If you want black coffee or plain
tea, ask for *teh/kopi kosong*, 'empty tea/coffee'.

coffee ...	*ko*-pee ...	*kopi ...*
without sugar	*tahn*-puh *goo*-luh	*tanpa gula*
without milk	o	*o*
without milk and sugar	o *ko*-song	*o kosong*
coffee with milk	*ko*-pee *soo*-soo	*kopi susu*
tea without sugar	teh *tahn*-puh *goo*-luh	*teh tanpa gula*
tea without milk	teh o	*teh o*
tea with milk	teh *soo*-soo	*teh susu*
frothed tea	teh *tah*-rik	*teh tarik*
boiled water	air *mah*-sah(k)	*air masak*
warm water	air swahm	*air suam*
ginger tea	teh *hah*-lee-uh	*teh halia*

TOO MUCH IS BARELY ENOUGH

Most Malaysians can't imagine drinking tea or coffee or
any other drink without a lot of sweeteners in it. Coffee
and tea, as well as iced tea, will be served with sweetened
condensed milk unless you specify *kopi o* or *teh o* which
will then be sweetened with sugar before it is brought to
you! In traditional restaurants and stalls, the milk used in
drinks is usually sweetened condensed milk. Drinks like
'ABC', *air batu campur*, 'mixed ice', are more of a dessert
than a drink, and are often served in a bowl. Drinks served
in Malaysian homes are almost always sweetened, too.

Cold Drinks		**Minuman Sejuk**
cincau		*chin*-chow
black *agar*, 'seaweed' jelly with fruit syrup and ice		
air limau		air *lee*-mow
citrus juice		
air kelapa muda		air ke-*lah*-puh *moo*-duh
coconut milk		
cendol		*chehn*-dol
coconut milk with rice jelly and ice		
air batu campur		air *bah*-too *chahm*-pur
ABC or coconut milk with fruit, jelly, nuts, sweet milk and shaved ice		
pekatan		*pe*-kah-tahn
cordial		
kopi ais		*ko*-pee ais
iced coffee with milk		
kopi o ais		*ko*-pee o ais
iced coffee without milk		
teh ais		teh ais
iced tea with milk		
teh o ais		teh o ais
iced tea without milk		
the o ais kosong		teh o ais *ko*-song
iced tea without milk or sugar		
teh o ais limau		teh o ais *lee*-mow
iced tea with lime		
Horlicks ais		*hor*-liks ais
iced milky malt drink		
Milo ais		*mi*-lo ais
iced chocolate milk		

milk	*susu*	*soo*-soo
water	*air*	air
bottled ...	... *botol*	... *bo*-tol

Alcohol

		Minuman Keras
beer	**bir**	*bir*
grape wine	**wain**	*wain*
palm tree spirits	*to*-dee	*todi*
rice wine	*too*-ah(k)	*tuak*

DI LUAR BANDAR
IN THE COUNTRY

CAMPING   BERKHEMAH

Malaysia offers cheap camping options: many of the national parks have camping grounds, and you can set up anywhere in the country. Sites near waterfalls and other jungle areas easily accessible by road are popular, so they can be crowded and a bit messy. Men and women can camp together, but again, it's best to say you're married to avoid any hassles.

The weather is wet, warm and humid and there are plenty of bugs. Make sure your tent has mosquito netting.

Can we camp here?
  bo-*leh(h)* ber-*kheh*-mah(h)
  dee *see*-nee?   *Boleh berkhemah di sini?*

How much is it per person/tent?
  be-*rah*-puh *hahr*-guh-nyuh
  oon-tu(k) *sah*-too o-rahng/   *Berapa harganya*
  kheh-mah(h)?   *untuk satu orang/*
                                          khemah?

Where can I hire a tent?
  kheh-mah(h) dee-*seh*-wuh
  dee *mah*-nuh?   *Khemah disewa di mana?*

Are there shower facilities?
  ah-duh tem-*paht*   *Ada tempat*
  mahn-dee tah(k)?   *mandi tak?*

backpack	behg *sahn*-dahr	*beg sandar*
campground	kah-*wah*-sahn	*kawasan*
	per-*kheh*-mah(h)-ahn	*perkhemahan*
camping	ber-*kheh*-mah(h)	*berkhemah*
campsite	*tah*-pah(k)	*tapak*
	per-*kheh*-mah(h)-ahn	*perkhemahan*
firewood	*kai*-yoo *ah*-pee	*kayu api*
mat	*tee*-kahr	*tikar*
mosquito net	ke-*lahm*-boo	*kelambu*
national park	*tah*-mahn ne-*gah*-ruh	*taman negara*
penknife	*pee*-sow *lee*-paht	*pisau lipat*
sleeping bag	*kahm*-tung *tee*-dur	*kantung tidur*
stove (burner)	*dah*-pur	*dapur*
tent	*kheh*-mah(h)	*khemah*
torch (flashlight)	*lahm*-poo *soo*-luh	*lampu suluh*

HIKING

MERENTAS HUTAN

Are there any tourist attractions near here?

ah-duh tem-*paht* tah-ree-kahn
pe-*lahn*-cong de-*kaht see*-nee?

*Ada tempat tarikan
pelancong dekat sini?*

Where's the nearest village?

dee *mah*-nuh *kahm*-pung
yahng *pah*-ling de-*kaht*?

*Di mana kampung
yang paling dekat?*

Is it safe to climb this mountain?

se-*lah*-maht-kah(h) *oon*-tu(k)
men-*dah*-kee *goo*-nung *ee*-nee?

*Selamatkah untuk
mendaki gunung ini?*

Is there a hut up there?

ah-duh pon-do(k)-kah(h) dee *ah*-tahs?

Ada pondokkah di atas?

Do I need a guide?

ah-duh-kah(h) *sai*-yuh per-*loo*
pe-*mahn*-doo pe-*lahn*-chong?

*Adakah saya perlu
pemandu pelancong?*

Where can I find out about hiking trails in the region?

dee *mah*-nuh *ah*-duh
mah(k)-loo-maht *tehm*-tahng
je-*jah*-kahn me-*rehn*-tahs
hoo-tahn dee dah-*eh*-rah(h) *ee*-nee?

*Di mana ada
maklumat tentang
jejakan merentas
hutan di daerah ini?*

I'd like to talk to someone who knows this area.

sai-yuh nah(k) ber-*chah*-kahp
de-ngahn se-se-*o*-rahng
yahng *tah*-hoo *tehm*-tahng
dah-*eh*-rah(h) *ee*-nee

*Saya nak bercakap
dengan seseorang
yang tahu tentang
daerah ini.*

How long is the trail?

be-*rah*-puh *pahn*-jahng
lo-rong me-*rehn*-tahs
hoo-tahn *ee*-nee?

*Berapa panjang
lorong merentas
hutan ini?*

Is the track well marked?

ah-duh-kah(h) *trehk*-nyuh
dee-*tahn*-duh *de*-ngahn bai(k)?

*Adakah treknya
ditanda dengan baik?*

How high is the climb?

be-*rah*-puh *ting*-gee
pen-dah-*kee*-ahn *ee*-nee?

*Berapa tinggi
pendakian ini?*

Which is the shortest/easiest route?
   yahng *mah*-nuh
   lah-loo-ahn yahng
   pah-ling che-*paht*/*moo*-dah(h)?

Yang mana
laluan yang
paling cepat/mudah?

When does it get dark?
   bee-luh-kah(h)
   hah-ree moo-luh ge-*lahp*?

Bilakah
hari mula gelap?

Is it very scenic?
   pe-*mahm*-dahng-ahn-nyuh
   in-*dah*(h) se-*kah*-lee tah(k)?

Pemandangannya
indah sekali tak?

Where can I hire mountain gear?
   ah-laht men-*dah*-kee
   goo-nung dee-*seh*-wuh
   dee *mah*-nuh?

Alat mendaki
gunung disewa
di mana?

Where can we buy supplies?
   be-*kah*-lahn dee-*joo*-ahl
   dee *mah*-nuh?

Bekalan dijual
di mana?

On the Path

Dalam Perjalanan

Where have you come from?
   ahn-duh *dah*-tahng
   dah-ree *mah*-nuh?

Anda datang
dari mana?

How long did it take you?
   be-*rah*-puh *lah*-muh
   per-*jah*-lah-nahn *ah*-wah(k)?

Berapa lama
perjalanan awak?

Does this path go to ...?
   ah-duh-kah(h) *jah*-lahn
   ee-nee me-*noo*-joo ke ...?

Adakah jalan
ini menuju ke ...?

Where can we spend the night?
   dee *mah*-nuh *kah*-mee
   bo-*leh*(h) ber-*mah*-lahm?

Di mana kami
boleh bermalam?

Can I leave some things
here for a while?
   bo-*leh*(h) *sim*-pahn bah-*rahng*
   dee *see*-nee se-ke-*jahp*?

Boleh simpan barang
di sini sekejap?

There's a cave here.
   ah-duh *goo*-ah dee *see*-nee

Ada gua di sini.

I'm lost.	*sai*-yuh ter-*seh*-saht	*Saya tersesat.*
altitude	ke-*ting*-gee-ahn	*ketinggian*
binoculars	te-*ro*-pong	*teropong*
candles	*lee*-lin	*lilin*
to climb	men-*dah*-kee/	*mendaki/*
	me-*nai*-kee	*menaiki*
compass	*kom*-pahs	*kompas*
downhill	*too*-roon *boo*-kit	*turun bukit*
first-aid kit	*ko*-tah(k)	*kotak*
	ke-che-*mah*-sahn	*kecemasan*
gloves	*sah*-rung tah-*ngahn*	*sarung tangan*
guide	pe-*mahn*-doo	*pemandu*
guided trek	trehk yahng	*trek yang*
	ber-*pahn*-doo	*berpandu*
hiking	me-*rehn*-tahs *hoo*-tahn	*merentas hutan*
hiking boots	*kah*-sut me-*rehn*-tahs	*kasut merentas*
	hoo-tahn	*hutan*
hunting	ber-*boo*-roo	*berburu*
ledge	*bi*-rai	*birai*
lookout	tem-*paht*	*tempat*
	me-*mahn*-dahng	*memandang*
map	*peh*-tuh	*peta*
mountain	men-*dah*-kee	*mendaki*
climbing	*goo*-nung	*gunung*
pick	be-*lee*-ung	*beliung*
provisions	be-*kah*-lahn	*bekalan*
rock climbing	me-*mahn*-jaht *bah*-too	*memanjat batu*
rope	*tah*-lee	*tali*
short cut	*jah*-lahn *pin*-tahs	*jalan pintas*
signpost	*tahn*-duh *jah*-lahn	*tanda jalan*
steep	*choo*-rahm	*curam*
track	trehk; *jah*-lahn	*trek; jalan*
	ke-*chil*; *lo*-rong	*kecil; lorong*
trek	trehk	*trek*
uphill	nai(k) *boo*-kit	*naik bukit*
to walk	ber-*jah*-lahn *kah*-kee	*berjalan kaki*

AT THE BEACH   DI PANTAI

Can we swim here?
> bo-*leh(h)* be-re-*nahng*   *Boleh berenang*
> dee *see*-nee?   *di sini?*

Is it safe to swim here?
> se-lah-*maht*-kah(h)   *Selamatkah*
> be-re-*nahng* dee *see*-nee?   *berenang di sini?*

What time is high/low tide?
> *poo*-kool be-*rah*-puh air   *Pukul berapa air*
> *pah*-sahng *ting*-gee/*rehm*-dah(h)?   *pasang tinggi/rendah?*

coast	*pahn*-tai	*pantai*
diving	me-nye-*lahm*	*menyelam*
fishing	me-*mahn*-ching	*memancing*
marine reserve	*tah*-mahn	*taman*
	sim-pah-nahn lowt	*simpanan laut*
reef	*bah*-too *kah*-rahng	*batu karang*
sand	*pah*-sir	*pasir*
sea	lowt	*laut*
snorkelling	*snor*-kel	*snorkel*
sunblock	pe-*lin*-dung	*pelindung*
	chah-*hai*-yuh	*cahaya*
	mah-tuh-*hah*-ree	*matahari*
sunglasses	cher-*min mah*-tuh	*cermin*
	hee-tahm	*mata hitam*
surf	*om*-bah(k)	*ombak*
surfboard	*pah*-pahn se-*lahn*-chahr	*papan selancar*
surfing	ber-se-*lahn*-chahr	*berselancar*
swimming	be-re-*nahng*	*berenang*
tide	air *pah*-sahng	*air pasang*
towel	*twah*-luh	*tuala*
waterski	skee air	*ski air*
waves	*om*-bah(k)	*ombak*
windsurfing	ber-se-*lahn*-chahr	*berselancar*
	ah-ngin	*angin*

Diving

Penyelaman

Are there good diving sites here?
ah-duh tem-*paht*
pe-nye-*lah*-mahn
yahng bah-*gus* dee *see*-nee?

Ada tempat
penyelaman
yang bagus di sini?

Can we hire a diving boat/guide?
bo-*leh(h)*-kah(h) *kah*-mee
me-*nyeh*-wuh bot/
pe-*mahn*-doo *oon*-tu(k)
me-nye-*lahm?*

Bolehkah kami
menyewa bot/
pemandu untuk
menyelam?

We'd like to hire diving equipment.
kah-mee nah(k) me-*nyeh*-wuh
ke-leng-*kah*-pahn
pe-nye-*lah*-mahn

Kami nak menyewa
kelengkapan
penyelaman.

I'm interested in exploring wrecks.
sai-yuh ber-*mee*-naht
oon-tuk men-*chah*-ree
kah-pahl *kah*-rahm

Saya berminat
untuk mencari
kapal karam.

WEATHER

CUACA

Weather reports in Malaysia are always the same. Rain in some places, dry in others. Hot during the day, slightly cooler at night. Humidity: high. In the Klang Valley (Kuala Lumpur and surrounding area) afternoon thunderstorms are common.

What's the weather like?
bah-gai-*mah*-nuh
choo-*ah*-chuh-nyuh?

Bagaimana
cuacanya?

Today it's ...	choo-*ah*-chuh *hah*-ree *ee*-nee ...	*Cuaca hari ini ...*
cloudy	*men*-dung/ be-*rah*-wahn	*mendung/ berawan*
cold	se-*joo*(k)	*sejuk*
flooding	*bahn*-jir	*banjir*
hot	*pah*-nahs	*panas*
humid/wet	lem-*bahb*	*lembab*
raining heavily	*hoo*-jahn leh-*baht*	*hujan lebat*
raining lightly	ge-*ree*-mis	*gerimis*
warm	koo-*rahng pah*-nahs	*kurang panas*
windy	be-*rah*-ngin	*berangin*

What time is ...?	*poo*-kool be-*rah*-puh ...?	*Pukul berapa ...?*
sunrise	mah-tuh-*hah*-ree ter-*bit*	*matahari terbit*
sunset	mah-tuh-*hah*-ree ter-*be*-nahm	*matahari terbenam*

cloud	*ah*-wahn	*awan*
fog	*kah*-boos	*kabus*
moon	*bu*-lahn	*bulan*
mud	*loom*-pur	*lumpur*
rain	hoo-*jahn*	*hujan*
sky	lah-*ngit*	*langit*
smoke	*ah*-sahp	*asap*
storm	*ree*-but	*ribut*
sun	mah-tuh-*hah*-ree	*matahari*
typhoon	*tow*-fahn	*taufan*

BLAME IT ON THE RAIN

Malaysia is monsoonal, but only the east coast has a clear season of rain, when it buckets down for days and days. The driest part of the Peninsula is Kuala Pilah, Negeri Sembilan.

musim hujan	the rainy (monsoon) season, October to March
musim kemarau	the dry season, April to September

GEOGRAPHICAL TERMS ISTILAH GEOGRAFI

atoll	*poo*-low *chin*-chin	*pulau cincin*
beach	*pahn*-tai	*pantai*
bridge	*jahm*-bah-tahn	*jambatan*
cave	*goo*-uh	*gua*
city	*bahn*-dahr	*bandar*
cliff	te-*bing ting*-gee	*tebing tinggi*
earth	*boo*-mee	*bumi*
earthquake	*gehm*-puh *boo*-mee	*gempa bumi*
estuary	moo-*ah*-ruh	*muara*
farm	*lah*-dahng/	*ladang/*
	ke-*bun*	*kebun*
footpath	*lo*-rong ber-*jah*-lahn	*lorong berjalan*
	kah-kee	*kaki*
forest	*hoo*-tahn/*rim*-buh	*hutan/rimba*
gap (narrow pass)	*lah*-loo-ahn sem-*pit*	*laluan sempit*
harbour	pe-*lah*-boo-hahn	*pelabuhan*
hill	*boo*-kit	*bukit*
hot spring	*mah*-tuh air *pah*-nahs	*mata air panas*
jungle	*hoo*-tahn/*rim*-buh	*hutan/rimba*
island	*poo*-low	*pulau*
lake	*tah*-si(k)	*tasik*
mountain (path)	(*lah*-loo-ahn)	(*laluan*)
	goo-nung	*gunung*
pass	*lah*-loo-ahn	*laluan*
peak	*poon*-chah(k)	*puncak*
plain	dah-*tah*-rahn	*dataran*
river	*soo*-ngai	*sungai*
rock	*bah*-too	*batu*
town	*ko*-tuh	*kota*
valley	*lehm*-bah(h)	*lembah*
village	*kahm*-pung/*deh*-suh	*kampung/desa*
volcano	*goo*-nung ber-*ah*-pee	*gunung berapi*
waterfall	air ter-*joon*	*air terjun*

FAUNA

bird	*boo*-rung	*burung*
buffalo	ker-*bow*	*kerbau*
cat	*koo*-ching	*kucing*
chicken	*ai*-yahm	*ayam*
civet cat	*moo*-sahng	*musang*
cow	*lehm*-boo	*lembu*
crocodile	boo-*ai*-yuh	*buaya*
dog	*ahn*-jing	*anjing*
fish	*ee*-kahn	*ikan*
frog	*kah*-tah(k)/*ko*-do(k)	*katak/kodok*
gecko	*chi(k)*-chah(k)	*cikcak*
goat	*kahm*-bing	*kambing*
horse	*koo*-duh	*kuda*
monitor lizard	bee-*ah*-wah(k)	*biawak*
monkey	*mo*-nyeht	*monyet*
mouse deer	*kahn*-chil	*kancil*
pig	*bah*-bee	*babi*
python	*sah*-wah(h)	*sawah*
rooster	*ai*-yahm *jahn*-tahn	*ayam jantan*
sheep	*bi*-ree-*bi*-ree	*biri-biri*
(poisonous) snake	*oo*-lahr (ber-*bee*-suh)	*ular (berbisa)*
tiger	*hah*-ree-mow	*harimau*

DUNIA BINATANG

TINY BUT CLEVER

The tales of *Sang Kancil,* sahng *kahn*-chil, the tiny but clever mouse deer, are favourites among Malay children. The mouse deer (which you can see at the National Zoo) weighs only a few pounds, but manages to outwit many other bigger predators in these traditional tales. The smallest of Malaysian-made cars is appropriately called the *Kancil.*

Insects

		Serangga
... ant	se-*mut* ...	*semut* ...
fire	*ah*-pee	*api*
biting	*gee*-git	*gigit*
butterfly	*koo*-poo-*koo*-poo/ *rah*-muh-*rah*-muh	*kupu-kupu/ rama-rama*
centipede	*lee*-pahn	*lipan*
cockroach	*lee*-pahs	*lipas*
fly	*lah*-laht	*lalat*
leech (large, in rivers)	*lin*-tah(h)	*lintah*
(small, in grass)	*pah*-chaht	*pacat*
mosquito	*nyah*-mu(k)	*nyamuk*
spider	*lah*-bah(h)-*lah*-bah(h)	*labah-labah*
termite	*ah*-nai-*ah*-nai	*anai-anai*

FLORA & AGRICULTURE

DUNIA TUMBUHTUMBUHAN & PERTANIAN

agriculture	per-*tah*-nee-ahn	*pertanian*
coconut palm	*po*-ko(k) ke-*lah*-puh	*pokok kelapa*
coconut	ke-*lah*-puh	*kelapa*
corn	*jah*-gung	*jagung*
flower	*boo*-nguh	*bunga*
fruit tree	*po*-ko(k) *boo*-ah(h)	*pokok buah*
to harvest	me-me-*ti(k)*	*memetik*
irrigation	*sah*-li-rahn	*saliran*
leaf	down	*daun*
oil palm	ke-*lah*-puh *sah*-wit	*kelapa sawit*
orchard	*doo*-sun	*dusun*
plantation	eh-*steht*/lah-*dahng*	*estet/ladang*
to plant	me-*nah*-nahm	*menanam*
rice field	*sah*-wah(h)	*sawah*
rice terrace	*peh*-tah(k) *sah*-wah(h)	*petak sawah*
rubber	*geh*-tah(h)	*getah*
sugar cane	*teh*-boo	*tebu*
tobacco	tem-*bah*-kow	*tembakau*

IN THE COUNTRY

PULL YOUR SOCKS UP!

When camping, be aware that South-East Asia has a tremendous number of venomous snakes and some enormous pythons. One was caught during the '90s with a grisly mouthful: the head and shoulders of a man. It had presumably dropped on him in an overgrown area near his house, and squeezed him into submission.

KESIHATAN HEALTH

Public health is generally excellent and you're unlikely to get seriously ill during your travels in Malaysia. If you do need to talk about illness, the all-purpose word is *sakit*, *sah*-kit, which means 'to feel sick' or 'to hurt'. Government clinics and hospitals can accommodate foreigners, although there is usually a long wait. Private clinics and hospitals are fast, do not generally require appointments and are reasonably priced.

AT THE DOCTOR DI KLINIK

Almost all doctors and most nurses speak English, even in rural areas. Most doctors dispense medicine and prescriptions as you need them, so there is seldom the need make an extra trip to a pharmacy. Malaysia enjoys a good standard of health, so as long as you observe the general guidelines for health in the tropics, you should be fine.

Where's a ...	... dee *mah*-nuh?	... *di mana?*
chemist	*fahr*-mah-see	*farmasi*
dentist	*dok*-tor *gee*-gee	*doktor gigi*
doctor	*dok*-tor	*doktor*
hospital	hos-*pi*-tahl	*hospital*
clinic	*kli*-nik	*klinik*

I'm sick.
   sai-yuh *sah*-kit   *Saya sakit.*
My friend is sick.
   kah-wahn *sai*-yuh *sah*-kit   *Kawan saya sakit.*
Is there a doctor here
who speaks English?
   ah-duh *dok*-tor yahng   *Ada doktor yang*
   ber-*bah*-hah-suh *ing*-ge-ris?   *berbahasa Inggeris?*
Could the doctor come to the hotel?
   bo-*leh*(h)-kah(h)   *Bolehkah*
   dok-tor *dah*-tahng ke *ho*-tehl?   *doktor datang ke hotel?*

HEALTH

I've had a blood test.
dah-rah(h) *sai*-yuh soo-dah(h)
dee-per-*eek*-suh

Darah saya sudah diperiksa.

I need a blood test.
sai-yuh me-mer-*loo*-kahn
pe-mer-*eek*-sah-ahn *dah*-rah(h)

Saya memerlukan pemeriksaan darah.

Is that a new syringe?
jah-*rum* soon-*ti*(k)
ee-too bah-*roo*-kah(h)?

Jarum suntik itu barukah?

Please use this syringe.
to-long *pah*-kai jah-*rum*
soon-*ti*(k) ee-nee

Tolong pakai jarum suntik ini.

What are you doing?
ahm-duh *boo*-aht *ah*-puh?

Anda buat apa?

What do you want to do?
ahm-duh *boo*-aht nah(k) *ah*-puh?

Anda buat nak apa?

I feel better/worse.
sai-yuh be-*rah*-suh le-*bi*(h)
bai(k)/te-*ru*(k)

Saya berasa lebih baik/teruk.

This is my usual medicine.
ee-nee oo-baht
bee-*ah*-suh *sai*-yuh

Ini ubat biasa saya.

I've been vaccinated.
sai-yuh soo-dah(h)
dee-i-moo-ni-*sah*-see

Saya sudah diimunisasi.

I don't want a
blood transfusion.
sai-yuh tah(k) nah(k)
pe-nahm-*bah*-hahn *dah*-rah(h)

Saya tak nak penambahan darah.

I need a receipt for
my insurance.
sai-yuh per-*loo*-kahn *reh*-sit
oon-tu(k) in-*soo*-rans *sai*-yuh

Saya perlukan resit untuk insurans saya.

THEY MAY SAY ...

sah-kit *ah*-puh?
  What's the matter?

Sakit apa?

ahn-duh ber-*rah*-suh
sah-kit dee *mah*-nuh?
  Where does it hurt?

Anda berasa
sakit di mana?

ahn-duh *ah*-duh *ah*-lah-hahn?
  Are you allergic to anything?

Anda ada alahan?

ahn-duh ... ?	Do you ...?	*Anda ...?*
me-*ro*-ko(k)	smoke	*merokok*
mee-num	drink	*minum*
mee-nu-mahn		*minuman*
ke-*rahs*		*keras*
men-*goo*-nah-kahn	take drugs	*mengunakan*
dah-dah(h)		*dadah*

ahn-duh de-*mahm pah*-nahs?
  Do you have a temperature?

Anda demam panas?

ah-duh-kah(h) *ahn*-duh
se-*dahng dah*-tahng haid?
  Are you menstruating?

Adakah anda
sedang datang haid?

ahn-duh me-*ngahn*-dung/
hah-mil?
  Are you pregnant?

Anda mengandung/
hamil?

ahn-duh te-*rah*-suh *sah*-kit?
  Do you feel any pain?

Anda terasa sakit?

per-nah(h) ke-*nuh*
pe-*nyah*-kit *ee*-nee tah(k)?
  Have you had this before?

Pernah kena
penyakit ini tak?

ahn-duh se-*dahng*
mah-kahn oo-*baht*?
  Are you on medication?

Anda sedang
makan ubat?

soo-dah(h) be-*rah*-puh
lah-muh *ahn*-duh
be-*rah*-suh be-*gee*-nee?
  How long have you been like this?

Sudah berapa
lama anda
berasa begini?

HEALTH

AILMENTS   **PENYAKIT**

I feel under the weather.
   sai-yuh *koo*-rahng   *Saya kurang*
   se-*dahp bah*-dahn   *sedap badan.*

I feel nauseous.
   sai-yuh *moo*-ahl   *Saya mual.*

I've been vomiting.
   sai-yuh *soo*-dah(h) *moon*-tah(h)   *Saya sudah muntah.*

I'm having a hard time sleeping.
   sai-yuh *soo*-sah(h) *tee*-dur   *Saya susah tidur.*

I feel ...	*sai*-yuh ber-*rah*-suh ...	*Saya berasa ...*
dizzy	pe-*ning*	*pening*
shivery	meng-*gee*-gil	*menggigil*
weak	le-*mah(h)*	*lemah*

My leg is broken.
   too-lahng *kah*-kee   *Tulang kaki saya patah.*
   sai-yuh *pah*-tah(h)

My foot is sprained.
   kah-kee *sai*-yuh   *Kaki saya tersiliuh.*
   ter-see-*lee*-u(h)

I have low/high blood pressure.
   sai-yuh *ah*-duh te-*kah*-nahn   *Saya ada tekanan*
   dah-rah(h) *rehn*-dah(h)/*ting*-gee   *darah rendah/tinggi.*

My ... hurts
   ... *sai*-yuh *sah*-kit   *... saya sakit.*

HEALTH

I'm suffering from (a/an) ...	*sai*-yuh *sah*-kit ...	*Saya sakit ...*
addiction	ke-*tah*-gee-hahn	*ketagihan*
allergy	*ah*-ler-gee/*ah*-lah-hahn	*alergi/alahan*
anaemia	ah-*nee*-mee-uh	*anemia*
asthma	*leh*-lah(h)	*lelah*
bite	*gee*-gee-tahn	*gigitan*
burns	ke-*nuh ah*-pee	*kena api*
cancer	*kan*-ser	*kanser*
cholera	*tah*-oon	*taun*
cold	sel-*seh*-muh	*selsema*
constipation	sem-be-*lit*	*sembelit*
cough	*bah*-tu(k)	*batuk*
cystitis	*sah*-kit *ken*-ching	*sakit kencing*
diarrhoea	*chir*-rit-*bir*-it	*cirit-birit*
dog bite	*gee*-gee-tahn *ahn*-jing	*gigitan anjing*
dysentery	*di*-sen-tree	*disentri*
fever	de-*mahm pah*-nahs	*demam panas*
food poisoning	ke-*rah*-choo-nahn *mah*-kah-nahn; *sah*-lah(h) *mah*-kahn	*keracunan makanan; salah makan*
gastroenteritis	*sah*-kit *gas*-trik	*sakit gastrik*
headache	*sah*-kit ke-*pah*-luh	*sakit kepala*
heart condition	mah-*sah*-ah-lah(h) *jahn*-tung	*masalah jantung*
hepatitis	heh-*pah*-tai-tis	*hepatitis*
high blood pressure	te-*kah*-nahn *dah*-rah(h) *ting*-gee	*tekanan darah tinggi*
indigestion	tah(k) *hah*-zahm *mah*-kah-nahn	*tak hazam makanan*
infection	in-*fehk*-see	*infeksi*
influenza	sel-*seh*-muh/floo	*selsema/flu*
itch	*gah*-tahl	*gatal*
lice	*koo*-too	*kutu*
malaria	mah-*lah*-ree-uh	*malaria*
migraine	*sah*-kit ke-*pah*-luh be-*raht*; *mai*-grehn	*sakit kepala berat; migraine*

pain	*sah*-kit	*sakit*
rabies	*ray*-bees; pe-*nyah*-kit *ahn*-jing *gee*-luh	*rabies; penyakit anjing gila*
rheumatism	*sah*-kit *sen*-dee	*sakit sendi*
sore throat	*sah*-kit te-*kah(k)*	*sakit tekak*
sprain	ter-se-*lee*-oo(h)	*terseliuh*
stomachache	*sah*-kit pe-*root*	*sakit perut*
sunburn	ter-*bah*-kar mah-tuh-*hah*-ree	*terbakar matahari*
travel sickness	*mah*-buk per-*jah*-lah-nahn	*mabuk perjalanan*
typhoid	de-*mahm* ke-pee-*ah*-loo	*demam kepialu*
urinary tract infection	*sah*-kit *ken*-ching	*sakit kencing*
venereal disease	pe-*nyah*-kit ke-*lah*-meen	*penyakit kelamin*
worms	*chah*-ching	*cacing*

WOMEN'S HEALTH KESIHATAN WANITA

Private maternity clinics would have information on specific matters to do with women's health. Testing for STDs is available at most clinics and larger hospitals.

Is there a female doctor here?
  ah-duh *dok*-tor
  wah-*nee*-tuh dee *see*-nee?

*Ada doktor
wanita di sini?*

Is there a doctor especially for women?
  ah-duh *dok*-tor *khoo*-soos
  oon-tu(k) wah-*nee*-tuh?

*Ada doktor khusus
untuk wanita?*

I'd like to use contraception.
  sai-yuh nah(k) *goo*-nuh *ah*-laht/
  oo-baht pen-*ceh*-gah(h) *hah*-mil

*Saya nak guna alat/
ubat pencegah hamil.*

I haven't menstruated for ... weeks.
  sai-yuh be-*lum dah*-tahng
  haid se-*lah*-muh ... *ming*-goo

*Saya belum datang
haid selama ... minggu.*

I'm on the Pill.
  sai-yuh *mah*-kahn pil
  men-*cheh*-gah(h) *hah*-mil
(Maybe) I'm pregnant.
  (*moong*-kin) *sai*-yuh
  me-*ngahn*-dung/*hah*-mil

*Saya makan pil
mencegah hamil.*

(*Mungkin*) *Saya
mengandung/hamil.*

abortion	peng-*goo*-goo-rahn *ah*-nah(k)	*pengguguran anak*
cystitis	*sah*-kit *ken*-ching	*sakit kencing*
diaphragm	*dai*-ah-frahm	*diaphram*
IUD	ai oo deh	*IUD*
mammogram	*mah*-mo-gram	*mamogram*
menstruation	*dah*-tahng haid	*datang haid*
miscarriage	ke-*goo*-goo-rahn	*keguguran*
pap smear	smir	*smear*
period pain	se-*goo*-gup	*segugup*
the Pill	pil pen-*cheh*-gah(h) *hah*-mil	*pil pencegah hamil*
premenstrual tension	ke-*teh*-gah-ngahn se-be-*lum* *dah*-tahng haid	*ketegangan sebelum datang haid*
thrush	*goo*-ahm	*guam*
ultrasound	*ul*-trah-sownd	*ultrasound*

THEY MAY SAY ...

pil *ee*-nee *mes*-tee
dee *ahm*-bil *tee*-guh
kah-lee se-*hah*-ree

*Pil ini mesti
di ambil tiga
kali sehari*

  These pills must be
  taken three times a day.

gon-chahng-kahn
bo-tol *doo*-loo
se-be-*lum mee*-num

*Goncangkan
botol dulu
sebelum minum.*

  Shake the bottle
  before taking.

HEALTH

SPECIAL HEALTH NEEDS

KEPERLUAN KHUSUS KESIHATAN

anaemia	ah-*nee*-mee-uh	*anaemia*
asthma	*leh*-lah(h)	*lelah*
diabetes	*ken*-ching *mah*-nis	*kencing manis*

I'm allergic to ...	*sai*-yuh ah-*ler*-jik *ke*-pah-duh ...	*Saya alergik kepada ...*
antibiotics	an-tai-bai-*o*-tik	*antibiotik*
aspirin	*as*-pi-rin	*aspirin*
bees	*leh*-bah(h)	*lebah*
codeine	ko-deen	*kodein*
dairy products	*pro*-duk ber-*soo*-soo	*produk bersusu*
penicillin	pe-ni-*si*-lin	*penisilin*
pollen	de-*boo*-nguh	*debunga*

I have a skin allergy.
  sai-yuh *ah*-duh
  ah-lah-hahn *koo*-lit
  Saya ada alahan kulit.

I have my own syringe.
  sai-yuh *ah*-duh *jah*-rum
  soon-*ti(k)* sen-*di*-ree
  Saya ada jarum suntik sendiri.

I need a new pair of glasses.
  sai-yuh per-*loo*-kahn
  cher-*min mah*-tuh *bah*-roo
  Saya perlukan cermin mata baru.

I'm on medication for ...
  sai-yuh se-*dahng pah*-kai
  oo-baht *oon*-tu(k) ...
  Saya sedang pakai ubat untuk ...

ALTERNATIVE TREATMENTS

PENGUBATAN ALTERNATIF

Although Western-style medical treatment is the norm, alternative treatments, including some that are unique to Malaysia, are widely practised.

aromatherapy	ah-ro-mah-*teh*-rah-pee	*aromaterapi*
acupuncture	ah-koo-*punk*-toor	*akupunktur*
faith healer	bo-mo(h)/*doo*-koon/ pah-wahng	*bomoh/dukun/ pawang*
herbalist	*ah*-lee *jah*-moo	*ahli jamu*
massage	oo-root	*urut*
masseur/masseuse	*too*-kahng oo-root	*tukang urut*
meditation	per-*tah*-pah-ahn	*pertapaan*
physiotherapy	fi-see-o-*tehr*-ah-pee	*fisioterapi*
reflexology	ree-flek-*so*-lo-gee	*refleksologi*
yoga	*yo*-guh	*yoga*

HEALTH

PARTS OF THE BODY

BAHAGIAN TUBUH

ankle	ke-*ting*	*keting*
anus	*doo*-bur	*dubur*
appendix	ah-*pehn*-dik	*apendik*
arm	*leh*-ngahn	*lengan*
back	be-*lah*-kahng	*belakang*
bladder	kahn-*du*-ngahn	*kandungan*
	ken-ching	*kencing*
blood	*dah*-rah(h)	*darah*
bone	*too*-lahng	*tulang*
breast	*boo*-ah(h) *dah*-duh	*buah dada*
buttocks	*pong*-gong	*ponggong*
chest	*dah*-duh	*dada*
chin	*dah*-goo	*dagu*
ear	te-*li*-nguh	*telinga*
eye	*mah*-tuh	*mata*
face	*moo*-kuh	*muka*
finger	*jah*-ree *tah*-ngahn	*jari tangan*
foot	*kah*-kee	*kaki*

HEALTH

hands	*tah*-ngahn	*tangan*
head	ke-*pah*-luh	*kepala*
heart	*jahn*-tung	*jantung*
hip	*ping*-gahn	*pinggan*
kidney	*boo*-ah(h) *ping*-gahng	*buah pinggang*
knee	*loo*-tut	*lutut*
leg	*kah*-kee	*kaki*
liver	*hah*-tee	*hati*
lung	*pah*-roo-*pah*-roo	*paru-paru*
mouth	*moo*-lut	*mulut*
muscle	*o*-tot	*otot*
neck	*leh*-hehr	*leher*
nose	*hee*-dung	*hidung*
penis	*zah*-kahr	*zakar*
ribs	*too*-lahng *roo*-su(k)	*tulang rusuk*
shoulder	*bah*-hoo	*bahu*
skin	*koo*-lit	*kulit*
stomach	pe-*root*	*perut*
testicles	*boo*-ah(h) *peh*-lir	*buah pelir*
throat	te-*kah(k)*	*tekak*
toes	*jah*-ree *kah*-kee	*jari kaki*
tooth	*gee*-gee	*gigi*
vagina	*fah*-rahj	*faraj*
vein	oo-*raht dah*-rah(h)	*urat darah*
	hah-loos	*halus*

AT THE CHEMIST   DI FARMASI

Some internationally known painkillers are not sold off the shelf in Malaysian pharmacies. Although you do not need a prescription, you will have to ask the chemist to dispense them to you.

I need medicine for ...
    sai-yuh per-*loo*-kahn   *Saya perlukan*
    oo-baht *oon*-tu(k) ...   *ubat untuk ...*
How many times a day?
    be-*rah*-puh *kah*-lee se-*hah*-ree?   *Berapa kali sehari?*

antibiotics	an-tai-bai-*o*-tik	*antibiotik*
antiseptic	an-ti-*sehp*-tik	*antiseptik*
aspirin	*as*-pi-rin	*aspirin*
Band-aids	*plas*-ter	*plaster*
bandage	*pem*-bah-loot	*pembalut*
condoms	*kon*-dom	*kondom*
contraceptives	ah-laht/*oo*-baht	*alat/ubat*
	pen-*ceh*-gah(h) *hah*-mil	*pencegah hamil*
cotton wool	*kah*-pahs	*kapas*
cough medicine	*oo*-baht *bah*-tu(k)	*ubat batuk*
gauze	kain *kah*-suh	*kain kasa*
gastrolyte	ga-*stroh*-leet	*gastrolyte*
headache tablets	*oo*-baht *sah*-kit	*ubat sakit*
	ke-*pah*-luh	*kepala*
laxatives	*joo*-lahp	*julap*
painkillers	*oo*-baht *tah*-hahn	*ubat tahan sakit*
	sah-kit	
penicillin	pe-ne-*si*-lin	*penisilin*
quinine	*kwee*-nin	*kuinin*
rubbing alcohol	*al*-ko-hol *go*-so(k)	*alkohol gosok*
sleeping pills	*oo*-baht *tee*-dur	*ubat tidur*
tablet	*tab*-leht	*tablet*
vitamins	vee-*tah*-min	*vitamin*

HEALTH

Useful Words

accident	ke-*mahl*-ah-ngahn	*kemalangan*
breath	*nah*-fahs	*nafas*
disease	pe-*nyah*-kit	*penyakit*
faeces	*tah*-hee	*tahi*
fast (n)	*pwah*-suh	*puasa*
to fast	ber-*pwah*-suh	*berpuasa*
health	ke-see-*hah*-tahn	*kesihatan*
injection	*soon*-tee-kahn	*suntikan*
injury	ke-che-de-*rah*-ahn	*kecederaan*
medicine	*oo*-baht	*ubat*
poisonous	be-*rah*-choon	*beracun*
urine	air *ken*-ching	*air kencing*
wound	*loo*-kuh	*luka*

AT THE DENTIST

DI DOKTOR GIGI

I have a toothache.
  sai-yuh *sah*-kit *gee*-gee

Saya sakit gigi.

I have a cavity.
  ah-duh *gee*-gee ber-*loo*-bahng

Ada gigi berlubang.

My tooth is broken.
  gee-gee *sai*-yuh *pah*-tah(h)

Gigi saya patah.

I've lost a filling.
  tahm-pah-lahn
  gee-gee *sai*-yuh *hee*-lang

*Tampalan
gigi saya hilang.*

My gums hurt.
  goo-see *sai*-yuh *sah*-kit

Gusi saya sakit.

Don't extract it.
  jah-*ngahn* *chah*-but

Jangan cabut.

Please give me an anaesthetic.
  to-long *kah*-si(h)
  oo-baht bee-*oos*

*Tolong kasih
ubat bius.*

Ouch!	ah-*doo*(h)!	*Aduh!*

KEPERLUAN KHUSUS

SPECIFIC NEEDS

DISABLED TRAVELLERS

ORANG CACAT

Few facilities cater to the disabled in Malaysia. In most cities and towns there are seldom any sidewalks, and if there are, the curbs tend to be high and uneven. Toilets for the disabled are few and far between. Some of the newer mass transit and train systems in Kuala Lumpur have more accessibility. Malays in particular tend to stare at any one who looks different (this includes most non-Asian travellers) so be prepared to be gawked at.

I'm disabled.
    sai-yuh *chah*-chaht   *Saya cacat.*
I need assistance.
    sai-yuh per-*loo*-kahn   *Saya perlukan bantuan.*
    bahn-*too*-ahn
What services do you
have for disabled people?
    ah-duh per-*kheed*-mah-tahn   *Ada perkhidmatan untuk*
    oon-tu(k) *o*-rahng *chah*-chaht?   *orang cacat?*
Is there wheelchair access?
    ah-duh *jah*-lahn *mah*-su(k)   *Ada jalan masuk untuk*
    oon-tu(k) ke-*roo*-see be-*ro*-duh?   *kerusi beroda?*
I'm deaf.
    sai-yuh pe-*kah(k)*   *Saya pekak.*
I can lipread.
    sai-yuh *dah*-paht mem-*bah*-chuh   *Saya dapat membaca*
    ge-*rah*-kahn *bee*-bir   *gerakan bibir.*
Does anyone here know
sign language?
    ah-duh *o*-rahng yahng *tah*-hoo   *Ada orang yang tahu*
    bah-*hah*-suh ee-*shah*-raht?   *bahasa isyarat?*
I have a hearing aid.
    sai-yuh *ah*-duh *ah*-laht   *Saya ada alat bantu*
    bahn-too de-*ngahr*   *dengar.*

Speak more loudly please.
to-long *chah*-kahp
kwaht see-*kit*

*Tolong cakap
kuat sikit.*

Are guide dogs permitted?
bo-*leh(h)*-kah(h) *sai*-yuh
mem-*bah*-wuh *mah*-su(k)
ahn-jing pe-*mahn*-doo?

*Bolehkah saya membawa
masuk anjing pemandu?*

Braille library	per-poos-tah-*kah*-ahn brehl	*perpustakaan Braille*
disabled person	o-rahng *chah*-chaht	*orang cacat*
guide dog	*ahn*-jing pe-*mahn*-doo	*anjing pemandu*
wheelchair	ke-*roo*-see be-ro-duh	*kerusi beroda*

GAY TRAVELLERS   ORANG HOMOSEKSUAL

Despite negative views of homosexuality and laws which allow for the punishment of homosexual acts by imprisonment or caning, Malaysia is amazingly tolerant of transvestites, *pondan*, *pon-dahn*. Public displays of affection are not okay, however.

There is a gay scene in Kuala Lumpur. The word 'gay', pronounced geh, will be understood.

Where are the gay hangouts?
dee *mah*-nuh tem-*paht*
ber-*koom*-pool o-rahng geh/
ho-mo-*sek*-soo-ahl?

*Di mana tempat
berkumpul orang
gay/homoseksual?*

Where are the gay clubs?
ke-*lahb mah*-lahm *oon*-tu(k)
o-rahng geh dee *mah*-nuh?

*Kelab malam untuk
orang gay di mana?*

[Are we; Am I] likely to be harassed?
ah-duh-kah o-rahng geh
se-*ring* de-*gahng*-goo dee
see-*nee*?

*Adakah orang gay
sering diganggu di sini?*

Is there a gay organisation
in Kuala Lumpur?
ah-duh or-gahn-i-*sah*-see geh
dee *kwah*-luh *loom*-pur tah(k)?

*Ada organisasi gay di
Kuala Lumpur tak?*

TRAVELLING WITH THE FAMILY

PERJALANAN DENGAN KELUARGA

Malaysians love children, and if you have some it can be a real icebreaker. Discounts are available for children at most attractions and on public transport. You will see children eating out with adults, even in pricey restaurants, at almost any time of day.

Are there facilities for babies?
    ah-duh ke-moo-*dah(h)*-ahn
    oon-tu(k) *bah*-yee tah(k)?

Ada kemudahan untuk bayi tak?

Do you have a childminding service?
    ah-duh per-*kheed*-mah-tahn
    pen-*jah*-gah-ahn *ah*-nah(k) tah(k)?

Ada perkhidmatan penjagaan anak tak?

Where can I find a/an
(English-speaking) babysitter?
    dee *mah*-nuh *sai*-yuh bo-*leh(h)*
    men-*chah*-ree pen-*jah*-guh
    ah-nah(k) (yahng *tah*-hoo
    ber-*chah*-kahp *dah*-lahm
    bah-*hah*-suh *ing*-ge-ris)?

Di mana saya boleh mencari penjaga anak (yang tahu bercakap dalam Bahasa Inggeris)?

Can you put an (extra)
bed/cot in the room?
    bo-*leh(h)* *sai*-yuh *min*-tuh
    sah-too (*lah*-gee) *kah*-til *oon*-tu(k)
    bee-li(k) *kah*-mee?

Boleh saya minta satu (lagi) katil untuk bilik kami?

I need a car with a child seat.
    sai-yuh per-*loo*-kahn ke-*reh*-tuh
    de-*ngahn* ke-*roo*-see
    kah-nah(k)-*kah*-nah(k)

Saya perlukan kereta dengan kerusi kanak-kanak.

Is it suitable for children?
    ah-duh-kah(h) *ee*-nee se-*swai*
    oon-tu(k) *kah*-nah(k)-*kah*-nah(k)?

Adakah ini sesuai untuk kanak-kanak?

Are there any activities for children?
    ah-duh ke-gee-*ah*-tahn *oon*-tu(k)
    kah-nah(k)-*kah*-nah(k)?

Ada kegiatan untuk kanak-kanak?

Is there a family discount?
ah-duh *dis*-kown *oon*-tu(k)
ke-loo-*ahr*-guh?

Ada diskaun untuk keluarga?

Are children allowed?
ah-duh-kah(h)
kah-nah(k)-*kah*-nah(k)
dee-be-*nahr*-kahn *mah*-su(k)?

Adakah kanak-kanak dibenarkan masuk?

Do you have a children's menu?
ah-duh meh-nyoo *oon*-tu(k)
kah-nah(k)-*kah*-nah(k) tah(k)?

Ada menu untuk kanak-kanak tak?

ON BUSINESS   PERJALANAN PERNIAGAAN

We're attending a ...	*kah*-mee meng-hah-*di*-ree ...	*Kami menghadiri ...*
conference	per-*see*-dah-ngahn/ kon-fer-*ehn*-see	*persidangan/ konferensi*
meeting	me-shoo-*ah*-raht	*mesyuarat*
trade fair	*pehs*-tuh per-*toon*-joo-kahn per-*dah*-gah-ngahn	*pesta pertunjukan perdagangan*

I'm on a course.
sai-yuh se-*dahng* ber-*koor*-sus

Saya sedang berkursus.

I have an appointment with ...
sai-yuh *ah*-duh te-moo-*jahn*-jee de-*ngahn* ...

Saya ada temujanji dengan ...

Here's my business card.
ee-nee kahd *nah*-muh *sai*-yuh

Ini kad nama saya.

I need an interpreter.
sai-yuh per-*loo* pen-ter-*jeh*-mah(h)

Saya perlu penterjemah.

I'd like to use a computer.
sai-yuh per-*loo* meng-*goo*-nuh kom-*poo*-ter

Saya perlu mengguna komputer.

I'd like to send [a fax; an email].
  sai-yuh nah(k) meng-*hahn*-tahr   *Saya nak menghantar*
  fahks/*ee*-mehl   *faks/e-mel.*

client	pe-*lahng*-gahn/*klai*-ehn	*pelanggan/klien*
colleague	*rah*-kahn se-*ker*-juh	*rakan sekerja*
distributor	pe-*ngeh*-dahr	*pengedar*
email	*ee*-mehl	*e-mel*
exhibition	*pah*-meh-rahn	*pameran*
manager	pe-*ngoo*-roos	*pengurus*
mobile phone	teh-*leh*-fon *bim*-bit	*telefon bimbit*
profit	*oon*-tung	*untung*
proposal	*oo*-sool/*chah*-dah-ngahn	*usul/cadangan*

FILM & TV CREWS

KRU FILEM & TELEVISYEN

Can we film here?
  bo-*leh(h)* kah-mee   *Boleh kami*
  me-rah-*kahm*-kahn   *merakamkan*
  fee-lem dee *see*-nee?   *filem di sini?*

We're filming!
  kah-mee se-*dahng*   *Kami sedang*
  mem-*boo*-aht *fee*-lem!   *membuat filem!*

We're making a ...   *kah*-mee   *Kami membuat ...*
  mem-*boo*-aht ...

film	*fee*-lem	*filem*
documentary	do-koo-*mehn*-tah-ree	*dokumentari*
TV series	si-ree *rahm*-chah-ngahn	*siri rancangan*
	teh-le-vi-shen	*televisyen*

PILGRIMAGE & RELIGION	**NAIK HAJI & KEAGAMAAN**

Malaysian Muslims can be a little touchy about discussing religion. Approach Islam with great respect. If you're asking questions it's better to ask a Chinese or Indian Malaysian who is less likely to be a Muslim. Talking too much to a Malay about religions other than Islam might be perceived as trying to convert them, which is against the law. Remember that in order to enter a mosque, a man must wear a shirt, preferably with sleeves, and pants (or a *sarong*) falling below the knees. Women must wear clothing that covers their head and body with the exception of their hands and face – usually a skirt rather than pants. Don't walk in front of people who are performing their prayers.

Can I attend this service?
bo-*leh(h)* meng-hah-*di*-ree
oo-pah-*chah*-ruh *ee*-nee?

Boleh menghadiri upacara ini?

Can I pray here?
bo-*leh(h)* sai-yuh
ber-sehm-*bai*-yahng dee *see*-nee?

Boleh saya bersembayang di sini?

Where can I pray/worship?
dee *mah*-nuh tem-*paht* yahng
sai-yuh bo-*leh(h)*
ber-sehm-*bai*-yahng?

Di mana tempat yang saya boleh bersembayang?

Where can I make confession
(in English)?
pe-*ngah*-koo-ahn (*dah*-lahm
bah-*hah*-suh *ing*-ge-ris)
dee-lah-*koo*-kahn dee *mah*-nuh?

Pengakuan (dalam Bahasa Inggeris) dilakukan di mana?

May I enter this mosque?
bo-*leh(h)* tah(k) *sai*-yuh
mah-su(k) *mahs*-jid *ee*-nee?

Boleh tak saya masuk masjid ini?

Where may I stand/
walk in the mosque?
dee *mah*-nuh *sai*-yuh bo-*leh(h)*
ber-*di*-ree/*jah*-lahn *dah*-lahm
mahs-jid?

Di mana saya boleh berdiri/jalan dalam masjid?

SPECIFIC NEEDS

baptism	*bahp*-tis	*baptis*
christening	*bahp*-tis	*baptis*
church	ge-*reh*-juh	*gereja*
communion	per-*jah*-moo-ahn soo-chee	*perjamuan suci*
confession	pe-*ngah*-koo-ahn	*pengakuan*
fasting month	*rah*-mah-dahn	*Ramadhan*
Friday prayers	sem-*bah(h)*-yahng joo-mah-aht	*sembahyang Jumaat*
funeral	pe-*mah*-kah-mahn	*pemakaman*
God (Muslim)	*too*-hahn/*ahl*-lah(h)	*Tuhan/Allah*
monk	*rah*-hib	*rahib*
mosque	*mahs*-jid	*masjid*
pilgrim (Muslim)	*hah*-jee/*haj*-jah(h)	*haji/hajjah* (m/f)
pilgrimage to Mecca	hahj	*hajj*
prayer	*do*-ah/*sem*-bah(h)-yahng	*doa/sembahyang*
priest (Catholic)	*pah*-dree	*padri*
pastor (Protestant)	*pah*-dree/*pahs*-tor	*padri/pastor*
relic	pe-*ning*-gah-lahn	*peninggalan*
religious	pe-*rah*-rah-kahn	*perarakan*
procession	*ah*-gah-muh	*agama*
religious tax	*zah*-kaht	*zakat*
saint	o-rahng *soo*-chee/*wah*-lee	*orang suci/wali*
shrine	tem-*paht soo*-chee	*tempat suci*
... temple	*to*-kong ...	*tokong ...*
Buddhist	*boo*-dah	*Buddha*
Chinese	*chee*-nah	*Cina*
Hindu	*koo*-il	*kuil*

BAREFOOT & FANCY FREE

All Malaysians take off their shoes before entering accommodation of any kind, so remember to remove yours and put them next to the pile. Footwear must also be removed when visiting mosques and some temples, and beware – expensive shoes can walk off on their own.

TRACING ROOTS & HISTORY

MENCARI ASAL-USUL & SEJARAH

I think my ancestors came from this area.

    sai-yuh *rah*-suh neh-*neh*(k) *mo*-yahng *sai*-yuh ber-*ah*-sahl *dah*-ree *kah*-wah-sahn *ee*-nee

Saya rasa nenek moyang saya berasal dari kawasan ini.

I'm looking for my relatives.

    sai-yuh men-*chah*-ree *ah*(h)-lee ke-loo-*ahr*-guh *sai*-yuh

Saya mencari ahli keluarga saya.

I have/had a relative who lives around here.

    doo-loo ke-loo-*ahr*-guh *sai*-yuh *ting*-gahl dee *kah*-wah-sahn *ee*-nee

Dulu keluarga saya tinggal di kawasan ini.

Is there anyone here by the name of ...?

    ah-duh *o*-rahng dee *see*-nee yahng ber-*nah*-muh ...?

Ada orang di sini yang bernama ...?

I'd like to go to the cemetery/ burial ground.

    sai-yuh *i*-ngin me-*lah*-waht per-*koo*-bu-rahn

Saya ingin melawat perkuburan.

My father used to work here.

    ai-yah(h) *sai*-yuh per-*nah*(h) ber-*ker*-juh dee *see*-nee

Ayah saya pernah berkerja di sini.

MASA, TARIKH & PERAYAAN

TIME, DATES & FESTIVALS

Malaysians, especially in the big cities, tend to be punctual for business (although heavy rain and traffic jams may wreak havoc with schedules from time to time). However, for social functions, it's okay to be fashionably late.

TELLING THE TIME   MENENTUKAN MASA

In Malay, 'am' and 'pm' are replaced by whole words.

8 am
    poo-kool *lah*-pahn *pah*-gee

pukul lapan pagi
(lit: hour eight morning)

8 pm
    poo-kool *lah*-pahn *mah*-lahm

pukul lapan malam
(lit: hour eight night)

morning (12 midnight – 12 noon)
    pah-gee

pagi

afternoon (12 noon – 3 pm)
    te-ngah-*hah*-ree

tengahari

evening (3 – 7 pm)
    pe-*tahng*

petang

night (7 pm – 12 midnight)
    mah-lahm

malam

o'clock	*poo*-kool	*pukul*
second	sa-*aht*/de-*ti(k)*	*saat/detik*
minute	*mi*-nit	*minit*
to	se-be-*lum*	*sebelum*
past	se-le-*pahs*	*selepas*
half	se-te-*ngah(h)*	*setengah*
quarter	*soo*-koo	*suku*
one hour	se-*jahm*	*sejam*
two hours	*doo*-uh jahm	*dua jam*

What time is it?
   poo-kool be-*rah*-puh
   (se-*kah*-rahng)?

*Pukul berapa
(sekarang)?*

It's three o'clock.
   poo-kool *tee*-guh

Pukul tiga.

It's a quarter to four.
   lah-gee *soo*-koo jahm
   poo-kool em-*paht*

*Lagi suku jam
pukul empat.*

It's ten past three.
   se-*poo*-lu(h) *mi*-nit se-le-*pahs*
   poo-kool *tee*-guh

*Sepuluh minit selepas
pukul tiga.*

It's five-thirty.
   poo-kool *lee*-muh
   se-te-*ngah*(h)

*Pukul lima
setengah.*

Half past one.
   poo-kool *sah*-too se-te-*ngah*(h)

Pukul satu setengah.

DAYS   HARI DALAM SEMINGGU

Monday	*hah*-ree *ees*-nin	*hari Isnin*
Tuesday	*hah*-ree se-*lah*-suh	*hari Selasa*
Wednesday	*hah*-ree *rah*-boo	*hari Rabu*
Thursday	*hah*-ree *khah*-mis	*hari Khamis*
Friday	*hah*-ree *joo*-mah-aht	*hari Jumaat*
Saturday	*hah*-ree *sahb*-too	*hari Sabtu*
Sunday	*hah*-ree *ah*-hahd	*hari Ahad*
on Monday	*pah*-duh *hah*-ree *ees*-nin	*pada hari Isnin*

MONTHS | BULAN

January	*jahn*-oo-ah-ree	*Januari*
February	*feh*-broo-ah-ree	*Februari*
March	mahch	*Mac*
April	*ah*-pril	*April*
May	may	*Mei*
June	joon	*Jun*
July	joo-lai	*Julai*
August	o-gos	*Ogos*
September	sehp-*tehm*-ber	*September*
October	ok-*to*-ber	*Oktober*
November	no-*vehm*-ber	*November*
December	dee-*sehm*-ber	*Disember*
during June	se-*mah*-suh *bu*-lahn joon	*semasa bulan Jun*

THE NIGHT BEFORE

Nights refer to the following day – 'Saturday night' is
expressed as 'the night before Sunday', rather like saying
'Christmas Eve'.

Thursday night
  mah-lahm *joo*-mah-aht   *malam Jumaat*
                                (lit: at-night Friday)

DATES | TARIKH

Date order in Malaysia is expressed as day, month, year, eg:

17 August 1945
  too-ju(h) be-*lahs* o-gos   *Tujuh belas Ogos*
  sem-*bee*-lahn be-*lahs* em-*paht* *sembilan belas*
  poo-lu(h) *lee*-muh   *empat puluh lima*
What date is it today?
  ah-puh *tah*-rikh *hah*-ree ee-nee?   *Apa tarikh hari ini?*
It's 28 June.
  hah-ree ee-nee *doo*-uh *poo*-lu(h)   *Hari ini dua puluh lapan*
  lah-pahn hah-ree-*bu*-lahn joon   *haribulan Jun.*

PRESENT

immediately	ser-*tah*-mer-*tah*	*serta-merta*
now	se-*kah*-rahng/*kee*-nee	*sekarang/kini*
currently	se-*dahng*	*sedang*
today	*hah*-ree ee-nee	*hari ini*
this morning	*pah*-gee ee-nee	*pagi ini*
during the day	*pah*-duh *hah*-ree ee-nee	*pada hari ini*
tonight	*mah*-lahm ee-nee;	*malam ini;*
	mah-lahm *nahn*-tee	*malam nanti*
this week	*ming*-goo ee-nee	*minggu ini*
this month	*boo*-lahn ee-nee	*bulan ini*
this year	*tah*-hoon ee-nee	*tahun ini*

PAST

SEKARANG

YANG LALU

just now	*bah*-roo *sah*-juh	*baru saja*
before	se-be-*lum*	*sebelum*
recently	*bah*-roo-*bah*-roo ee-nee	*baru-baru ini*
already	*soo*-dah(h)	*sudah*
yesterday	se-*mah*-lahm	*semalam*
yesterday morning	*pah*-gee se-*mah*-lahm	*pagi semalam*
yesterday afternoon	te-ngah-*hah*-ree se-*mah*-lahm	*tengahari semalam*
last night	*mah*-lahm se-*mah*-lahm	*malam semalam*
day before yesterday	kel-*mah*-rin	*kelmarin*
last week	*ming*-goo le-*pahs*	*minggu lepas*
two weeks ago	*doo*-uh *ming*-goo le-*pahs*	*dua minggu lepas*
last month	*boo*-lahn le-*pahs*	*bulan lepas*
last year	*tah*-hoon le-*pahs*	*tahun lepas*
ago	yahng *lah*-loo; le-*pahs*	*yang lalu; lepas*
a while ago	se-*dee*-kit *mah*-suh doo-*loo*	*sedikit masa dulu*
long ago	*lah*-muh doo-*loo*	*lama dulu*

FUTURE

MASA DEPAN

as soon as possible	se-che-*paht* *moong*-kin	secepat mungkin
soon	se-*geh*-ruh	segera
not yet	be-*lum lah*-gee	belum lagi
later	ke-*moo*-dee-ahn/ *nahn*-tee	kemudian/ nanti
after	se-le-*pahs*/se-*soo*-dah(h)	selepas/sesudah
tomorrow	eh-so(k)	esok
morning	eh-so(k) *pah*-gee	esok pagi
afternoon	eh-so(k) te-ngah-*hah*-ree	esok tengahari
evening	eh-so(k) pe-*tahng*	esok petang
day after tomorrow	*loo*-suh	lusa
next week	*ming*-goo de-*pahn*	minggu depan
next month	*boo*-lahn de-*pahn*	bulan depan
next year	*tah*-hoon de-*pahn*	tahun depan
forever	se-*lah*-muh-*lah*-muh-nyuh	selama-lamanya

moment	se-*behn*-tahr	sebentar
minute	*mi*-nit	minit
hour	jahm	jam
day	*hah*-ree	hari
week	*ming*-goo	minngu
month	*boo*-lahn	bulan
year	*tah*-hoon	tahun
decade	*deh*-kahd	dekad
century	*ah*-bahd	abad
millennium	mi-*leh*-nee-um	milenium

DURING THE DAY

dawn	*sen*-juh	senja
day	*hah*-ree	hari
early	*ah*-wahl	awal
early morning	*ah*-wahl *pah*-gee	awal pagi
midday	te-ngah-*hah*-ree	tengahari
midnight	te-*ngah(h)* mah-lahm	tengah malam
sunrise	mah-tuh-*hah*-ree ter-*bit*	matahari terbit
sunset	mah-tuh-*hah*-ree	matahari
	ter-*be*-nahm	terbenam

SEPANJANG HARI

SEASONS

spring	*moo*-sim *boo*-nguh	musim bunga
summer	*moo*-sim *pah*-nahs	musim panas
autumn	*moo*-sim *loo*-ru(h);	musim luruh;
	goo-gur	gugur
winter	*moo*-sim se-*joo(k)*	musim sejuk
dry season	*moo*-sim ke-*mah*-row/	musim kemarau/
	ke-*ring*	kering
rainy season	*moo*-sim *hoo*-jahn	musim hujan

MUSIM

LIKE A PRAYER

Malays sometimes refer to prayer times, rather than the time of day. If you hear a Malay saying the following, they mean:

Selepas zohor
following the midday prayers, which usually occur around 12:30 – 1:00 pm

Selepas asar
after the mid-afternoon prayers, which usually start around 3:30 – 4:30 pm

Selepas mahgrib
following the sunset prayers; sunset on the Peninsula usually falls between 7:00 – 7:30 pm

Selepas isyak
after the commencement of night prayers, which is usually about one hour after sunset. 'After *isyak*' could actually mean any time before dawn the next morning!

HOLIDAYS & FESTIVALS

PERCUTIAN & PERAYAAN

Malaysia loves a festival! There are many religious dates observed and celebrated by various communities. The dates on which Muslim holidays fall change from year to year, because they follow the (lunar) Islamic calendar.

Some festivals will affect your stay. Almost everything shuts down during Chinese New Year. For *Hari Raya Aidl Fitri*, there's a big parade and lots of flag waving in Kuala Lumpur. Travel before and during *Hari Raya Puasa* can be difficult, as the whole country endeavours to *balik kampung*, *bah*-li(k) *kahm*-pung, (lit: go-back village) get home for celebrations. Flights will be full, trains will be packed and traffic will be jammed.

Chinese New Year

Chinese New Year is a major national event which falls in January or February. Dragon dances are held and Chinese families have a reunion dinner on the eve of Chinese New Year, opening their homes for family and friends during the first two days of the festival. Children and unmarried relatives receive *ang pow*, ahng pow, (money in small red envelopes) and everyone wishes you *Gong Si Fatt Choy* (a happy and prosperous New Year). In a true overlapping of cultures, the Malays have adopted the use of a green *ang pow* envelope for giving money (also a Muslim tradition during *Hari Raya*, *hah*-ree rai-yuh). These envelopes are widely available for free at banks throughout Malaysia, before the festive periods.

Deepavali

Deepavali, dee-pah-*vah*-lee, the Hindu 'Festival of Lights', celebrates *Rama's* victory over the demon *Ravana*. It's the most important of Hindu festivals in Malaysia. Oil lamps are lit to celebrate this victory and to invite *Lakshmi*, the goddess of wealth, into the home. The Malaysian Indians who celebrate *Deepavali* also hold open houses.

Hari Kebangsaan

Hari Kebahngsaan, *hah*-ree ke-bahng-*sah*-ahn, Malaysia's Independence Day, falls on 31 August and is marked with a national holiday.

Hari Raya Aidil Adha/Hari Raya Haji

Hari Raya, *hah*-ree *rai*-yuh, literally means 'day celebration'. This Muslim festival commemorates Ibrahim's devotion to God. On being ordered by God to kill his son, Isaac, Ibrahim was about to do the deed when God put a stop to it and told him to kill a sheep instead. It's the day upon which the Muslim pilgrims to Mecca complete their pilgrimage. Almost every Muslim in Malaysia has some member of the family in Mecca every year.

The sacrifice – of a goat or a sheep – is re-enacted throughout the Muslim areas of Malaysia on *Aidil Adha*, followed by great feasting. Muslims hold open houses, *rumah terbuka*, roo-mah(h) ter-*boo*-kuh, for friends and families, with a smorgasbord of delicious foods.

Hari Raya Aidil Fitri/Hari Raya Puasa

The first day of the tenth month marks the end of *Ramadan*, *rah*-mah-dahn, and the celebration of *Hari Raya Puasa*, *hah*-ree *rai*-yuh *pwah*-suh – also known as *Aidil Fitri*, *ai*-dil *fee*-tree. It begins with mass prayers at mosques and in city squares, followed by two days of open houses, family visits and culinary engorgement.

> ### BODY & SOUL
>
> During *Aidl Fitri*, children ask forgiveness from their parents for any wrongdoings, using the words *Maaf zahir batin*, mah-*ahf* zah-*hir* bah-*tin*, 'I apologise with my body and soul'.

Ramadan

The ninth month of the Muslim calendar is the month of *Ramadan*, *rah*-mah-dahn, also known as *bulan puasa*, *bu*-lahn *pwah*-suh, 'the fasting month'. During *Ramadan*, most adult Muslims don't drink, eat, smoke, have sex or indulge in other pleasures during daylight hours. The fast is symbolic of a person's faith, and is also a way for Muslims to feel an affinity with those who are too poor to afford food.

Children, pregnant or menstruating women, and people who are sick or elderly aren't expected to fast. However, some women 'make up' for missed fasting days later in the year. No one is forced to fast, but it's best to eat indoors, out of sight. Many restaurants and food stalls remain open, with a shade-cloth over the door.

Thaipusam

During *Thaipusam*, tai-*poo*-sahm, in January, Hindu devotees honor Lord *Subramaniam* with acts of physical endurance. The festival is celebrated primarily in Kuala Lumpur, at Batu Caves, and in Penang, at the Waterfall Hilltop Temple. The devotees march in a procession carrying *kavadi*, *kah*-vah-dee, heavy metal frames decorated with fruit, flowers and feathers. The *kavadi* are hung from their bodies with metal hooks and spikes driven through their flesh.

CROWDED HOUSE

Selamat Hari   se-*lah*-maht *hah*-ree   (lit: safe ... day)

If you arrive near a festival period, and express interest in the traditions and practices of any Malaysian, you might get a flag to an 'open house', a Malaysian tradition practised by all races and religions. Traditional foods are prepared, and every guest is treated to full hospitality. You're not expected to bring a gift – however it is appropriate to give small quantities of money to children and unmarried adults. Just feel free to go and enjoy the food and company.

    This is one tradition during which racial tensions are often put aside. You'll see people of all origins at each other's homes. Chinese families who are expecting Muslim guests will often prepare food that is *halal* (allowed) for Muslims. If you don't get an invitation on *Hari Raya Puasa*, you can always go to the Prime Minister's house, where everyone in the nation is welcome!

Happy/Merry (festival name)!	se-*lah*-maht ...!	*Selamat ...!*
ang pow	ahng pow	*ang pow*
open house	*roo*-mah(h) ter-*boo*-kuh	*rumah terbuka*
Please come in.	*see*-luh mah-su(k)	*Sila masuk.*
Please help yourself.	*see*-luh mah-kahn/ *mee*-num	*Sila makan/ minum.* (lit: please eat/drink)
Thank you.	te-*ree*-muh kah-si(h)	*Terima kasih.*
What are these?	mah-kah-nahn *ah*-puh nee?	*Makanan apa ni?*

WEDDINGS   PERKAHWINAN

Weddings are big business in Malaysia, often with hundreds of guests. Whole streets can be blocked off, tents set up and tables and decorations set on the road. Depending on the faith and/or wealth of the family, weddings can last for days. Even if you've never met the couple, it's not uncommon to be invited to the reception and wedding feast, *kenduri*, ken-*doo*-ree, rather than the actual religious ceremony, *nikah*, *nee*-kah(h).

Although offering gifts is acceptable, it's customary to give money in an envelope to the parents who are hosting the reception.

Congratulations!	*tah(h)*-nee-ah(h)!	*Tahniah!*
wedding	per-*kah(h)*-wi-nahn/ per-*nee*-kah(h)-ahn	*perkahwinan/ pernikahan*
reception	ken-*doo*-ree	*kenduri*

THEY SAY IT'S YOUR BIRTHDAY

Birthdays aren't a big deal once people have finished school. Malaysians sing the same happy birthday song that Westerners do – usually in English.

Happy Birthday!	
se-*lah*-maht *hah*-ree *jah*-dee!	*Selamat Hari Jadi!*
When is your birthday?	
bee-luh *hah*-ree *jah*-dee ahn-duh?	*Bila hari jadi anda?*
My birthday's on ...	
hah-ree *jah*-dee *sai*-yuh *pah*-duh ...	*Hari jadi saya pada ...*
How old are you?	
oo-mur be-*rah*-puh-kah(h)?	*Umur berapakah?*

FUNERALS   PEMAKAMAN/PERKEBUMIAN

Muslims believe that the corpse must be buried as soon as possible, and burial usually occurs within 24 hours of death. Chinese and Indian funerals, which sometimes feature processions with professional mourners, tend to be more public.

My condolences.	*tahk*-zee-ah(h)	*Takziah.*
When did he/ she die?	*bee*-luh *dee*-uh me-*ning*-gahl?	*Bila dia meninggal?*

BILANGAN & JUMLAH

NUMBERS & AMOUNTS

In Malay, numbers from 12 to 19 are comprised of the numbers one to nine plus *(-)belas*, (-)be-*lahs*. Numbers from 20 to 99 are counted with *(-)puluh*, (-)*poo*-lu(h), '10'. The number 10 is *sepuluh*, se-*poo*-lu(h), 20 is *dua puluh*, *doo*-uh *poo*-lu(h), and so on.

In the hundreds, *(-)ratus*, (-)*rah*-toos, is used. So, *seratus*, se-*rah*-toos, is 100, *duaratus*, *doo*-uh *rah*-toos, is 200, and so on. For thousands, use *(-)ribu*, (-)*ree*-boo, and for millions, use *(-)juta*, (-)*joo*-tuh.

CARDINAL NUMBERS   BILANGAN POKOK

0	*ko*-song/see-*fahr*	*kosong/sifar*
1	*sah*-too	*satu*
2	*doo*-uh	*dua*
3	*tee*-guh	*tiga*
4	em-*paht*	*empat*
5	*lee*-muh	*lima*
6	e-*nahm*	*enam*
7	*too*-ju(h)	*tujuh*
8	*lah*-pahn	*lapan*
9	sem-*bee*-lahn	*sembilan*
10	se-*poo*-lu(h)	*sepuluh*
11	se-be-*lahs*	*sebelas*
12	*doo*-uh be-*lahs*	*dua belas*
13	*tee*-guh be-*lahs*	*tiga belas*
14	em-*paht* be-*lahs*	*empat belas*
15	*lee*-muh be-*lahs*	*lima belas*
16	e-*nahm* be-*lahs*	*enam belas*
17	*too*-ju(h) be-*lahs*	*tujuh belas*
18	*lah*-pahn be-*lahs*	*lapan belas*
19	sem-*bee*-lahn be-*lahs*	*sembilan belas*
20	*doo*-uh *poo*-lu(h)	*dua puluh*
21	*doo*-uh *poo*-lu(h) *sah*-too	*dua puluh satu*
22	*doo*-uh *poo*-lu(h) *doo*-uh	*dua puluh dua*
30	*tee*-guh *poo*-lu(h)	*tiga puluh*
40	em-*paht* *poo*-lu(h)	*empat puluh*

NUMBERS & AMOUNTS

50	*lee*-muh *poo*-lu(h)	lima puluh
100	se-*rah*-toos	seratus
200	*doo*-uh *rah*-toos	dua ratus
268	*doo*-uh *rah*-toos e-*nahm* *poo*-lu(h) *lah*-pahn	dua ratus enam puluh lapan
300	*tee*-guh *rah*-toos	tiga ratus
1000	se-*ree*-boo	seribu
2000	*doo*-uh *ree*-boo	dua ribu
3000	*tee*-guh *ree*-boo	tiga ribu
51,783	*lee*-muh *poo*-lu(h) *sah*-too *ree*-boo, *too*-ju(h) *rah*-toos *lah*-pahn *poo*-lu(h) *tee*-guh	lima puluh satu ribu, tujuh ratus lapan puluh tiga
1 million	se-*joo*-tuh	sejuta
2 million	*doo*-uh *joo*-tuh	dua juta

ORDINAL NUMBERS · BILANGAN TINGKAT

1st	per-*tah*-muh	pertama
2nd	ke-*doo*-uh	kedua
3rd	ke-*tee*-guh	ketiga
4th	ke-em-*paht*	keempat
5th	ke-*lee*-muh	kelima
6th	ke-e-*nahm*	keenam
7th	ke-*too*-ju(h)	ketujuh
8th	ke-*lah*-pahn	kelapan
9th	ke-sem-*bee*-lahn	kesembilan
10th	ke-se-*poo*-lu(h)	kesepuluh

the first bus
    bahs (yahng) per-*tah*-muh   bas (yang) pertama
the third building
    bah-*ngoo*-nahn (yahng) ke-*tee*-guh   bangunan (yang) ketiga

FRACTIONS · PECAHAN

1/3	se-per-*tee*-guh	sepertiga
1/4	*soo*-koo	suku
1/2	se-te-*ngah*(h)	setengah
3/4	*tee*-guh pe-rem-*paht*	tiga perempat

QUANTITY

QUANTITY   JUMLAH

Quantity can either be indicated by a number, or by a quantity word placed before a noun.

all	se-*moo*-uh	*semua*
both	ke-*doo*-uh-nyuh/	*keduanya/*
	ke-*doo*-uh-*doo*-uh-nyuh	*kedua-duanya*
double	*doo*-uh *kah*-lee *gahm*-duh	*dua kali ganda*
each	se-*tee*-ahp/	*setiap/tiap-tiap*
	tee-ahp-*tee*-ahp	
enough	*choo*-kup	*cukup*
every	se-*tee*-ahp/	*setiap/*
	mah-sing-*mah*-sing	*masing-masing*
few	be-be-*rah*-puh	*beberapa*
a little	se-*dee*-kit	*sedikit*
many (for things)	*bah*-nyah(k)	*banyak*
(for people)	rah-*mai*	*ramai*
much	*bah*-nyah(k)	*banyak*
one more	*sah*-too *lah*-gee	*satu lagi*

There are many people.
ah-duh rah-*mai* o-rahng   *Ada ramai orang.*
(lit: there-are many person)

about	le-*bi(h)* koo-rahng/	*lebih kurang/*
	ki-ruh-*ki*-ruh	*kira-kira*
amount	*jum*-lah(h)	*jumlah*
to count	me-*ngi*-ruh	*mengira*
minus	*to*-lah(k)/*koo*-rahng	*tolak/kurang*
more	le-*bi(h)*	*lebih*
number	*nom*-bor/*ahng*-kuh/	*nombor/angka/*
	bee-*lah*-ngahn	*bilangan*
a pair	se-*pah*-sahng	*sepasang*
percent	pe-*rah*-toos	*peratus*
plus	*tahm*-bah(h)	*tambah*
quantity	bee-*lah*-ngahn/	*bilangan/*
	koo-*ahm*-ti-tee	*kuantiti*
some	be-be-*rah*-puh	*beberapa*

**NUMBERS &
AMOUNTS**

COUNT DOWN

Malay uses 'counters' before most numbers (see page 36, under Classifiers), like in English when we say 'a *piece* of paper'. However, in Malay these counters are used nearly all the time for specific numbers of things or people.

Common counters include:

batang   *bah*-tahng
   long, roundish things such as pencils, rivers, trees, cigarettes
biji   *bee*-jee
   small round things such as fruit, sweets, beans
buah   *boo*-ah(h)
   large objects such as cars, houses, furniture, airplanes, buildings, mountains, planets
ekor   *eh*-kor
   animals
helai   *heh*-lai
   flat, thin, saggy things such as clothing and paper
keping   *ke*-ping
   flat, thin, hard things such as a sheet of metal or wood
kotak   *ko*-tah(k)
   box shaped things, like a cigarette carton or box
orang   *o*-rahng
   people
potong   *po*-tong
   a piece of something you can cut, eg, cake

I want to buy three shirts.
   sai-yuh nah(k) be-*lee* tee-guh   *Saya nak beli tiga helai*
   heh-lai *bah*-joo   *baju.*
                            (lit: I want buy three *helai* shirt)

KECEMASAN   EMERGENCIES

Ambulance and paramedic services in Malaysia are slow at best. It's often better to get yourself to the nearest hospital if you need medical services.

Help!	*to*-long!	*Tolong!*
Stop!	ber-*hehn*-tee!	*Berhenti!*
Go away!	*per*-gee/be-*lah(h)!*	*Pergi/Belah!*
Watch out!	*ah*-wahs/	*Awas/*
	ber-*hah*-ti-*hah*-ti!	*Berhati-hati!*
Thief!	pen-*choo*-ree!	*Pencuri!*
Pickpocket!	pe-nye-*luk sah*-koo!	*Penyeluk saku!*
Fire!	ke-*bah*-kah-rahn!	*Kebakaran!*
It's an emergency!	ke-che-*mah*-sahn!	*Kecemasan!*

There's been an accident.
    ah-duh ke-*mah*-lah-ngahn!   *Ada kemalangan!*
Help me please!
    min-tuh *to*-long!   *Minta tolong!*
Could I use the telephone?
    bo-*leh(h)* goo-nai teh-*leh*-fon?   *Boleh gunai telefon?*
I'm lost.
    sai-yuh ter-*seh*-saht   *Saya tersesat.*
Where are the toilets?
    tahn-duhs dee *mah*-nuh?   *Tandas di mana?*
Call the police!
    pahng-gil *po*-lis!   *Panggil polis!*
I'll get the police!
    sai-yuh ah-*kahn pahng*-gil *po*-lis!   *Saya akan panggil polis!*
Where's the police station?
    bah-lai *po*-lis dee *mah*-nuh?   *Balai polis di mana?*
I've been robbed!
    sai-yuh te-*lah(h)* dee-rom-*pah(k)!*   *Saya telah dirompak!*
I speak English.
    sai-yuh *tah*-hoo ber-*chah*-kahp   *Saya tahu bercakap*
    bah-*hah*-suh *ing*-ge-ris   *bahasa Inggeris.*

EMERGENCIES

I've lost my ...	... *sai-yuh hee*-lahng	... *saya hilang.*
My ... was/were stolen.	... *sai-yuh* dee-*choo*-ree	... *saya dicuri.*
backpack	behg *sahn*-dahr	*beg sandar*
bags	behg	*beg*
handbag	behg *tah*-ngahn	*beg tangan*
money	*doo*-it/wahng	*duit/ wang*
papers	*do*-koo-mehn/ ker-*tahs*	*dokumen/ kertas*
passport	*pahs*-port	*pasport*
travellers cheques	chehk kem-*bah*-ruh	*cek kembara*
wallet	*dom*-peht	*dompet*

DEALING WITH THE POLICE

BERURUSAN DENGAN POLIS

Good manners go a long way in Malaysia. As a foreign visitor you are considered a guest, and guests are on best behaviour! At least be patient and try to keep your voice low.

My possessions are insured.	
sai-yuh *ah*-duh in-*soo*-rahns *oon*-tu(k) *bah*-rahng-*bah*-rahng *sai*-yuh	*Saya ada insurans untuk barang-barang saya.*
What am I accused of?	
sai-yuh dee-*too*-du(h) *ah*-puh?	*Saya dituduh apa?*
I (don't) understand.	
sai-yuh (tah(k)) *fah*-hahm	*Saya (tak) faham.*
I didn't realise I was doing anything wrong.	
sai-yuh tah(k) se-*dahr sai*-yuh ber-*sah*-lah(h)	*Saya tak sedar saya bersalah.*

I didn't do it.
    sai-yuh *tee*-dah(k)
    me-lah-*koo*-kahn ee-too

Saya tidak melakukan itu.

I'm sorry; I apologise.
    sai-yuh me-nye-*sahl*;
    sai-yuh *min*-tuh mah-*ahf*

Saya menyesal; Saya minta maaf.

We're innocent.
    kah-mee *tee*-dah(k)
    ber-sah-*lah(h)*

Kami tidak bersalah.

We're foreigners.
    kah-mee *o*-rahng *ah*-sing

Kami orang asing.

Can I call someone?
    bo-*leh(h)*-kah(h) *sai*-yuh
    me-neh-*leh*-fon se-se-*o*-rahng?

Bolehkah saya menelefon seseorang?

Can I see a lawyer
who speaks English?
    bo-*leh(h)*-kah(h) *sai*-yuh
    ber-*jum*-puh de-*ngahm*
    pe-*gwahm* yahng
    ber-bah-*hah*-suh *ing*-ge-ris?

Bolehkah saya berjumpa dengan peguam yang berbahasa Inggeris?

Is there a fine we
can pay to clear this?
    bo-*leh(h)*-kah(h) *kah*-mee
    mem-*bai*-yahr *den*-duh
    oon-tu(k) me-nye-le-*sai*-kahn
    mah-*sah*-luh(h) ee-nee?

Bolehkah kami membayar denda untuk menyelesaikan masalah ini?

Can we pay an on-the-spot fine?
    bo-*leh(h)* bai-yahr *den*-duh
    se-*kah*-rahng?

Boleh bayar denda sekarang?

I know my rights.
    sai-yuh *tah*-hoo hahk *sai*-yuh

Saya tahu hak saya.

I want to contact my
embassy/consulate.
    sai-yuh nah(k)
    meng-hoo-*boo*-ngee
    ke-*doo*-tah-ahn/*kon*-soo-laht
    sai-yuh

Saya nak menghubungi kedutaan/konsulat saya.

EMERGENCIES

THE POLICE MAY SAY ...

ahn-duh dee-*too*-duh me-lah-*koo*-kahn ...	*Anda dituduh melakukan ...*	You'll be charged with ...
dee-uh dee-*too*-duh me-lah-*koo*-kahn ...	*Dia dituduh melakukan ...*	She'll/He'll be charged with ...
be-*ker*-juh *tahn*-puh ee-zin	*bekerja tanpa izin*	working without a permit
ke-*gee*-ah-tahn sub-*ver*-sif	*kegiatan subversif*	anti-government activity
mah-su(k) *tahn*-puh ee-zin *mah*-su(k) *tahn*-puh vee-suh	*masuk tanpa izin masuk tanpa visa*	illegal entry entry without a visa
meng-*gahng*-goo ke-*ah*-mah-nahn	*mengganggu keamanan*	disturbing the peace
me-*mee*-li-kee *bah*-rah-ngahn hah-rahm	*memiliki barangan haram*	possession of illegal substances
pe-*lahng*-gah-rahn pe-*rah*-tu-rahn lah-loo-*lin*-tahs	*pelanggaran peraturan lalulintas*	traffic violation
pem-*boo*-noo-hahn	*pembunuhan*	murder
pen-*choo*-ree-ahn	*pencurian*	theft
pen-*choo*-ree-ahn dee ke-*dai*	*pencurian di kedai*	shoplifting
pe-*rom*-pah-kahn	*perompakan*	robbery
pe-*ro*-go-lahn	*perogolan*	rape
se-*rahng*-ahn	*serangan*	assault
me-le-*bee*-hee *tehm*-po(h) sah(h) vee-suh	*melebihi tempoh sah visa*	overstaying your visa

arrested	dee-*tahng*-kahp	*ditangkap*
cell	sehl	*sel*
consulate	*kon*-soo-laht	*konsulat*
court	*mah(h)*-khah-mah(h)	*mahkamah*
embassy	ke-*doo*-tah-ahn	*kedutaan*
fine	*dehm*-duh	*denda*
(not) guilty	(*tee*-dah(k)) ber-sah-*lah(h)*	*(tidak) bersalah*
lawyer	pe-*gwahm*	*peguam*
police officer	pe-*gah*-wai *po*-lis	*pegawai polis*
police station	*bah*-lai *po*-lis	*balai polis*
prison	pen-*jah*-ruh	*penjara*
trial	pe-*ngah*-di-lahn	*pengadilan*

EMERGENCIES

THE BILL

It's best to address the police as 'sir' or 'ma'am'.

Sir	twahn/en-*chi(k)*	*tuan/encik*
Ma'am	pwahn/chi(k)	*puan/cik*

HEALTH   KESIHATAN

For common ailments head to a walk-in clinic; go to a private hospital if you're really ill.

I'm ill.
sai-yuh *sah*-kit   *Saya sakit.*
My friend is ill.
kah-wahn *sai*-yuh *sah*-kit   *Kawan saya sakit.*
Call an ambulance!
to-long *pang*-gil *ahm*-boo-lahns!   *Tolong panggil ambulans!*
Call a doctor!
pang-gil *dok*-tor!   *Panggil doktor!*

EMERGENCIES

Please take me/us to a hospital.
to-long *hahn*-tahr-kahn
sai-yuh/*kah*-mee ke *hos*-pi-tahl

*Tolong hantarkan
saya/kami ke hospital.*

My blood group is
(A, B, O, AB) positive/negative.
koom-poo-lahn *dah*-ruh *sai*-yuh
ee-*ah*-lah(h) (ay, bee, oh, ay bee)
po-si-tif/*neh*-gah-tif

*Kumpulan darah saya
ialah (A, B, O, AB)
positif/negatif.*

My contact number is ...
nom-bor teh-*leh*-fon *sai*-yuh ...

Nombor telefon saya ...

The number of my next of kin is ...
nom-bor teh-*leh*-fon *oon*-tu(k)
ke-loo-*ahr*-guh *sai*-yuh
ee-*ah*-lah(h) ...

*Nombor telefon untuk
keluarga saya ialah ...*

I have medical insurance.
sai-yuh *ah*-duh in-*soo*-rahns
ke-see-*hah*-tahn

*Saya ada insurans
kesihatan.*

Please get medicine from
the chemist for me.
to-long be-*lee* oo-baht *oon*-tu(k)
sai-yuh dee *fahr*-mah-see

*Tolong beli ubat untuk
saya di farmasi.*

Root words are given in square brackets after verbs. (Root words are often used in place of active verbs by Malay speakers.) Verbs are preceded by 'to' to distinguish them from nouns of similar spelling.

to look	me-*lee*-haht [*lee*-haht]	melihat [lihat]

Remember that nouns don't change their form according to whether they're singular or plural. When a word can be either a noun or an adjective, the adjective form is followed by the marking (adj).

Bullets separate more than one alternative word and slashes words that are interchangeable.

A

to be able (can)	bo-*leh*(h)	boleh

Can (may) I take your photo?
bo-*leh*(h) ahm-bil *fo*-to ahn-duh? — *Boleh ambil foto anda?*

Can you show me (on the map)?
to-long toon-*joo*(k)-kahn (dee pe-*tuh*)? — *Tolong tunjukkan (di peta)?*

aboard	dee ah-*tahs*	di atas
abortion	peng-goo-*goo*-rahn	pengguguran
above	dee ah-*tahs*	di atas
to accept	me-ne-*ree*-muh [te-ree-*muh*]	menerima [terima]
accident	ke-mah-*lah*-ngahn	kemalangan
accommodation	pe-*ngee*-nah-pahn	penginapan
to accompany	me-ne-*mah*-nee	menemani
across	se-be-*rahng*	seberang
activist	*ahk*-ti-vis	aktivis
adaptor (electric)	a-*dap*-ter eh-*lehk*-trik	adapter elektrik
address (of house)	*ah*-lah-maht	alamat
admission (entry)	ke-mah-*su*(k)-kahn	kemasukan
adult	deh-*wah*-suh	dewasa
aeroplane	*kah*-pahl ter-bahng	kapal terbang
afraid	tah-*kut*	takut
after	se-le-*pahs* • se-te-*lah*(h) • se-soo-*dah*(h)	selepas • setelah • sesudah
afternoon	te-ngah-*hah*-ree • pe-*tahng*	tengahari • petang
in the afternoon	pah-*duh wahk*-too te-ngah-*hah*-ree/pe-*tahng*	pada waktu tengahari/petang
this afternoon	te-ngah-*hah*-ree/pe-*tahng ee*-nee	tengahari/petang ini
again	se-*moo*-luh	semula
against (opposed)	me-*nen*-tahng	menentang
age	*oo*-mur	umur
ago	le-*pahs*	lepas
(half an hour) ago	(se-te-*ngah*(h) jahm) le-*pahs*	(setengah jam) lepas
(three days) ago	(tee-*guh* hah-ree) le-*pahs*	(tiga hari) lepas

to agree	ber-se-*too*-joo [se-*too*-joo]	*bersetuju [setuju]*

I don't agree. *sai*-yuh *tee*-dah(k) se-*too*-joo		*Saya tidak setuju.*
Agreed. se-*too*-joo		*Setuju.*

ahead	dee de-*pahn*/hah-dah-*pahn*	*di depan/hadapan*
straight ahead	te-*rus* ke hah-dah-*pahn*	*terus ke hadapan*
AIDS	ehds	*AIDS*
air	oo-*dah*-ruh	*udara*
air-conditioner	pen-*dee*-ngin oo-*dah*-ruh	*pendingin udara*
airmail	mehl oo-*dah*-ruh	*mel udara*
airport	lah-*pah*-ngahn ter-*bahng*	*lapangan terbang*
airport tax	*choo*-kai pe-ner-*bah*-ngan	*cukai penerbangan*
alarm clock	jahm *lo*-chehng	*jam loceng*
alive	*hee*-dup	*hidup*
all	se-*moo*-uh	*semua*
allergy	ah-*ler*-jee • ah-lah-*hahn*	*alergi • alahan*
alley	lo-*rong*	*lorong*
to allow	mem-be-*nahr*-kahn • me-*ngee*-zin-kahn	*membenarkan • mengizinkan*

It's (not) allowed. dee-*lah*-rahng		*Dilarang.*

almost	*hahm*-pir • *nyah*-ris-*nyah*-ris	*hampir • nyaris-nyaris*
alone	ber-*sen*-dee-ree-ahn	*bersendirian*
already	*soo*-dah(h) • te-*lah*(h) • per-*nah*(h)	*sudah • telah • pernah*
also	*joo*-guh • pun	*juga • pun*
altitude	ke-*teeng*-gee-ahn	*ketinggian*
always	se-*lah*-loo • *sen*-tee-ah-sah	*selalu • sentiasa*
ambassador	doo-*tah*	*duta*
among	dee *ahn*-tah-ruh/kah-*lah*-ngahn	*di antara/kalangan*
anarchist	hoo-roo-*hah*-ruh	*huru-hara*
ancient	*pur*-buh • *koo*-no • *too*-uh	*purba • kuno • tua*
and	dahn	*dan*
angry	mah-*rah*(h)	*marah*
animal	bee-*nah*-tahng • *hai*-wahn	*binatang • haiwan*
to annoy	meng-*gahng*-goo [gahng-goo]	*mengganggu [ganggu]*
to answer	men-*jah*-wahb [*jah*-wahb]	***menjawab [jawab]***
ant	se-*mut*	*semut*
antibiotics	an-tai-bai-o-tik	*antibiotik*
antiques	*bah*-rahng *ahn*-tik	*barang antik*
antiseptic	pem-*bahs*-mee koo-*mahn*	*pembasmi kuman*
any	*ah*-puh pun • se-*bah*-rahng	*apa pun • sebarang*
anything	*ah*-puh-*ah*-puh	***apa-apa***
anytime	*bee*-luh-*bee*-luh	*bila-bila*
anywhere	mah-*nuh*-mah-*nuh*	*mana-mana*
apple	eh-pahl	*epal*

appointment	te-moo-*jahn*-jee	temujanji
appropriate	se-soo-ai	sesuai
approximately	*kee*-ruh-*kee*-ruh	kira-kira
archaeological	kah-jee-*pur*-buh • *ahr*-kee-o-lo-ji	kajipurba • arkeologi
architecture	se-nee-*bee*-nuh	senibina
to argue	mem-*bahn*-tah(h) [bahn-tah(h)]	membanta [bantah]
arm (of body)	le-*ngahn*	lengan
to arrive	dah-tahng • tee-buh • sahm-pai	datang • tiba • sampai
arrivals	ke-dah-*tah*-ngahn [dah-tahng] • ke-*tee*-buh-an [tee-buh]	kedatangan [datang] • ketibaan [tiba]
art	se-nee	seni
artist	se-nee-mahn/se-nee-wah-tee (m/f)	seniman/seniwati
artwork	ka-ri-*ah* se-nee	karya seni
ashtray	be-*kahs* ah-boo ro-ko(k)	bekas abu rokok
to ask for something	me-*min*-tuh [min-tuh]	meminta [minta]
to ask a question	ber-*tah*-nyuh [tah-nyuh]	bertanya [tanya]
asleep	tee-dur	tidur
assault	se-*rah*-ngahn	serangan
assistance	per-*to*-lo-ngan • bahn-too-ahn	pertolongan • bantuan
asthma	*sah*-kit le-*lah(h)*	sakit lelah
at (location)	dee • de-*kaht*	di • dekat
at (time)	pah-*duh*	pada
ATM	ay tee ehm	ATM
atmosphere (of place)	*swah*-sah-nuh	suasana
atmosphere (of planet)	*aht*-mos-fe-rah	atmosfera
aunt	e-*mah(k)* sow-*dah*-ruh	emak saudara
autumn	*moo*-sim *loo*-ru(h)	musim luruh
avenue	*jah*-lahn	jalan
avocado	ah-vo-*kah*-do	avokado

B

baby	bah-yee	bayi
babysitter	pen-*jah*-guh ah-*nah*(k)	penjaga anak
back (of body)	*ping*-gahng	pinggang
at the back (behind)	dee be-*lah*-kahng	di belakang
backpack	behg *sahn*-dahr	beg sandar
bad	boo-*ru(k)*	buruk
bad (attitude)	see-*kahp*	sikap
bad (weather)	coo-*ah*-chuh	cuaca
bag	behg	beg
baggage	bah-*gah*-see • bah-rahng-*bah*-rahng	bagasi • barang-barang
baggage claim	*toon*-tu-tahn bah-*gah*-see	tuntutan bagasi
bakery	ke-*dai* ro-tee	kedai roti
ball (for sport)	bo-luh	bola
banana	pee-sahng	pisang
band (music)	*koom*-poo-lahn	kumpulan
bandage	kain *pem*-bah-lut	kain pembalut

bank	bank	bank
bank clerk	ke-*rah*-nee bank	kerani bank
bar (drinks)	bahr	bar
barber	peng-*gun*-ting *rahm*-but	penggunting rambut
to bargain	tah-wahr-me-*nah*-wahr [tah-wahr]	tawar-menawar [tawar]
basket	*bah*-kul	bakul
to bathe	mahn-dee	mandi
bathing suit	*bah*-joo re-*nahng*	baju renang
bathroom	*bee*-li(k) air	bilik air
battery	*bah*-te-ree	bateri
to be (see Grammar, page 29)		
beach	*pahn*-tai	pantai
bean	*kah*-chahng	kacang
beautiful (scenery)	*in*-dah(h)	indah
beautiful (woman or object)	chahn-*ti(k)*	cantik
because	se-*bahb* • ke-*rah*-nuh	sebab • kerana
bed	*kah*-til	katil
bedroom	*bee*-li(k) *tee*-dur	bilik tidur
beef	*dah*-ging *lem*-boo	daging lembu
beer	bir • ah-*ra(k)*	bir • arak
before	se-*be*-lum	sebelum
beggar	pe-*nge*-mis	pengemis
to begin	moo-*luh*-kahn	mulakan
behind	dee be-*lah*-kahng	di belakang
below	dee bah-*wah(h)*	di bawah
beside	dee te-*pee/sahm*-ping	di tepi/samping
best	ter-bai(k)	terbaik
bet	tah-*ru*-hahn	taruhan
better	le-*bi(h)* bai(k)	lebih baik
between	*ahn*-tah-ruh	antara
bicycle	bah-*see*-kahl	basikal
big	be-*sahr*	besar
bill (account)	bil	bil
binoculars	te-*ro*-pong	teropong
bird	boo-*rung*	burung
birth certificate	soo-*raht* be-rah-*nah(k)*	surat beranak
birthday (cake)	(kehk) *hah*-ree *jah*-dee/*lah*-hir	(kek) hari jadi/lahir
to bite	meng-*gee*-git [*gee*-git]	menggigit [gigit]
bite (dog, insect)	*gee*-gee-tahn	gigitan
black	*hee*-tahm	hitam
blanket	se-*lee*-mut	selimut
to bleed	ber-*dah*-rah(h) [*dah*-rah(h)]	berdarah [darah]
blood	*dah*-rah(h)	darah
blood group	*koom*-poo-lahn *dah*-rah(h)	kumpulan darah
blood pressure	te-*kah*-nahn *dah*-rah(h)	tekanan darah
blood test	*oo*-jee-ahn *dah*-rah(h)	ujian darah
blue	*bee*-roo	biru

English	Pronunciation	Malay
to board (ship, etc)	nai(k)	naik
boarding pass	pahs nai(k)	pas naik
boat	bot • pe-rah-hoo • sahm-pahn	bot • perahu • sampan
body	bah-dahn	badan
boiled water	air mah-sah(k)	air masak
bone	too-lahng	tulang
book	boo-koo	buku
to make a booking	mem-boo-aht tem-pah-hahn	membuat tempahan
bookshop	ke-dai boo-koo	kedai buku
boots	boot • kah-sut boot	but • kasut but
border	sem-pah-dahn	sempadan
bored	bo-sahn	bosan
to borrow	me-min-jahm [pin-jahm]	meminjam [pinjam]
both	ke-doo-uh-doo-uh	kedua-dua

Don't bother.
bee-ahr-lah(h)   Biarlah.

English	Pronunciation	Malay
bottle	bo-tol	botol
bottle opener	pem-boo-kuh bo-tol	pembuka botol
(at the) bottom	(dee) bah-hah-gee-ahn bah-wah(h) • dee dah-sahr	(di) bahagian bawah • di dasar
box (package)	ko-tah(k)	kotak
boy	ah-nah(k) le-lah-kee	anak lelaki
boyfriend	te-mahn le-lah-kee • pah(k)-we	teman lelaki • pakwe (col)
brain	o-tah(k)	otak
bread	ro-tee	roti
break (fracture)	pe-chah	pecah
breakfast	sah-rah-pahn pah-gee	sarapan pagi
to bribe	me-rah-soo-ah(h)	merasuah
bridge	jahm-bah-tahn	jambatan
brilliant	bah-gus	bagus
to bring	mem-bah-wuh [bah-wuh]	membawa [bawa]
broken	pah-tah(h)	patah
older brother	ah-bahng	abang
brown	chok-laht	coklat
bruise	tahn-duh le-bahm	tanda lebam
bucket	bahl-dee	baldi
Buddhist	pe-ngah-nut boo-duh	penganut Buda
bug (insect)	se-rahng-guh	serangga
to build	mem-bee-nuh [bee-nuh]	membina [bina]
building	bah-ngoo-nahn	bangunan
burn	bah-kahr	bakar
... bus	bahs ...	bas ...
city	bahn-dahr	bandar
intercity	ahn-tah-ruh bahn-dahr	antara bandar
bus station	steh-sehn bahs	stesen bas
bus stop	per-hen-tee-ahn bahs	perhentian bas

business	per-nee-ah-*gah*-ahn	*perniagaan*
busker	*peng*-hi-bur *jah*-lah-nahn	*penghibur jalanan*
busy (place/party)	rah-*mai*	*ramai*
(time)	si-*bu(k)*	*sibuk*
but	te-*tah*-pee	*tetapi*
butter	men-*teh*-guh	*mentega*
butterfly	koo-poo-koo-poo	*kupu-kupu*
buttons	boo-*tahng*	*butang*
to buy	mem-be-*lee* [be-*lee*]	*membeli [beli]*

C

cabin	*bee*-li(k)	*bilik*
calm	te-*nahng*	*tenang*
camera (shop)	(ke-*dai*) ka-me-rah	*(kedai) kamera*
to camp	ber-*keh* mah(h) [*keh*-mah(h)]	*berkhema [khemah]*
campsite	kah-*wah*-sahn per-*keh*-mah-han	*kawasan perkhemahan*
can (able)	bo-*leh(h)* • *dah*-paht • *mahm*-poo	*boleh • dapat • mampu*

> **Can we camp here?**
> bo-*leh(h)* ta(k) *kah*-mee
> ber-*keh*-mah(h) dee *see*-nee?
>
> *Boleh tak kami*
> *berkhemah di sini?*

to cancel	mem-bah-*tahl*-kah [bah-*tahl*]	*membatalka [batal]*
candle	*lee*-lin	*lilin*
can opener	pem-*boo*-kuh tin	*pembuka tin*
car (park)	tem-*paht* le-*tah(k)* ke-*reh*-tuh	*(tempat letak) kereta*
cards (playing)	down te-*rup*	*daun terup*
careful	ber-*hah*-tee-*hah*-tee	*berhati-hati*
to carry	mem-*bah*-wuh [bah-*wuh*]	*membawa [bawa]*
cash	wahng *too*-nai	*wang tunai*
cashier	joo-roo-*wahng*	*juruwang*
cassette	*kah*-seht	*kaset*
cat	koo-*ching*	*kucing*
cave	*goo*-uh	*gua*
CD	see dee	*CD*
to celebrate	me-*rah*-yuh-kahn [*rah*-yuh]	*merayakan [raya]*
chair	ke-*roo*-see	*kerusi*
chance	ke-*mung*-ki-nahn • pe-loo-*ahng*	*kemungkinan • peluang*
to change	me-*noo*-kahr [*too*-kahr]	*menukar [tukar]*
changing rooms	*bee*-li(k) too-*kahr* pah-kai-*ahn*	*bilik tukar pakaian*
to chat up	me-*ngoo*-ruht	*mengurat*
cheap	*moo*-rah(h)	*murah*

> **Cheat!**
> pe-nee-*poo*!
>
> *Penipu!*

| to check | me-me-*rik*-sah [pe-*rik*-sah] | *memeriksa [periksa]* |

English	Pronunciation	Malay
check-in (desk)	*(kown-*ter) pen-*dahf*-tah-rahn	*(kaunter) pendaftaran*
cheese	*keh-*joo	*keju*
chemist (pharmacy)	*fahr-*mah-see	*farmasi*
cheque	chehk	*cek*
chess	*chah-*tur	*catur*
chewing gum	gahm koo-*nyah(h)*	*gam kunyah*
chicken	ai-yahm	*ayam*
child	*ah-*nah(k)-*ah-*nah(k) • boo-*dah(k)*	*anak-anak • budak*
childminding	pen-*jah-gah-*ahn *ah-*nah(k)	*penjagaan anak*
chilli	*chee-*lee	*cili*
chocolate	*chok-*laht	*coklat*
to choose	me-*mee-*li(h) [*pee-*li(h)]	*memilih [pilih]*
Christmas Day	*hah-*ree *kris-*muhs	*Hari Krismas*
Christmas Eve	*mah-*lahm *kris-*muhs	*Malam Krismas*
church	ge-*reh-*juh	*gereja*
cigarette (papers)	(ker-*tahs*) ro-ko(k)	*(kertas) rokok*
clove cigarettes	*kreh-*teh(k)	*kretek*
cinema	*pahng-*gung *wai-*yahng	*panggung wayang*
citizenship	ke-*wahr-*guh-ne-gah-rah-ahn	*kewarganegaraan*
city	*bahn-*dahr	*bandar*
civil rights	ha(k) ah-*sah-*see mah-*noo-*see-uh	*hak asasi manusia*
(1st) class	ke-*lahs* (per-*tah-*muh)	*kelas (pertama)*
(2nd) class	ke-*lahs* (ke-*doo-*uh)	*kelas (kedua)*
to clean	mem-ber-*si(h)*-kahn [ber-*si(h)*]	*membersihkan [bersih]*
cliff	te-*bing ting-*gee	*tebing tinggi*
clock	jahm	*jam*
to close	me-*noo-*tup [*too*-tup]	*menutup [tutup]*
clothing (store)	(ke-*dai*) pah-*kai-*ahn	*(kedai) pakaian*
cloudy	men-dung • be-*rah-*wahn	*mendung • berawan*
(night)club	ke-*lahb* (*mah-*lahm)	*kelab (malam)*
coast	*ping-*gir lowt	*pinggir laut*
cocaine	ko-*kehn*	*kokain*
coconut	ke-*lah-*puh	*kelapa*
coffee	*ko-*pee	*kopi*
coins	*shee-*ling	*syiling*
cold	se-*ju(k)*	*sejuk*
(to have a) cold	*ah-*duh sel-*se-*muh	*ada selsema*

It's cold here.
se-*ju(k)* dee *see-*nee

Sejuk di sini.

cold water	air se-*ju(k)*	*air sejuk*
college	ko-*lehj*	*kolej*
colour	*wahr-*nuh	*warna*
to come (arrive)	dah-*tahng* • *tee-*buh	*datang • tiba*
to come from (origin)	be-rah-*sahl [ah-*sahl]	*berasal [asal]*

Come on!
joom! — *Jum!*

comfortable	se-*leh*-suh	selesa
company (friends)	kah-*wahn*-kah-*wahn*	kawan-kawan
(business)	*sha*-ree-kaht	syarikat
compass	*kom*-pahs	kompas
to complain	me-*ngah*-doo [*ah*-doo]	mengadu [adu]
computer game	per-*mai*-nahn kom-*piu*-ter	permainan komputer
concert	*kon*-sert	konsert
condom	*kon*-dom	kondom
to confirm (a booking)	me-nge-*sah(h)*-kahn [*sah(h)*]	mengesahkan [sah]

Congratulations!
tah(h)-nee-ah(h)! — *Tahniah!*

constipation	*sem*-be-lit • *kons*-tee-pah-see	sembelit • konstipasi
contraceptive	kon-trah-*sehp*-see	kontrasepsi
to cook	*mah*-sah(k)	masak
cool (temperature)	dee-*ngin*	dingin

Cool!
bah-gus! — *Bagus!*

corner	soo-*dut* • *pen*-joo-roo	sudut • penjuru
corrupt (adj)	soo-kuh me-ne-*ree*-muh rah-soo-ah(h)	suka menerima rasuah
cost (of object/service)	*hahr*-guh • kos	harga • kos
cotton	*kah*-pahs	kapas
cough (n/v)	*bah*-tu(k)	batuk
to count	me-*ngee*-ruh [*kee*-ruh]	mengira [kira]
country	ne-*gah*-ruh	negara
countryside	kah-*wah*-sahn loo-ahr *bahn*-dahr	kawasan luar bandar
court (legal)	mah(h)-*kah*-mah(h)	mahkamah
(tennis)	*pah*-dahng teh-*nis*	padang tenis
cow	*lem*-boo	lembu
crab	ke-*tahm*	ketam
crazy	*gee*-luh	gila
credit card	kahd *kreh*-dit	kad kredit
crossroad	sim-*pahng jah*-lahn	simpang jalan
crowded	pe-*nuh(h)* se-*sa(k)*	penuh sesak
cucumber	*tee*-mun	timun
cup	chah-*wahn*	cawan
custom (tradition)	*ah*-daht	adat
customs (border)	*kahs*-tahm	kastam
to cut	me-*mo*-tong [*po*-tong]	memotong [potong]
cute (baby)	cho-*mehl*	comel

D

daily	hah-ree-*ahn*	*harian*
to dance	ber-*dahn*-sah [*dahn*-sah]	*berdansa [dansa]*
dangerous	bah-*hah*-yuh	*bahaya*
dark	ge-*lahp*	*gelap*
date (appointment)	te-*moo*-jahn-jee	*temujanji*
(time)	tah-*rikh*	*tarikh*
date of birth	tah-*rikh* lah-*hir*	*tarikh lahir*
daughter	ah-nah(k) pe-*rem*-pwahn	*anak perempuan*
dawn (sunrise)	fah-*jahr* (mah-tuh-*hah*-ree ter-*bit*)	*fajar (matahari terbit)*
day	hah-ree	*hari*
day after tomorrow	*loo*-suh	*lusa*
day before yesterday	kel-*mah*-rin •	*kelmarin •*
	doo-uh hah-ree le-*pahs*	*dua hari lepas*
in (six) days	dah-*lahm* (e-*nahm*) hah-ree	*dalam (enam) hari*
dead (battery/animal)	*mah*-tee	*mati*
dead (person)	me-*ning*-gahl *doo*-ni-uh	*meninggal dunia*
deaf	pe-*kah(k)* • *too*-lee	*pekak • tuli*
death	ke-*mah*-tee-ahn	*kematian*
to decide	me-moo-*tus*-kahn [poo-*tus*]	*memutuskan [putus]*
deep	dah-*lahm*	*dalam*
deer	*roo*-suh	*rusa*
deforestation	pe-ne-*bah*-ngahn hoo-*tahn*	*penebangan hutan*
delay	ke-*leh*-wah-tahn •	*kelewatan •*
	pe-*nahng*-gu-hahn	*penangguhan*
delicious	se-*dahp*	*sedap*
delirious	*gee*-luh	*gila*
democracy	deh-mo-*krah*-see	*demokrasi*
demonstration	toon-*ju(k)* pe-rah-*sah*-ahn	*tunjuk perasaan*
dentist	*dok*-tor *gee*-gee	*doktor gigi*
to deny	me-nah-*fee*-kahn [nah-*fee*]	*menafikan [nafi]*
deodorant	di-o-do-rahn	*deodoran*
depart	be-*rahng*-kaht [*ahng*-kaht]	*berangkat [angkat]*
department stores	poo-*saht* mem-be-*lee*-be-*lah(h)*	*pusat membeli-belah*
departure	pe-le-*pah*-sahn	*pelepasan*
desert	*goo*-run • *pah*-dahng *pah*-sir	*gurun • padang pasir*
destination	*dehs*-tee-nah-see	*destinasi*
develop (film)	men-*choo*-chee [*choo*-chee]	*mencuci [cuci]*
diabetes	*ken*-ching *mah*-nis	*kencing manis*
diarrhoea	*chi*-rit-*bi*-rit	*cirit-birit*
diary	*boo*-koo *chah*-tah-tahn	*buku catatan*
dictionary	*kah*-mus	*kamus*
to die (person)	me-*ning*-gahl [*ting*-gahl]	*meninggal [tinggal]*
different	ber-*beh*-zuh	*berbeza*
difficult	soo-*sah(h)* • soo-*kahr*	*susah • sukar*
dinner	*mah*-kahn *mah*-lahm	*makan malam*
director (of film)	pe-*ngah*-rah(h) (*fee*-lem)	*pengarah (filem)*

dirty	ko-tor	kotor
disabled	cha-chat	cacat
disco	dis-ko	disko
discount	dis-kown	diskaun
to discover	men-joom-pah-ee [joom-pah]	menjumpai [jumpa]
disease	pe-nyah-kit	penyakit
distance (length)	jah-rah(k)	jarak
to dive	me-nye-lahm [se-lahm]	menyelam [selam]
diving equipment	ah-laht se-lahm	alat selam
dizzy	pe-ning	pening
to do	me-lah-koo-kahn [lah-koo] •	melakukan [laku] •
	mem-boo-aht [boo-aht]	membuat [buat]

> What are you doing?
> boo-aht ah-puh?
>
> Buat apa?
>
> I didn't do it.
> boo-kahn sai-yuh
>
> Bukan saya.

doctor	dok-tor	doktor
documentary	do-kiu-men-tah-ree	dokumentari
dog	ahn-jing	anjing
door	peen-too	pintu
dope (drugs)	dah-dah(h)	dadah
double bed	kah-til ke-lah-min	katil kelamin
drama (arts)	(se-nee) drah-mah	(seni) drama
to dream	ber-mim-pee	bermimpi [mimpi]
dress	bah-joo gown	baju gaun
drink	mee-nu-mahn	minuman
to drink	mee-num	minum
to drive	me-mahn-doo	memandu [pandu]
drivers licence	leh-sehn me-mahn-doo	lesen memandu
drug (prescription)	oo-baht	ubat
(illegal)	dah-dah(h)	dadah
drug dealer	pen-joo-ahl dah-dah(h)	penjual dadah
drums	drahm • gen-dahng	dram • gendang
to be drunk	mah-bu(k)	mabuk
to dry	me-nge-ring-kahn [ke-ring]	mengeringkan [kering]
duck	ee-ti(k)	itik
dysentery	pe-nyah-kit beh-ra(k) dah-rah(h)	penyakit berak darah

E

each	se-tee-ahp • tee-ahp-tee-ahp	setiap • tiap-tiap
ear	te-lee-nguh	telinga
early	ah-wahl	awal

> It's early.
> mah-si(h) ah-wahl
>
> Masih awal

to earn	men-dah-paht [dah-paht]	mendapat [dapat]

E

earrings	soo-*bahng* • *ahn*-ting-*ahn*-ting	*subang* • *anting-anting*
earth	boo-*mee*	*bumi*
east	*tee*-mur	*timur*
easy	se-*nahng* • moo-*dah(h)*	*senang* • *mudah*
eat	*mah*-kahn	*makan*
economy (class)	(ke-*lahs*) ee-ko-*no*-mee	*(kelas) ekonomi*
editor	pe-*nyun*-ting	*penyunting*
to educate	men-dee-*di(k)* [dee-*di(k)*]	*mendidik [didik]*
education	pen-dee-*di(k)*-kahn	*pendidikan*
egg	te-*lur*	*telur*
elections	pee-lee-*hahn*-rah-yuh	*pilihanraya*
electricity	eh-*lehk*-trik	*elektrik*
embarassment	*mah*-loo	*malu*
embassy	ke-*doo*-tah-ahn	*kedutaan*
emergency	ke-che-*mah*-sahn • dah-*roo*-raht	*kecemasan* • *darurat*
employee	pe-*ker*-juh	*pekerja*
employer	mah-*ji(k)*-kahn	*majikan*
empty	*ko*-song	*kosong*
to end	me-ngah-*khi*-ree [*ah*-khir]	*mengakhiri [akhir]*
endangered species	bee-*nah*-tahng *hahm*-pir poo-*pus*	*binatang hampir pupus*
engine	*ehn*-jin	*enjin*
engineer	joo-*roo*-te-ruh	*jurutera*
English	*ing*-ge-ris	*Inggeris*
to enjoy (oneself)	me-*nik*-mah-tee [*nik*-maht]	*menikmati [nikmat]*

Enough!		
dah(h) *choo*-kup!		*Dah cukup!*

to enter	mah-*su(k)*	*masuk*
entertaining	meng-hee-*bur*-kahn [hee-*bur*]	*menghiburkan [hibur]*
entrance	*jah*-lahn/*peen*-too mah-*su(k)*	*jalan/pintu masuk*
envelope	sahm-*pul* soo-*raht*	*sampul surat*
environment	soo-ah-*sah*-nuh	*suasana*
epilepsy	sah-*wahn* bah-*bee* • eh-*pee*-lehp-see	*sawan babi* • *epilepsi*
equal opportunity	hah(k) *sah*-muh tah-*rahf*	*hak sama taraf*
equipment	ke-*leng*-kah-pahn [*leng*-kahp]	*kelengkapan [lengkap]*
essential	pah-*ling* pen-*ting*	*paling penting*
European	o-rahng eh-ro-*pah(h)*	*orang Eropah*
evening	pe-*tahng* • *mah*-lahm	*petang* • *malam*
every	se-*tee*-ahp • *tee*-ahp-*tee*-ahp	*setiap* • *tiap-tiap*
everyone	se-*moo*-uh o-rahng	*semua orang*
every day	se-*tee*-ahp hah-*ree*	*setiap hari*
everything	se-moo-*uh*-nyuh	*semuanya*
example	chon-*to(h)* • mi-*sah*-lahn	*contoh* • *misalan*

For example ...		
mi-*sahl*-nyuh .../chon-*to(h)*-nyuh ...		*Misalnya ... /Contohnya ...*

excellent	sa-*ngaht* bai(k)/*oo*-lung	*sangat baik/ulung*
exchange (rate)	(kah-*dahr*) per-too-*kah*-rahn	*(kadar) pertukaran*

D
I
C
T
I
O
N
A
R
Y

Excuse me. mah-*ahf*-kahn *sai*-yuh		Maafkan saya.
exhibition	pah-*meh*-rahn	pameran
exit	ke-*loo*-ahr	keluar
expensive	mah-*hahl*	mahal
exploitation	ehks-*ploy*-tah-see	eksploitasi
to export	me-*ngehks*-port [*ehks*-port]	mengeksport [eksport]
express mail	mehl *ehks*-prehs	mel ekspres
eye	*mah*-tuh	mata

F

face	*moo*-kuh	muka
factory	kee-*lahng*	kilang
to faint	*pehng*-sahn	pengsan
to fall	jah-*tuh(h)* • *goo*-gur	jatuh • gugur
family	ke-loo-*ahr*-guh	keluarga
famous	ter-ke-*nahl*	terkenal
fan (machine)	kee-*pahs*	kipas
(of a team)	pe-*nyo*-kong [*so*-kong]	penyokong [sokong]

Fantastic! bah-*gus*!		Bagus!
far	jow(h)	jauh

Is it far? jow(h) tah(k)		Jauh tak?
farm	lah-*dahng* • ke-*bun*	lading • kebun
farmer	pe-*tah*-nee	petani
fart	*ken*-tut	kentut
fast (quick)	che-*paht*	cepat
fat	ge-*mu(k)*	gemuk
father	ah-*yah(h)* • bah-*puh*	ayah • bapa
fault (someone's)	sah-*lah(h)*	salah
fear	ke-tah-*ku*-tahn	ketakutan
feelings	pe-*rah*-sah-ahn [*rah*-suh]	perasaan [rasa]
female (human)	pe-*rem*-pwahn	perempuan
(animal)	be-*tee*-nuh	betina
festival	pe-rah-*yah*-ahn • *pehs*-tah	perayaan • pesta
fever	de-*mahm*	demam
few	be-be-*rah*-puh	beberapa
fiance(e)	too-*nah*-ngahn	tunangan
fiction	*fik*-shen	fiksyen
fight	per-gah-*du(h)*-hahn	pergaduhan
to fight	ber-gah-*du(h)* [gah-*du(h)*]	bergaduh [gaduh]
to fill	me-*ngee*-see [*ee*-see]	mengisi [isi]
film (speed)	(ke-*lah*-joo-ahn) *fee*-lem	(kelajuan) filem
filtered	ber-*tah*-pis	bertapis

to find	men-*joom*-pah-ee *[joom*-pah]	menjumpai [jumpa]
finger	*jah*-ree	jari
finished	*hah*-bis	habis
fire	ah-*pee*	api
first	per-*tah*-muh	pertama
first-aid kit	ko-*tah(k)* per-to-*lo*-ngahn ke-che-*mah*-sahn	kotak pertolongan kecemasan
first name	*nah*-muh per-*tah*-muh	nama pertama
fish	ee-*kahn*	ikan
to fish	me-*mahn*-ching *[pahn*-ching]	memancing [pancing]
flag	ben-*deh*-ruh	bendera
flea	koo-*too*	kutu
flight	pe-ner-*bah*-ngahn	penerbangan
floor (of room)	*lahn*-tai	lantai
(storey)	*ting*-kaht	tingkat
flower (seller)	(pen-*joo*-ahl) *boo*-nguh	(penjual) bunga
fluent	*fah*-si(h)	fasih
fly	*lah*-laht	lalat
foggy	ber-*kah*-bus	berkabus
to follow (join in)	me-*ngee*-ku-tee *[ee*-kut]	mengikuti [ikut]
food	mah-*kah*-nahn	makanan
food stall	ge-*rai* • wah-*rung*	gerai • warung
foot	*kah*-kee	kaki
football (soccer)	*bo*-luh *seh*-pah(k)	bola sepak
footpath	*jah*-lahn pe-*jah*-lahn kah-*kee*	jalan pejalan kaki
for (purpose)	oon-*tu(k)* • boo-*aht*	untuk • buat
(length of time)	se-*lah*-muh	selama
foreigner	o-rahng *ah*-sing	orang asing
forest	hoo-*tahn*	hutan
forever	se-*lah*-muh-*lah*-muh-nyuh	selama-lamanya
to forget	*loo*-puh	lupa

I forget.
sai-yuh ter-*loo*-puh

Saya terlupa.

Forget about it!
tah(k) ah-puh!

Tak apa!

to forgive	me-mah-*ahf*-kahn [mah-*ahf*]	memaafkan [maaf]
fork	*gahr*-foo	garfu
fortune teller	too-*kahng* te-nung/tee-*li(k)*	tukang tenung/tilik
free (not bound)	beh-*bahs*	bebas
(of charge)	per-*choo*-muh	percuma
to freeze	mem-*be*-koo [*be*-koo]	membeku [beku]
fresh	se-*gahr*	segar
Friday	*hah*-ree *joo*-mah-aht	hari Jumaat
fried	go-*rehng*	goreng
friend	kah-*wahn* • te-*mahn*	kawan • teman
frog	kah-*tah(k)* • *ko*-do(k)	katak • kodok
from	dah-*ree* • dah-ree-*pah*-duh	dari • daripada

F

D
I
C
T
I
O
N
A
R
Y

fruit	boo-ah(h)-boo-ah-hahn	buah-buahan
full	pe-nu(h)	penuh
full (of food)	ke-nyahng	kenyang
fun	se-ro-no(k)	seronok
to have fun	oon-tu(k) ber-se-ro-no(k)	untuk berseronok
to make fun of	me-ngeh-jeh(k)	mengejek
funeral	pe-mah-kah-mahn	pemakaman
funny	lah-wah(k) • ke-lah-kahr • loo-choo	lawak • kelakar • lucu
future	mah-suh de-pahn	masa depan

G

game (boardgame)	per-mai-nahn	permainan
(sport)	per-mai-nahn	permainan
game show	kuiz	kuiz
garage	gah-rahj	garaj
garden	ke-bun	kebun
gardens (botanical)	ke-bun bo-tah-nee	kebun botani
garlic	bah-wahng poo-ti(h)	bawang putih
gay	geh	gay
general	oo-mum • ahm	umum • am
generous	moo-rah(h) hah-tee	murah hati
gentle	lem-but	lembut
geography	ji-o-grah-fee	geografi
gift	pem-be-ree-ahn [be-ree]	pemberian [beri]
girl	boo-dah(k)/ah-nah(k)	budak/anak
	pe-rem-pwahn	perempuan
girlfriend	te-mahn wah-nee-tah • mah(k)-we	teman wanita • makwe
give	mem-be-ree [be-ree]	memberi [beri]

Could you give me ...?
to-long bah-gee ...? — Tolong bagi ...?

glass	kah-chuh	kaca
glasses (eye)	cher-min mah-tuh	cermin mata
glue	gahm	gam
to go	per-gee	pergi

Let's go.
joom per-gee — Jum pergi.

We'd like to go to ...
kah-mee nah(k) per-gee ke ... — Kami nak pergi ke ...

Go straight ahead.
per-gee te-rus — Pergi terus.

to go home	poo-lahng	pulang
to go out with	ke-loo-ahr ber-sah-muh	keluar bersama
goal	gol	gol

goalkeeper	pen-jah-*guh* gol	*penjaga gol*
goat	*kahm*-bing	*kambing*
God (Muslim)	too-*hahn* • ahl-*luh(h)*	*Tuhan* • *Allah*
gold	e-*mahs*	*emas*
good	bai(k)	*baik*

Good afternoon.
se-*lah*-maht te-ngah-*hah*-ree/pe-*tahng*   *Selamat tengahari/petang*

Goodbye. (speaker leaving)
se-*lah*-maht *ting*-gahl   *Selamat tinggal.*

Goodbye. (speaker staying)
se-*lah*-maht *jah*-lahn   *Selamat jalan.*

Goodbye. (inf)
bai   *Bye.*

Good evening.
se-*lah*-maht pe-*tahng*   *Selamat petang.*

Good morning.
se-*lah*-maht *pah*-gee   *Selamat pagi.*

Good night.
se-*lah*-maht *mah*-lahm   *Selamat malam.*

government	ke-rah-*jah*-ahn	*kerajaan*
gram	*grahm*	*gram*
grammar	tah-tah-bah-*hah*-suh	*tatabahasa*
grandchild	choo-*choo*	*cucu*
grandfather	dah-*tu(k)* • ah-*tu(k)*	*datuk* • *atuk*
grandmother	neh-*neh(k)*	*nenek*
grape	*ahng*-gur	*anggur*
grass	*room*-put	*rumput*
grave	koo-*bur*	*kubur*

Great!
bah-*gus!*   *Bagus!*

green	*hee*-jow	*hijau*
grey	ke-*lah*-boo	*kelabu*
ground	tah-*na(h)*	*tanah*
group	*koom*-poo-lahn •	*kumpulan* •
	ke-*lom*-po(k)	*kelompok*
to guess	me-ne-*kuh* [te-*kuh*]	*meneka [teka]*
guest	te-*tah*-moo	*tetamu*
guide (person or audio)	pe-*mahn*-doo	*pemandu*
guidebook	*boo*-koo *pahn*-dwahn	*buku panduan*
guide dog	*ahn*-jing pe-*mahn*-doo	*anjing pemandu*
guided trek	trehk ber-*pahn*-doo	*trek perbandu*
guitar	gee-*tahr*	*gitar*

H

habit	ke-bee-ah-*sah*-ahn	*kebiasaan*
hair	*rahm*-but	*rambut*
hairbrush	be-*rus* rahm-but	*berus rambut*
half	se-te-*ngah(h)*	*setengah*
half a litre	se-te-*ngah(h)* lee-ter	*setengah liter*
to hallucinate	ber-*khah*-yahl [*khah*-yahl]	*berkhayal* [*khayal*]
ham	*dah*-ging bah-*bee*	*daging babi*
hammock	boo-*ai*-ahn	*buaian*
hand	tah-*ngahn*	*tangan*
handbag	behg tah-*ngahn*	*beg tangan*
handicrafts	*krahf*-tah-ngahn	*kraftangan*
handmade	boo-*ah*-tahn tah-*ngahn*	*buatan tangan*
handsome (male)	hehnd-sem • kah-*chah(k)*	*hendsem • kacak*
happy	gem-*bee*-ruh	*gembira*

Happy birthday! se-*lah*-maht hah-ree *jah*-dee!	*Selamat hari jadi!*

harbour	pe-*lah-bu*-hahn	*pelabuhan*
hard (not soft)	ke-*rahs*	*keras*
(difficult)	soo-*sah(h)* • soo-*kahr*	*susah • sukar*
harassment	*gahng*-goo-ahn	*gangguan*
hashish	*gahn*-jah • *hah*-sis	*ganja • hasis*
hat	*to*-pee	*topi*
to have	ah-duh • mem-*poo*-nyah-ee [*poo*-nyah]	*ada • mempunyai* [*punya*]

Do you have ...? *ahn*-dah *ah*-duh ... tah(k)	*Anda ada ... tak?*
I have ... *sai*-yuh mem-*poo*-nyah-ee ...	*Saya mempunyai ...*

he	*dee*-uh	*dia*
head	ke-*pah*-luh	*kepala*
headache	*sah*-kit ke-*pah*-luh	*sakit kepala*
healthy	si-*haht*	*sihat*
to hear	men-de-*ngahr* [de-*ngahr*]	*mendengar* [*dengar*]
heart	*jahn*-tung	*jantung*
heat	hah-*buh* • *pah*-nahs	*haba • panas*
heavy	be-*raht*	*berat*

Hello. *heh*-lo	*Helo.*

helmet	*to*-pee ke-leh-*dahr*	*topi keledar*
to help	me-*no*-long [*to*-long] • mem-*bahn*-too [*bahn*-too]	*menolong* [*tolong*] • *membantu* [*bantu*]

English	Pronunciation	Malay
herbs	*her*-bah	herba
herbalist (person)	*sin*-seh(h)	sinseh
herbalist shop	ke-*dai* oo-*baht* chee-nuh	kedai ubat Cina
here	dee *see*-nee	di sini
heroin (addict)	(pe-*nah*-gi(h)) *heh*-ro-in	(penagih) heroin
high	*teeng*-gee	tinggi
high school	se-ko-*lah*(h) me-ne-*ngah*(h)	sekolah menengah (SM)
to hike	ber-*jah*-lahn kah-*kee*	berjalan kaki
hiking boots	boot *jah*-lahn	but jalan
hill	boo-*kit*	bukit
Hindu	hin-*doo*	Hindu
to hire (rent)	me-*nyeh*-wuh [*seh*-wuh]	menyewa [sewa]
historical ruins	run-*tu*-hahn ber-se-*jah*-rah(h)	runtuhan bersejarah
history	se-*jah*-rah(h)	sejarah
to hitchhike	me-*noom*-pahng	menumpang
HIV positive	ehch ai vee *po*-si-tif	HIV positif
holiday	coo-*tee*	cuti
homeless	pe-*ngahng*-gur	pengangur
homosexual	ho-mo-*sehk*-soo-ahl	homoseksual
honest	*joo*-jur	jujur
honeymoon	boo-lahn mah-*doo*	bulan madu
horny	gah-*tahl*	gatal
horrible	*dah*(h)-shaht • me-nge-*ree*-kahn	dahsyat • mengerikan
horse (riding)	(pe-*nung*-gah-ngahn) *koo*-duh	(penunggangan) kuda
hospital	hos-*pee*-tahl	hospital
hospitality	ke-rah-*mah*(h)-tah-*mah*(h)-hahn	keramah-tamahan
hot (temperature)	*pah*-nahs	panas
(spicy)	pe-*dahs*	pedas

It's hot here.
pah-nahs dee *see*-nee — Panas di sini.

to be hot	ke-*pah*-nahs-sahn [*pah*-nahs]	kepanasan [panas]
hotel	ho-*tehl*	hotel
hour	jahm	jam
house	roo-*mah*(h)	rumah
how	mah-chahm *mah*-nuh • bah-*gai*-mah-nuh	macam mana • bagaimana

How can I get to ...?
mah-chahm *mah*-nuh sai-yuh bo-*leh*(h) per-*gee* ke ...? — Macam mana saya boleh pergi ke ...?

How do you say ... in Malay?
mah-chahm *mah*-nuh chah-*kahp* ... ah-*lahm* bah-*hah*-suh me-*lah*-yoo? — Macam mana cakap ... alam bahasa Melayu?

How many? (animals)		
be-*rah*-puh *eh*-kor?		*Berapa ekor?*

How many? (goods)		
be-*rah*-puh *bah*-nya(k)?		*Berapa banyak?*

How much?		
be-*rah*-puh?		*Berapa?*

hug	pe-*lu(k)*	peluk
human rights	ha(k) ah-sah-*see* mah-*noo*-si-uh	hak asasi manusia
humid	*lem*-bahb	lembab
a hundred	se-*rah*-tus	seratus
hungry	*lah*-pahr	lapar
to hunt	ber-*boo*-roo [boo-roo]	berburu [buru]
husband	soo-*ah*-mee	suami

I

I	*sai*-yuh • *ah*-koo	saya • aku

I'm (Chris).		
sai-yuh (kris)		*Saya (Chris).*

ice	ais	ais
ice cream	ais krim	ais krim
idea	*ai*-deh-ah	idea
identification	pe-*nge*-nah-lahn	pengenalan
ID	kahd pe-*nge*-nah-lahn	kad pengenalan
idiot	bo-*do(h)*	bodoh
if	kah-*low*	kalau
imagine	mem-bah-*yahng*-kahn	membayangkan
immediately	de-*ngahn* ser-*tah*-mer-*tah*	dengan serta-merta
immigration	ee-mee-*greh*-sen	imigresen
important	*pen*-ting	penting

It's (not) important.		
(tah(k)) *pen*-ting		*(Tak) penting.*

in	dah-*lahm*	dalam
in a hurry	ter-boo-*roo*-boo-*roo*	terburu-buru
in front of	dee de-*pahn*	di depan
included	ter-*mah*-su(k)	termasuk
income tax	*choo*-kai pen-dah-*pah*-tahn	cukai pendapatan
indigenous	*ahs*-lee	asli
indigestion	*sah*-kit pe-*rut*	sakit perut
infection	*jahng*-ki-tahn	jangkitan
information	*mahk*-loo-maht • in-for-*mah*-see	maklumat • informasi
to inject	me-nyun-*ti(k)*-kahn	menyuntikkan [suntik]
injection	sun-*ti(k)*-kahn	suntika [suntik]
injury	ke-che-de-*rah*-ahn [che-de-*rah*]	kecederaan [cedera]
insect	se-*rahng*-guh	serangga

inside	dee dah-*lahm*	*di dalam*
instructor	joo-roo-*lah*-ti(h) • goo-*roo*	*jurulatih* • *guru*
insurance	in-soo-*rahns*	*insurans*
intense	*sah*-ngaht • men-*dah*-lahm	*sangat* • *mendalam*
interesting	me-*nah*-ri(k)	*menarik*
international	ahn-tah-rah-*bahng*-suh	*antarabangsa*
intersection	per-*sim*-pah-ngahn	*persimpangan*
interview	wah-wahn-*chah*-ruh	*wawancara*
island	poo-*low*	*pulau*
itch	gah-*tahl*	*gatal*
itinerary	jah-*doo*-ahl per-jah-*lah*-nahn	*jadual perjalanan*
ivory	gah-*ding*	*gading*

J

jacket	ja-*keht*	*jaket*
jail	pen-*jah*-ruh	*penjara*
jar	*bo*-tol	*botol*
jeans	jeen	*jean*
jeep	jeep	*jip*
jewellery	*bah*-rahng ke-*mahs*	*barang kemas*
job	pe-ker-*jah*-ahn	*pekerjaan*
joke	lah-*wah(k)* • ke-lah-*kahr*	*lawak* • *kelakar*
to joke	ber-lah-*wah(k)* [lah-*wah(k)*]	*berlawak [lawak]*
journalist	wahr-*tah*-wahn	*wartawan*
journey	per-jah-*lah*-nahn	*perjalanan*
judge (court)	hah-*kim*	*hakim*
juice	joos	*jus*
jump (across)	lom-*paht*	*lompat*
(high)	lon-*chaht*	*loncat*
jumper (sweater)	*bah*-joo se-*ju(k)*	*baju sejuk*
just one	sah-*too* sah-juh	*satu saja*
justice	ke-ah-*di*-lahn	*keadilan*

K

key	*koon*-chee	*kunci*
keyboard	pah-*pahn* ke-*koon*-chee	*papan kekunci*
kick	*ten*-dah-ngahn *[ten-dahng]*	*tendangan [tendang]*
kick off	me-moo-*lah*-ee *[moo-luh]*	*memulai [mula]*
to kill	mem-boo-*nuh(h)* [boo-*nuh(h)*]	*membunuh [bunuh]*
kilogram	kee-lo-*grahm*	*kilogram*
kilometre	*ki*-lo-*mee*-ter	*kilometer*
kind (adj)	bai(k) hah-*tee*	*baik hati*
kindergarten	tah-*dee*-kah	*tadika*
kiss	*chee*-um	*cium*
to kiss	men-*chee*-um *[chee*-um]	*mencium [cium]*
kitchen	dah-*pur*	*dapur*
knee	loo-*tut*	*lutut*

L

knife	*pee*-sow	*pisau*
to know (someone)	ke-*nahl*	*kenal*
(something)	*tah*-hoo	*tahu*

I (don't) know.
sai-yuh *(tee*-dah(k)) *tah*-hoo

Saya (tidak) tahu.

L

lake	tah-*si(k)*	*tasik*
lamb	*ah*-nah(k) bee-*ree*-bee-*ree*	*anak biri-biri*
land (ground)	tah-*nah(h)*	*tanah*
landscape	lahns-*kahp*	*lanskap*
language	bah-*hah*-suh	*bahasa*
large	loo-*ahs* • be-*sahr*	*luas • besar*
last (final)	te-rah-*khir*	*terakhir*
last month	*boo*-lahn le-*pahs*	*bulan lepas*
last night	*mah*-lahm se-*mah*-lahm	*malam semalam*
last week	ming-*goo* le-*pahs*	*minggu lepas*
last year	*tah*-hoon le-*pahs*	*tahun lepas*
late (not on time)	leh-*waht* • *lahm*-baht	*lewat • lambat*
later	ke-*moo*-dee-ahn • *nahn*-tee	*kemudian • nanti*
laugh	ge-*lah(k)* • ke-tah-*wuh*	*gelak • ketawa*
laundry (shop)	ke-*dai* do-bee	*kedai dobi*
law	oon-*dahng*-oon-*dahng*	*undang-undang*
lawyer	pe-*gwahm*	*peguam*
laxatives	oo-*baht* pen-*choo*-chee pe-*rut*	*ubat pencuci perut*
lazy	mah-*lahs*	*malas*
leader	pe-*meem*-pin *[peem*-pin]	*pemimpin [pimpin]*
leak	bo-*chor*	*bocor*
to learn	be-*lah*-jahr *[ah*-jahr]	*belajar [ajar]*
leather	koo-*lit*	*kulit*
lecture	koo-lee-*ah(h)* • *shah*-rah-hahn	*kuliah • syarahan*
lecturer	pen-shah-*rah(h)*	*pensyarah*
left, (behind/over)	dee-*ting*-gahl-kahn *[ting*-gahl]	*ditinggalkan [tinggal]*
left (not right)	ki-ree	*kiri*
left-handed	ki-dahl	*kidal*
left luggage	bah-*gah*-see yahng dee-*ting*-*gahl*-kahn	*bagasi yang ditinggalkan*
left-wing	sah-*yahp* ki-ree	*sayap kiri*
leg (body)	*kah*-kee	*kaki*
(in race)	poo-si-ngahn	*pusingan*
lemon	*lee*-mow nee-pis	*limau nipis*
length	*pahn*-jahng	*panjang*
lens	kahn-*tuh* • lehn-*sah*	*kanta • lensa*
lesbian	lehs-*bee*-uhn	*lesbian*
less	koo-*rahng*	*kurang*
letter	soo-*raht*	*surat*
library	per-poos-*tah*-kah-ahn	*perpustakaan*

lice	*koo-too*	kutu
to lie	me-*nee*-poo [tee-poo]	menipu [tipu]
life	*hee*-dup	hidup
lift (elevator)	lif	lif
light (electric)	*lahm*-poo	lampu
(not dark)	te-*rahng*	terang
(not heavy)	ri-*ngahn*	ringan
light bulb	*mehn*-tul	mentul
lighter	pe-me-*ti(k)* ah-pee	pemetik api
to like	*soo*-kuh • ge-*mahr*	suka • gemar
lips	*bee*-bir	bibir
lipstick	*gin*-choo	gincu
to listen	men-de-ngahr [de-ngahr]	mendengar [dengar]
little (small)	ke-*chil*	kecil
(amount)	se-*dee*-kit	sedikit
to live (life)	*hee*-dup	hidup
(somewhere)	*ting*-gahl	tinggal
liver	*hah*-tee	hati
local	tem-*pah*-tahn	tempatan
local (city) bus	bahs *(bahn*-dahr) tem-*pah*-tahn	bas (bandar) tempatan
location	tem-*paht*	tempat
to lock	me-*ngun*-chee [koon-chee]	mengunci [kunci]
long (measurement)	*pahn*-jahng	panjang
(time)	*lah*-muh	lama
long distance	jah-*rah(k)* pahn-jahng	jarak panjang
long-distance bus	bahs jah-*rah(k)* jow(h)	bas jarak jauh
to look	me-*lee*-haht [lee-haht]	melihat [lihat]
to look after	men-*jah*-guh [jah-guh]	menjaga [jaga]
to look for	men-*chah*-ree [chah-ree]	mencari [cari]
loose	*long*-gahr	longgar
to lose (something)	meng-hee-*lahng*-kahn [hee-lahng]	menghilangkan [hilang]
loss	ke-kah-*lah*-hahn [kah-lah(h)]	kekalahan [kalah]
lost	ter-se-*saht* [se-saht]	tersesat [sesat]

Get lost!
per-*gee*-lah(h)/be-*lah(h)*-lah(h) — *Pergilah!/Belahlah!*

a lot (quantity)	*bah*-nya(k)	banyak
loud	*bee*-sing	bising
lounge (room)	roo-*ahng tah*-moo	ruang tamu
love	kah-*si(h)* • *chin*-tuh • *sah*-yahng	kasih • cinta • sayang

I love you.
sai-yuh me-nyin-tah-*ee* moo — *Saya menyintai mu.*

lover	ke-*kah*-si(h)	kekasih
low	ren-*dah(h)*	rendah
loyal	se-*tee*-uh	setia
luck	nah-*sib*	nasib
lucky	be-*roon*-tung	beruntung
luggage	bah-*gah*-see	bagasi

luggage lockers	ahl-*mah*-ree bah-*gah*-see	*almari bagasi*
lunch	*mah*-kahn te-ngah-*hah*-ree	*makan tengahari*
lunchtime	*wak*-too *mah*-kahn te-ngah-*hah*-ree	*waktu makan tengahari*
luxury	ke-meh-*wah*-hahn	*kemewahan*

M

machine	me-*sin*	*mesin*
mad (angry)	*mah*-rah(h)	*marah*
made (of)	dee-per-*boo*-aht (dah-ree-*pah*-duh)	*diperbuat (daripada)*
magazine	mah-jah-*lah*(h)	*majalah*
mail	mehl	*mel*
main ...	... oo-*tah*-muh	*... utama*
road	*jah*-lahn	*jalan*
square	dah-*tah*-rahn	*dataran*
majority	mah-*jo*-ree-tee	*majoriti*
to make	mem-*boo*-aht [*boo*-aht]	*membuat [buat]*
make-up	ah-*laht* so-*leh*(k)-kahn	*alat solekan*
malaria	mah-lah-*ree*-ah	*malaria*
Malay	bah-*hah*-suh me-*lah*-yoo	*Bahasa Melayu*

I (don't) speak Malay.
sai-yuh *(tee*-dah(k)) *tah*-hoo *chah*-kahp
bah-*hah*-suh me-*lah*-yoo

*Saya (tidak) tahu cakap
bahasa Melayu*

Malaysia	mah-*lay*-see-ah	*Malaysia*
male (person)	le-*lah*-kee	*lelaki*
(animal)	*jahn*-tahn	*jantan*
man	le-*lah*-kee	*lelaki*
manager	pe-*ngoo*-rus	*pengurus*
mango	*mang*-guh	*mangga*
many	*bah*-nya(k)	*banyak*
map	pe-*tuh*	*peta*

Can you show me ... on the map?
to-long toon-*joo*(k)-kahn ... dee pe-*tuh*?

Tolong tunjukkan ... di peta?

market (night)	pah-*sahr* (*mah*-lahm)	*pasar (malam)*
marriage	per-*kah*(h)-wi-nahn	*perkahwinan*
to marry	ber-*kah*(h)-win • ber-*nee*-kah(h)	*berkahwin • bernikah*
mask (face)	to-*pehng*	*topeng*
massage	*oo*-ru-tahn	*urutan*
to massage	me-*ngoo*-rut [*oo*-rut]	*mengurut [urut]*
mat	*tee*-kahr	*tikar*
matches	*mahn*-chis	*mancis*
material (for clothing)	kain	*kain*

It doesn't matter.
ta(k) *ah*-puh

Tak apa.

What's the matter?
ke-*nah*-puh be-*gee*-nee?

Kenapa begini?

mattress	tee-*lahm*	tilam
may (can)	bo-*leh(h)*	boleh
maybe	*moong*-kin	mungkin
meaning	*mahk*-nuh • er-tee	makna • erti
meat	*dah*-ging	daging
mechanic	me-*ka*-nik	mekanik
medicine	oo-*baht*	ubat
meditation	tah-*fah*-kur	tafakur
to meet	ber-te-moo [te-*moo*]	bertemu [temu]
meeting	per-te-*moo*-ahn • me-*shoo* ah-raht	pertemuan • mesyuarat
menthol (cigarettes)	(ro-ko(k)) *mehn*-tol	(rokok) mentol
menu	*meh*-noo	menu
message	pe-*sah*-nahn	pesanan
metal	lo-*gahm*	logam
metre	*mee*-ter	meter
midnight	te-*ngah(h)* mah-lahm	tengah malam
migraine	*mai*-grehn	migraine
milk	soo-*soo*	susu
millimetre	mi-lee-*mee*-ter	milimeter
million	joo-*tuh*	juta
mineral water	air mi-*ne*-rahl	air mineral
(with/without gas)	(ber-*kar*-bo-naht/bee-*ah*-suh)	(berkarbonat/biasa)
minibus	bahs mee-*nee*	bas mini
minute	*mi*-nit	minit

Just a minute.
se-ke-*jahp*   Sekejap.

in (five) minutes
dah-*lahm* (lee-muh) *mi*-nit lah-*gee*   dalam (lima) minit lagi

mirror	*cher*-min	cermin
to miss (feel absence)	me-*rin*-doo-ee [rin-*doo*]	merindui [rindu]
Miss	chi(k)	Cik
mistake	ke-see-lah-*pahn* • ke-sah-*lah*-hahn	kesilapan • kesalahan
misunderstanding	sah-*lah(h)* fah-hahm	salah faham
to mix	men-*cham*-pur-kahn [chahm-*pur*]	mencampurkan [campur]
mobile phone	teh-*leh*-fon *bim*-bit	telefon bimbit
modem	mo-*dem*	modem
moisturising cream	krim pe-*lem*-bahb	krim pelembab
monastery	bee-*ah*-ruh	biara
Monday	*hah*-ree ees-*nin*	hari Isnin
money	*doo*-it • *wahng*	duit • wang
monk	bee-*ah*-rah-wahn	biarawan
monkey	mo-*nyeht* • ke-*ruh*	monyet • kera
month (this)	*boo*-lahn (ee-nee)	bulan (ini)
moon	*boo*-lahn	bulan
more	le-*bi(h)*	lebih
morning	*pah*-gee	pagi
Moslem	o-*rahng* ees-lahm	orang Islam

mosque	*mahs*-jid	masjid
mosquito (net)	*nyah*-mu(k) (ke-*lahm*-boo)	nyamuk (kelambu)
most (the)	(yahng) *pah*-ling	(yang) paling
mother	e-*mah(k)* • ee-boo	emak/ibu
mother-in-law	ee-boo mer-*too*-uh	ibu mertua
motorboat	bot ber-*mo*-tor	bot bermotor
motorcycle	mo-to-*see*-kahl	motosikal
motorway (tollway)	*jah*-lahn ber-tol	jalan bertol
mountain	goo-nung	gunung
mountain bike	bah-*see*-kahl goo-nung	basikal gunung
mountaineering	men-*dah*-kee goo-nung	mendaki gunung
mountain hut	pon-*do(k)*	pondok
mountain path	*jah*-lahn goo-nung	jalan gunung
mountain range	per-goo-*nu*-ngah	pergunungan
mouth	*moo*-lut	mulut
movie	*fee*-lem	filem
Mr	en-*chi(k)* • *too*-ahn	Encik • Tuan
Mrs	pwahn	Puan
much	*bah*-nya(k)	banyak
mud	*loom*-pur	lumpur
muscle	o-*tot*	otot
museum	moo-*zee*-um	muzium
music	*moo*-zik	muzik
musician	pe-*main moo*-zik	pemain muzik
Muslim	o-*rahng* ees-lahm	orang Islam
must	*mes*-tee • hah-*rus*	mesti • harus

N

name	*nah*-muh	nama

What's your name?	
see-*ah*-puh *nah*-muh *ahn*-dah	*Siapa nama anda?*

nappy	kain *lahm*-pin	kain lampin
nappy rash	roo-*ahm bah*-yee	ruam bayi
nationality	*bahng*-suh	bangsa
national park	tah-*mahn* ne-*gah*-ruh	taman negara
nature	ah-*lahm* se-moo-luh-*jah*-dee	alam semulajadi
nausea	*moo*-ahl	mual
near	de-*kaht*	dekat

Is it near here?	
de-*kaht*-kuh dah-*ree* see-*nee*?	*Dekatkah dari sini?*

necessary	per-*loo*	perlu
necklace	*rahn*-tai	rantai
need	per-*loo*	perlu
needle	*jah*-rum	jarum
(sewing, syringe)		

neighbour	*jee-rahn*	*jiran*
nervous	*che-mahs • coo-ah(k)*	*cemas • cuak*
never	*tee-dah(k) per-nah(h)*	*tidak pernah*
never mind	*ta(k) ah-puh*	*tak apa*
new	*bah-roo*	*baru*
news	*be-ree-tuh*	*berita*
newspaper	*soo-raht kah-bahr*	*surat khabar*
next	*yahng be-ree-kut-nyah • de-pahn*	*yang berikutnya • depan*

Next time.	*lain kah-lee*	*Lain kali.*

next to	*dee se-be-lah(h)*	*di sebelah*
nickname	*nah-muh pang-gi-lahn*	*nama panggilan*
night	*mah-lahm*	*malam*
Saturday night	*sab-too mah-lahm*	*Sabtu malam*
no	*tee-dah(k)*	*tidak*
noise	*boo-nyee*	*bunyi*
noisy	*bee-sing*	*bising*
none	*tee-ah-duh*	*tiada*
noodles	*mee*	*mee*
noon	*te-ngah-hah-ree*	*tengahari*
north	*oo-tah-ruh*	*utara*
nose	*hee-dung*	*hidung*
not	*boo-kahn*	*bukan*
not yet	*be-lum lah-gee*	*belum lagi*
notebook	*boo-koo chah-tah-tahn*	*buku catatan*
nothing	*tee-dah(k) ah-puh-ah-puh*	*tidak apa-apa*
novel (book)	*no-vel*	*novel*
now	*se-kah-rahng*	*sekarang*
nuclear energy	*te-nah-guh noo-klee-er*	*tenaga nuklear*
nuclear testing	*oo-jee-ahn noo-klee-er*	*ujian nuklear*
nude	*bo-gehl • te-lahn-jahng*	*bogel • telanjang*
number	*nom-bor*	*nombor*
nun	*bee-ah-rah-wah-tee*	*biarawati*
nurse	*joo-roo-rah-waht*	*jururawat*
nut (food)	*kah-chahng*	*kacang*

O

occupation	*pe-ker-jah-ahn*	*pekerjaan*
ocean	*low-tahn*	*lautan*
offer	*tah-wah-rahn*	*tawaran*
office worker	*pe-ker-juh pe-jah-baht*	*pekerja pejabat*
offside	*of-said*	*offside*
often	*se-ring • ke-rahp*	*sering • kerap*
oil (cooking)	*min-ya(k) mah-sah(k)*	*minyak masak*

OK.		
oh-kay/bai(k)		OK./Baik.

old (person)	*too*-uh	tua
(building)	*lah*-muh	lama
older sister	kah-*kah(k)*	kakak
older brother	ah-*bahng*	abang
Olympic Games	ke-*soo*-kah-nahn o-*lim*-pik	Kesukanan Olimpik
on (location)	dee	di
on time	te-*paht pah*-duh mah-*sah*-nyuh	tepat pada masanya
once	se-*kah*-lee	sekali
once again	se-*kah*-lee lah-*gee*	sekali lagi
one-way (ticket)	(tee-*keht*) se-*hah*-luh	(tiket) sehala
onion	*bah*-wahng	bawang
only	hah-*nyuh*	hanya
open	*boo*-kuh	buka
to open	mem-*boo*-kuh *[boo*-kuh]	membuka [buka]
operation	o-pe-*rah*-see	operasi
(telephone) operator	o-pe-*ray*-tor (teh-*leh*-fon)	operator (telefon)
opinion	pen-*dah*-paht	pendapat
opposite	lah-*wahn*	lawan
or	ah-*tow*	atau
oral	lee-*sahn*	lisan
orange (colour)	o-*rehn* • *jeeng*-gah	oren • jingga
(food)	o-*rehn*	oren
orchestra	or-*kehs*-truh	orkestra
to order	me-*nehm*-pah(h) *[tehm*-pah(h)]	menempah [tempah]
to organise	me-*ngah*-tur *[ah*-tur]	mengatur [atur]
orgasm	or-*gahs*-mah	orgasma
original	*ahs*-lee	asli
other	lain	lain
outgoing	rah-*mah(h)*-tah-*mah(h)*	ramah-tamah
outside	*loo*-ahr	luar
over (above)	dee ah-*tahs*	di atas
overdose	ter-*lah*-loo bah-*nyu*(k)	terlalu banyak
	mah-kahn oo-baht	makan ubat
over here	dee *see*-nee	di sini
over there	dee *sah*-nuh	di sana
to we	ber-*hoo*-tahng	berhutang
owner	pe-*mee*-li(k)	pemilik
oxygen	ok-*see*-jen	oksigen

P

package	*boong*-ku-sahn	bungkusan •
padlock	me-*mahng*-guh •	memangga •
	mang-guh	mangga (col)
pain	*sah*-kit	sakit
pain in the neck	me-nyoo-*sah(h)*-kahn	menyusahkan

painful	me-nyah-*kit*-kahn	*menyakitkan*
painkillers	oo-*baht* tah-*hahn sah*-kit	*ubat tahan sakit*
painter (artist)	pe-*loo*-kis • *ahr*-tis • se-*nee*-mahn	*pelukis • artis • seniman*
painting (activity)	me-*loo*-kis	*melukis*
(picture)	loo-*ki*-sahn	*lukisan*
pair (a couple)	se-*pah*-sahng	*sepasang*
palace	ees-tah-nuh	*istana*
pap smear	smir	*smir*
paper	ker-*tahs*	*kertas*
paraplegic	*loom*-pu(h) kah-*kee*	*lumpuh kaki*
parents	ee-boo *bah*-puh • o-rahng *too*-uh	*ibu bapa • orang tua*
parliament	*pahr*-lee-men	*parlimen*
part (n)	bah-*hah*-gee-ahn	*bahagian*
party (fiesta)	*pehs*-tuh	*pesta*
(political)	*pahr*-tee	*parti*
to pass (give)	mem-*be*-ree *[be*-ree*]*	*memberi [beri]*
passenger	pe-*noom*-pahng	*penumpang*
passport (number)	(*nom*-bor) *pahs*-port	*(nombor) pasport*
past (before)	dah-*hoo*-loo • yahng *lah*-loo	*dahulu • yang lalu*
path	jah-*lahn* ke-*chil* • lo-*rong*	*jalan keci • lorong*
patient (adj)	sah-*bahr*	*sabar*
to pay	mem-*bah*-yahr *[bah*-yahr*]*	*membayar [bayar]*
payment	bah-*yah*-rahn	*bayaran*
peace	ah-*mahn* • dah-*mai*	*aman • damai*
peak (of mountain)	*pun*-chah(k)	*puncak*
pedestrian	pe-*jah*-lahn *kah*-kee	*pejalan kaki*
pen	pehn	*pen*
penalty	hoo-*koo*-mahn	*hukuman*
penis	zah-*kahr*	*zakar*
penknife	*pee*-sow *lee*-paht	*pisau lipat*
pensioner	pe-*sah*-ruh	*pesara*
people	o-rahng	*orang*
perfect	sem-*pur*-nuh	*sempurna*
performance	per-toon-*ju(k)*-kahn	*pertunjukan*
perhaps	*moong*-kin	*mungkin*
period pain	sah-kit haid	*sakit haid*
permission	ee-zin	*izin*
permit	per-*mit*	*permit*
person	o-rahng	*orang*
personality	pe-ree-*bah*-dee	*peribadi*
to perspire	ber-pe-*lu(h)* *[pe-lu(h)]*	*berpeluh [peluh]*
petrol	*peh*-trol • *min*-yah(k)	*petrol • minyak*
pharmacy	fahr-*mah*-see	*farmasi*
phone book	*boo*-koo teh-*leh*-fon	*buku telefon*
phone box	teh-*leh*-fon ah-wahm	*telefon awam*
phonecard	kahd teh-*leh*-fon	*kad telefon*
photograph	*gahm*-bahr • *fo*-to	*gambar • foto*

May I take a photograph? bo-*leh*(h) sai-yuh *ahm*-bil *gahm*-bahr/fo-to?		Boleh saya ambil gambar/foto?
photograph	*gahm*-bahr • *fo*-to	gambar • foto
photographer	joo-roo-*gahm*-bahr	jurugambar
photography	se-*nee* fo-to	senifoto
to pick up	me-*ngahm*-bil [*ahm*-bil]	mengambil [ambil]
pickpocket	pe-nye-*lu*(k) sah-*koo*	penyeluk saku
picture	*gahm*-bahr	gambar
piece	*po*-tong	potong
pig	*bah*-bee	babi
pill	pil	pil
the Pill	oo-*baht* pen-che-*gah*(h) hah-mil	ubat pencegah hamil
pillow	*bahn*-tahl	bantal
pillowcase	sah-*rung bahn*-tahl	sarung bantal
pineapple	*nah*-nahs • *neh*-nahs	nanas • nenas
pink	*meh*-rah(h) *jahm*-boo	merah jambu
pipe (plumbing)	paip	paip
piss	ken-*ching*	kencing
to piss	boo-*ahng* air ke-*chil*	buang air kecil
place	tem-*paht*	tempat
place of birth	tem-*paht* ke-la-*hi*-rahn	tempat kelahiran
plain (adj)	se-*der*-hah-nuh	sederhana
plan	pe-*lahn*	pelan
planet	plah-*neht*	planet
plant	tah-*nah*-mahn	tanaman
plastic	*plahs*-tik	plastik
plate	*peeng*-gahn	pinggan
plateau	dah-*tah*-rahn *teeng*-gee	dataran tinggi
play (theatre)	*drah*-mah	drama
to play (a game, music)	ber-*main* [main]	bermain [main]
(cards)	main kahd • main down te-*rup*	main kad • main daun terup
player	pe-*main*	pemain
please	see-*lah*-kahn • *to*-long	silakan • tolong
plug (electricity)	pluhg	plug
plus	*tahm*-bah(h)	tambah
pocket	po-*keht* • sah-*koo* • ko-*cheh*(k)	poket • saku • kocek
poetry	sah-*jah*(k) • poo-*ee*-see	sajak • puisi
poisonous	be-*rah*-chun	beracun
poker (the game)	*po*-ker	poker
police	*po*-lis	polis
political speech	oo-*chah*-pahn • pee-*dah*-to po-*lee*-tik	ucapan/pidato politik
politicians	*ah*-lee po-*lee*-tik	ahli politik
pollen	de-*boo*-nguh	debunga
pollution	pen-che-*mah*-rahn	pencemaran
pool (swimming)	ko-*lahm* re-*nahng*	kolam renang
(game)	per-*mai*-nahn bee-*lee*-uhrd	permainan biliard

poor	*mis*-kin	miskin
popular	po-*piu*-luhr	popular
pork	*dah*-ging bah-*bee*	daging babi
port (harbour)	pe-lah-*bu*-hahn	pelabuhan
portrait sketcher	pe-*loo*-kis po-*treht*	pelukis potret
possible	bo-*leh(h)*	boleh

It's not possible.
tee-dah(k) bo-leh(h)/dee-lah-rahng   Tidak boleh./Dilarang.

postage	bah-*yah*-rahn pos	bayaran pos
postcard	pos-*kahd*	poskad
postcode	pos-*kod*	poskod
poster	*pos*-ter	poster
post office	pe-*jah*-baht pos	pejabat pos
pot (cooking)	pe-*ree*-u(k)	periuk
(dope)	*gahn*-jah	ganja
potato	ken-*tahng*	kentang
pottery	se-*nee* tem-*bee*-kahr	seni tembikar
poverty	ke-*mees*-ki-nahn	kemiskinan
power	koo-ah-*suh*	kuasa
prayer	do-*ah* • sem-*bah*-yahng	doa • sembahyang
prayer book	*boo*-koo do-*ah*	buku doa
to prefer	le-*bi(h)* soo-*kuh*	lebih suka
pregnant	hah-*mil* • me-*ngahn*-dung	hamil • mengandung
prehistoric art	se-*nee* prah-se-jah-*rah(h)*	seni prasejarah
premenstrual tension	pee em es	PMS
to prepare	me-nye-dee-*ah*-kahn [se-dee-*uh*]	menyediakan [sedia]
prescription	ah-*rah*-hahn dok-tor ber-*too*-lis	arahan doktor bertulis
present (time)	se-*kah*-rahng • *kee*-nee	sekarang • kini
(gift)	pem-be-*ree*-ahn [be-*ree*] •	pemberian [beri] •
	hah-dee-ah(h)	hadiah
presentation	pe-*nyahm*-pai-ahn [*sahm*-pai]	penyampaian [sampai]
presenter (TV, etc)	pe-*nyahm*-pai	penyampai
president	preh-*see*-den	presiden
pressure	te-*kah*-nahn	tekanan
pretty (adj)	chahn-*ti(k)* • een-*dah(h)* •	cantik • indah •
	lah-*wah*	lawa
to prevent	men-che-*gah(h)*	mencegah
price (of goods or service)	*hahr*-guh	harga
pride	ke-*bahng*-gah-ahn [*bahng*-guh]	kebanggaan [bangga]
priest (Catholic, Protestant)	pah-de-*ree*	paderi
prime minister	per-*dah*-*nuh* men-te-ree	perdana menteri
print (artwork)	cheh-*ta(k)*-kahn (kar-*yah* se-*nee*)	cetakan (karya seni)
prison	pen-*jah*-ruh	penjara
prisoner	bahn-*doo*-ahn	banduan
private	per-sen-dee-*ree*-ahn •	persendirian •
	pe-ree-*bah*-dee	peribadi
private hospital	hos-*pee*-tahl *swahs*-tah	hospital swasta
problem	mah-sah-ah-*lah(h)*	masalah

to produce	meng-*hah*-sil-kahn [*hah*-sil]	menghasilkan [hasil]
producer (film)	pe-*ner*-bit [ter-*bit*] (fee-lem)	penerbit [terbit] (filem)
profession	pe-ker-*jah*-ahn	pekerjaan
program (TV)	rahn-*chah*-ngahn	rancangan
projector	pro-*jehk*-tor	projektor
promise	*jahn*-jee	janji
proposal	chah-*dah*-ngahn • *ahn*-joo-rahn	cadangan • anjuran
prostitute	pe-*lah*-chur • soon-*dahl*	pelacur • sundal
to protect	me-*lin*-du-ngee [*lin*-dung]	melindungi [lindung]
protected forest	hoo-*tahn* sim-*pahn*	hutan simpan
protected species	hai-*wahn* ter-*leen*-dung	haiwan terlindung
to protest	mem-*bahn*-tah(h) [bahn-*tah(h)*]	membantah [bantah]
public toilet	tahn-*dahs* ah-*wahm*	tandas awam
to pull	me-*nah*-ri(k) [*tah*-ri(k)]	menarik [tarik]
pump	pahm	pam
puncture	ke-bo-*cho*-rahn	kebocoran
to punish	meng-*hoo*-kum [*hoo*-kum]	menghukum [hukum]
puppet (leather)	(*koo*-lit) bo-neh-*kah*	(kulit) boneka
(wooden)	pah-tung kah-*yoo*	patung kayu
puppy	ah-nah(k) *ahn*-jing	anak anjing
pure	*moor*-nee • soo-*chee* • too-*lehn*	murni • suci • tulen
purple	oo-*ngoo*	ungu
purse	dom-peht • puhrs	dompet • purse
to push	me-no-*lah(k)* [to-*lah(k)*]	menolak [tolak]
to put	me-le-*tah(k)*-kahn [le-*tah(k)*]	meletakkan [letak]

qualifications	ke-lah-*yah(k)*-kahn	kelayakan
quality	moo-*too* • kwah-lee-*tee*	mutu • kualiti
quantity	joom-*lah(h)*	jumlah
quarantine	kwah-*rahn*-teen	kuarantin
quarter	soo-*koo*	suku
question	per-*tah*-nyuh-ahn • so-*ah*-lahn	pertanyaan • soalan
to question	ber-*tah*-nyuh [*tah*-nyuh]	bertanya [tanya]
queue	be-*rah*-tur	beratur
quick	che-*paht* • pahn-*tahs*	cepat • pantas
quickly	de-*ngahn* che-*paht*/pahn-*tahs*	dengan cepat/pantas
quiet	se-*nyahp* • soo-*nyee* • se-*pee*	senyap • sunyi • sepi
quinine	kui-*nin*	kuinin
to quit	ber-*hen*-tee [*hen*-tee]	berhenti [henti]

race (breed)	*bahng*-suh • kowm	bangsa • kaum
(sport)	per-*loom*-bah-ahn	perlumbaan
racism	rah-*sis*-mah	rasisme
racquet	rah-*keht*	raket
radiator	rah-*dee*-ah-tor	radiator

railroad	jah-lahn ke-reh-tah-ah-pee	jalan keretapi
railway station	steh-sehn ke-reh-tah-ah-pee	stesen keretapi
rain	hoo-jahn	hujan

It's raining heavily.
hoo-*jahn* le-*baht.*   Hujan lebat.

rally (demonstration)	per-*him*-pu-nahn	perhimpunan
rape	pe-ro-go-lahn [ro-*gohl*]	perogolan [rogol]
rare (uncommon)	jah-*rahng*	jarang
rash	roo-*ahm*	ruam
rat	tee-kus	tikus
rate of pay	kah-*dahr* pem-bah-*yah*-rahn	kadar pembayaran
raw (food)	men-*tah(h)*	mentah
razor	pee-sow choo-kur	pisau cukur
to read	mem-*bah*-chah [*bah*-chuh]	membaca [baca]
ready	se-dee-*uh* • see-*ahp*	sedia • siap
to realise	me-nye-*dah*-ree [se-*dahr*]	menyedari [sedar]
reason	se-*bahb* • ah-*lah*-sahn	sebab • alasan
receipt	re-*sit*	resit
to receive	me-ne-ree-muh [te-ree-muh]	menerima [terima]
recent	bah-*roo* ber-*lah*-koo	baru berlaku
to recognise	ke-*nahl* • me-ngah-*koo*-ee [ah-*koo*-ee]	kenal • mengakui [akui]
to recommend	me-nge-*shor*-kahn [shor]	mengesyorkan [syor]
recording	rah-*kah*-mahn	rakaman
to recycle	meng-goo-*nah*-kahn kem-*bah*-lee	menggunakan kembali
red	meh-rah(h)	merah
referee	pe-*ngah*-dil	pengadil
reforestation	pe-nah-*nah*-mahn hoo-*tahn* se-*moo*-luh	penanaman hutan semula
refrigerator	pe-*tee* se-*ju(k)*	peti sejuk
refugee	pe-lah-*ree*-ahn	pelarian
to refund	pe-ngem-*bah*-lee-ahn wahng	pengembalian wang
to refuse	me-no-*la(k)* [to-*la(k)*] • *eng*-gahn	menolak[tolak] • enggan
region	kah-*wah*-sahn • dah-eh-rah(h)	kawasan • daerah
registered mail	soo-*raht* ber-*dahf*-tahr	surat berdaftar
to regret	me-nye-*sahl* [se-*sahl*]	menyesal [sesal]
relationship	hoo-*bu*-ngahn	hubungan
to relax	be-reh-*haht* [reh-*haht*]	berehat [rehat]
religion	ah-*gah*-muh	agama
religious	ke-ah-*gah*-mah-ahn • be-*ree*-mahn	keagamaan • beriman
to remember	ee-*ngaht*	ingat
remote	jow(h) • ter-pen-*chil*	jauh • terpencil
to rent	me-*nyeh*-wuh [*seh*-wuh]	menyewa [sewa]
to repair	mem-per-*bai*-kee	memperbaiki [baik]
repeat	me-ngoo-*lah*-ngee [oo-*lahng*]	mengulangi [ulang]
reply	jah-*wah*-pahn • bah-lah-*sahn*	jawapan • balasan
to reply	men-jah-*wahb* [jah-*wahb*]	menjawab [jawab]

to report	me-lah-*por*-kahn [lah-*por*]	melaporkan [lapor]
republic	ree-*puhb*-lik	republik
reservation	tem-*pah(h)*-hahn	tempahan
to reserve	me-nem-*pah(h)* [tem-*pah(h)*]	menempah [tempah]
respect	hor-*maht*	hormat
responsibility	tang-gung-*jah*-wahb	tanggungjawab
rest (relaxation)	reh-*haht*	rehat
(what's left)	*see*-suh	sisa
to rest	be-reh-*haht* [reh-*haht*]	berehat [rehat]
restaurant	rehs-*to*-rahn	restoran
result	*hah*-sil • ah-*kee*-baht	hasil • akibat
resumé	reh-siu-*meh* • *see*-vee	resume • CV
return	kem-*bah*-lee	kembali
return ticket	ti-*keht* per-gee *bah*-li(k)	tiket pergi balik
review	pe-me-*rik*-sah-ahn kem-*bah*-lee	pemeriksaan kembali
rheumatism	pe-*nyah*-kit se-*ngahl*-se-*ngahl*	penyakit sengal-sengal
	too-lahng	tulang
rhythm	ren-*tah(k)*	rentak
rice (cooked)	nah-*see*	nasi
(uncooked)	be-*rahs*	beras
rich (food)	sah-*ngaht* le-*mah(k)*	sangat lemak
(wealthy)	*kah*-yuh	kaya
to ride (bike, horse)	me-*nai(k)*-kee [*nai(k)*]	menaiki [naik]
(bus, car,	me-*noong*-gahng	menunggang
plane, train)	[*toong*-gahng]	[tunggang]
right (not left)	*kah*-nahn	kanan
(correct)	be-*tul*	betul

You're right.
*ahn-*dah be-*tul*   Anda betul.

right now	se-*kah*-rahng *joo*-guh	sekarang juga
right-wing	sah-*yahp kah*-nahn	sayap kanan
ring (on finger)	*chin*-chin	cincin
(sound)	boo-*nyee*	bunyi

I'll give you a ring.
sai-yuh teh-*leh*-fon *ahn*-dah nahn-*tee*   Saya telefon anda nanti.

ripe	*mah*-sah(k)	masak
rip-off	ter-*lah*-loo mah-*hahl*	terlalu mahal
risk	ree-*see*-ko	risiko
river	soo-*ngai*	sungai
road	*jah*-lahn	jalan
road map	pe-*tuh jah*-lahn	peta jalan
roasted	*pahng*-gahng	panggang
to rob	me-rom-*pa(k)* [rom-*pa(k)*]	merompak [rompak]
rock	*bah*-too	batu
rock climbing	pen-dah-*kee*-ahn te-*bing bah*-too	pendakian tebing batu
rock group	koom-*pu*-lahn rok	kumpulan rock
rolling	ber-goo-*ling*	berguling

romance	per-*chin*-tah-ahn	percintaan
roof	ah-*tahp* • *boom*-bung	atap • bumbung
room (number)	(*nom*-bor) bee-li(k)	(nombor) bilik
rope	tah-*lee*	tali
rotten	boo-*su*(k) • ro-*sah*(k)	busuk • rosak
round (shape)	boo-*laht*	bulat
(at the) roundabout	(dee) boo-*lah*-tahn	(di) bulatan
to row	men-*dah*-yung	mendayung
rubbish	sahm-*pah*(h)	sampah
rug	per-*mai*-dah-nee	permaidani
ruins	run-*tu*-hahn	runtuhan
rules	pe-*rah*-tu-rahn	peraturan
run	lah-*ree*	lari

S

sad	se-*di*(h)	sedih
safe (secure)	se-*lah*-maht	selamat
safe (vault)	pe-*tee* be-*see*	peti besi
safe sex	sehks se-*lah*-maht	seks selamat
sail	lah-*yahr*	layar
sailor	ah-nah(k) *kah*-pahl	anak kapal
saint	o-rahng soo-*chee*	orang suci
(on) sale	joo-*ah*-lahn moo-*ra*(h)	jualan murah
sales department	bah-*hah*-gee-ahn pen-joo-*ah*-lahn	bahagian penjualan
salt	gah-*rahm*	garam
salty	*mah*-sin	masin
same	*sah*-muh	sama
sand	*pah*-sir	pasir
sandals	se-*lee*-pahr	selipar
sanitary napkins	too-*ah*-luh wah-*nee*-tah	tuala wanita
Saturday	*hah*-ree *sab*-too	hari Sabtu
to save	me-nye-*lah*-maht-kahn [se-*lah*-maht]	menyelamatkan [selamat]
to say	ber-*kah*-tuh [*kah*-tuh]	berkata [kata]
scared	tah-*kut*	takut
scenery	pe-*mahn*-dah-ngahn	pemandangan
school	se-ko-*lah*(h)	sekolah
science	sains	sains
scientist	*sain*-tis	saintis
scissors	*goon*-ting	gunting
scoreboard	pah-*pahn mah*-tuh/*mahr-kah*(h)	papan mata/markah
screen (film)	lah-*yahr* pe-*rah*(k)	layar perak
script	mah-*niu*-skrip • nahs-*kah*(h)	manuskrip • naskhah
sculpture	se-*nee* oo-kir	seni ukir
sea	lowt	laut
to search	men-*chah*-ree [*chah*-ree]	mencari [cari]
seasick	mah-*bu*(k) lowt	mabuk laut
seaside	te-*pee* lowt	tepi laut

season	moo-sim	musim
seat	tem-paht doo-du(k)	tempat duduk
seat belt	tah-lee peeng-gahng ke-leh-dahr	tali pinggang keledar
second (unit of time)	sah-aht	saat
(in order)	ke-doo-uh	kedua
secretary	se-tee-uh-oo-suh-huh	setiausaha
to see	lee-haht	lihat

I see. (understand)
sai-yuh fah-hahm   Saya faham.

See you later.
joom-*puh* lah-*gee*   Jumpa lagi.

See you tomorrow.
joom-*puh* eh-so(k)   Jumpa esok.

self-employed	be-ker-juh sen-dee-ree	bekerja sendiri
selfish	me-mee-kir-kahn dee-ree	memikirkan diri
	sen-dee-ree sah-juh	sendiri saja
self-service	lah-yahn dee-ree	layan diri
to sell	men-joo-ahl [joo-ahl]	menjual [jual]
to send	meng-hahn-tahr [hahn-tahr]	menghantar [hantar]
sensible	ah-rif • moo-nah-sah-bah(h)	arif • munasabah
sentence (words)	ah-yaht	ayat
(prison)	hoo-ku-mahn	hukuman
to separate	me-mee-sah(h)-kahn [pee-sah(h)]	memisahkan [pisah]
serious	see-ree-uhs	serius
servant	o-rahng gah-jee	orang gaji
to serve	me-lah-yah-nee [lah-yahn]	melayani [layan]
service (assistance)	khid-maht • jah-suh	khidmat • jasa
several	be-be-rah-puh	beberapa
to sew	jah-hit	jahit
sex	sehks	seks
sexism	sehk-sis-muh	seksisme
sexy	mem-be-rah-hee-kahn	memberahikan
	[be-rah-hee]	[berahi]
shade	te-du(h)	teduh
to shampoo	men-shehm-poo [shem-poo]	mensyempu [syempu]
shape	ben-tu(k)	bentuk
to share (with)	ber-kong-see (de-ngahn)	berkongsi (dengan)
to share a dorm	ber-kong-see bee-li(k)/dorm	berkongsi bilik/dorm
to shave	choo-kur	cukur
she	dee-uh	dia
sheet (bed)	chah-dahr	cadar
(of paper)	he-lai	helai
shell (sea)	koo-lit	kulit
ship	kah-pahl	kapal
shirt	bah-joo • ke-meh-juh	baju • kemeja
shit	tai(k)	tahi

to shit	boo-*ahng* air be-*sahr*	buang air besar
shoelaces	tah-*lee* kah-sut	tali kasut
shoes	kah-sut	kasut
to shoot	me-*nehm*-ba(k) [tehm-ba(k)]	menembak [tembak]
shop	ke-*dai*	kedai
to go shopping	mem-be-*lee*-be-*lah(h)* [be-*lee*]	membeli-belah [beli]
short (length, height)	pehn-deh(k)	pendek
short film	fee-lem pehn-deh(k)	filem pendek
short story	cher-*pehn*	cerpen
shortage	ke-koo-*rah*-ngahn	kekurangan
shorts (clothes)	se-loo-*ahr* pehn-*de(k)*	seluar pendek
shoulders	bah-*hoo*	bahu
to shout	men-je-*rit* [je-*rit*]	menjerit [jerit]
show	per-toon-*joo(k)*-kahn [toon-*joo(k)*]	pertunjukan [tunjuk]
to show	me-noon-*joo(k)*-kahn [toon-*joo(k)*]	menunjukkan [tunjuk]

Please show me (on the map).
to-long toon-*joo(k)*-kahn (dee pe-*tuh*)   Tolong tunjukkan (di peta).

to shower	*mahn*-dee	mandi
shrimp	oo-*dahng*	udang
shrine	tem-*paht* soo-chee	tempat suci
shut	*too*-tup	tutup
shy	*mah*-loo • se-*gahn*	malu • segan
sick	sah-kit	sakit
sickness	pe-nyah-*kit*	penyakit
side (of a street)	te-*pee* (jah-lahn)	tepi (jalan)
sign	tahn-duh	tanda
to sign	me-nahn-duh-*tah*-ngah-nee [tahn-duh-*tah*-ngahn]	menandatangani [tandatangan]
signature	tahn-duh-*tah*-ngahn	tandatangan
silk	soo-te-ruh	sutera
silver	peh-*ra(k)*	perak
of silver	dah-ree-*pah*-duh peh-*ra(k)*	daripada perak
similar	se-*mah*-chahm • se-*roo*-puh	semacam • serupa
simple	se-der-*hah*-nuh	sederahana
sin	do-*suh*	dosa
since	se-*jah(k)*	sejak
to sing	me-*nyah*-nyee [*nyah*-nyee]	menyanyi [nyanyi]
singer	pe-*nyah*-nyee	penyanyi
single room	*bee*-li(k) se-o-rahng	bilik seorang
to sit	*doo*-du(k)	duduk
size	saiz	saiz
skin	*koo*-lit	kulit
skinny	*koo*-rus	kurus
sky	lah-*ngit*	langit
sleazy (person)	ko-*tor* • *tee*-dah(k) ke-*mahs*	kotor • tidak kemas
to sleep	*tee*-dur	tidur
sleeping bag	kahn-*tung tee*-dur	kantung tidur

sleeping pills	oo-*baht* tee-dur	ubat tidur
sleepy	me-*ngahn*-tu(k)	mengantuk
to slice	meng-*hee*-ris	menghiris [hiris]
slide (film)	ge-*lahn*-sahr fee-*lem*	gelansar filem
slow	per-*lah*-hahn	perlahan
small	ke-*chil*	kecil
smell	bow	bau
to smell	meng-*hee*-doo [*hee*-doo]	menghidu [hidu]
to smile	se-*nyum*	senyum
smoke	ah-*sahp*	asap
to smoke	me-*ro*-ko(k) [*ro*-ko(k)]	merokok [rokok]
snake	oo-*lahr*	ular
soap	sah-*bun*	sabun
soap opera	drah-mah sah-*bun*	drama sabun
soccer	bo-luh seh-*pah*(k)	bola sepak
social welfare	ke-bah-*jii(k)*-kahn so-see-*ahl*	kebajikan sosial
socialist	so-see-*ah*-lis	sosialis
society	mah-*shah*-rah-kaht	masyarakat
socks	sto-*king*	stoking
soft	*lem*-but	lembut
some	be-be-*rah*-puh	beberapa
someone	se-se-o-rahng	seseorang
something	se-soo-*ah*-too	sesuatu
sometimes	kah-*dahng*-kah-*dahng*	kadang-kadang
son	*ah*-nah(k) le-lah-*kee*	anak lelaki
song	lah-*goo*	lagu
soon	se-ke-*jahp* lah-*gee*	sekejap lagi
sorry	mah-*ahf*	maaf

I'm sorry. mah-*ahf*		*Maaf.*

sound	boo-*nyee*	bunyi
sour	*mah*-sahm	masam
south	se-la-*tahn*	selatan
souvenir	chen-de-ruh-*mah*-tuh	cenderamata
souvenir shop	ke-*dai* chen-de-ruh-*mah*-tuh	kedai cenderamata
soy sauce	kee-*chahp*	kicap
space (area)	roo-*ahng*	ruang
speak	chah-*kahp*	cakap
to speak (Malay)	ber-bah-*hah*-suh me-*lah*-yoo	berbahasa Melayu
special	ees-tee-*meh*-wuh • khahs	istimewa • khas
specialist	pah-*kahr*	pakar
speed (limit)	(hahd) lah-*joo*	(had) laju
spicy	pe-*dahs*	pedas
spoon	soo-*doo*	sudu
sport	soo-*kahn*	sukan
sportsplayer	pe-*main* soo-*kahn*	pemain sukan
sprain	ter-se-*lee*-uh(h)	terseliuh

spring (season)	*moo*-sim *boo*-nguh	musim bunga
(coil)	pe-*gahs* • spring	pegas • spring
square (shape)	se-gee-*em*-paht	segiempat
(plaza)	dah-*tah*-rahn	dataran
stadium	stah-*dee*-um	stadium
stage	pen-*tahs*	pentas
stairs	*tahng*-guh	tangga
stale	bah-*see*	basi
stamp	se-*tehm*	setem
standard (adj)	stahn-*dahrd* • tah-*rahf*	standard • taraf
standard of living	tah-*rahf* ke-hee-*du*-pahn	taraf kehidupan
starfruit	be-*lim*-bing	belimbing
stars (in the sky)	bin-*tahng*	bintang
to start	me-moo-*luh*-kahn [moo-*luh*]	memulakan [mula]
station	steh-*sehn*	stesen
stationmaster	pe-gah-*wai* pe-*ngah*-wahs	pegawai pengawas
	steh-sehn ke-reh-tah-*ah*-pee	stesen keretapi
statue	*pah*-tung	patung
to stay (remain)	*ting*-gahl	tinggal
(overnight)	ber-*mah*-lahm [mah-lahm]	bermalam [malam]
to steal	men-*choo*-ree [choo-ree]	mencuri [curi]
steam	wahp	wap
steep (hill)	choo-*rahm*	curam
step	lang-*kah(h)*	langkah
still (yet)	*mah*-si(h)	masih
stomach	pe-*rut*	perut
stomachache	*sah*-kit pe-*rut*	sakit perut
stone	bah-*too*	batu
stoned (drugged)	mah-*bu(k)*	mabuk
to stop	ber-*hen*-tee [hen-tee]	berhenti [henti]

Stop!		
ber-*hen*-tee!		*Berhenti!*

storm	ree-*but*	ribut
story	che-*ree*-tuh	cerita
stove	dah-*pur*	dapur
straight (line)	(gah-*ri*-sahn) loo-*rus*	(garisan) lurus
strange	pe-*li(k)* • *gahn*-jil • ah-*neh(h)*	pelik • ganjil • aneh
stranger	o-rahng yahng tee-*dah(k)*	orang yang tidak
	dee-ke-*nah*-lee	dikenali
stream (small river)	soo-*ngai*	sungai
street	*jah*-lahn	jalan
strength	ke-koo-*ah*-tahn	kekuatan
(on) strike	mo-*go(k)*	mogok
string	*tah*-lee	tali
stroll	*jah*-lahn-*jah*-lahn • *see*-*ahr*-*see*-*ahr*	jalan-jalan • siar-siar
strong	koo-*aht*	kuat
student (school)	pe-*lah*-jahr • *moo*-rid	pelajar • murid
student (university)	mah-*hah*-sis-wah • pe-lah-*jahr*	mahasiswa • pelajar

studio	stoo-*dee*-o	*studio*
stupid	bo-*do(h)*	*bodoh*
style	*gah*-yuh	*gaya*
subtitles	tehks	*teks*
suburb	*ping*-gir bahn-dahr	*pinggir bandar*
suburbs of Kuala Lumpur	*ping*-gir bahn-dahr koo-*ah*-luh *loom*-pur	*pinggir bandar* *Kuala Lumpur*
success	ke-jah-*yah*-ahn	*kejayaan*
to suffer	men-de-*ree*-tuh [de-*ree*-tuh]	*menderita [derita]*
sugar	*goo*-luh	*gula*
summer	*moo*-sim *pah*-nahs	*musim panas*
sun	*mah*-tuh-*hah*-ree	*matahari*
sunblock	krim pe-*leen*-dung	*krim pelindung*
	chah-*hah*-yuh mah-tuh-*hah*-ree	*cahaya matahari*
sunburnt	*koo*-lit ter-bah-*kahr*	*kulit terbakar*
Sunday	*hah*-ree ah-*hahd*	*hari Ahad*
sunglasses	cher-*min mah*-tuh *hee*-tahm	*cermin mata hitam*
sunny	che-*rah(h)*	*cerah*
sunrise	mah-tuh-*hah*-ree ter-*bit*	*matahari terbit*
sunset	mah-tuh-*hah*-ree ter-be-*nahm*	*matahari terbenam*
supermarket	pah-sah-*rah*-yuh	*pasaraya*

Sure.		
bo-*leh(h)*		*Boleh.*

surface mail	mehl bee-*ah*-suh	*mel biasa*
to surf	ber-se-*lahn*-chahr [se-*lahn*-chahr]	*berselancar [selancar]*
surfboard	pah-*pahn* se-*lahn*-chahr	*papan selancar*
surname	*nah*-muh ke-loo-*ahr*-guh	*nama keluarga*
surprise	ke-joo-*tahn*	*kejutan*
to survive	hee-*dup*	*hidup*
to sweat	ber-pe-*lu(h)* [pe-*lu(h)*]	*berpeluh [peluh]*
sweet (adj)	mah-*nis*	*manis*
sweets	*goo*-luh-*goo*-luh	*gula-gula*
to swim	be-re-*nahng* [re-*nahng*]	*berenang [renang]*
swimming pool	ko-*lahm* re-*nahng*	*kolam renang*
swimsuit	*bah*-joo re-*nahng*	*baju renang*
sword	pe-*dahng*	*pedang*
sympathetic	ber-sim-*pah*-tee	*bersimpati*
synagogue	ge-*reh*-juh yah-*hoo*-dee	*gereja Yahudi*
synthetic	sin-*teh*-tik	*sintetik*
syringe	*jah*-rum soon-*ti(k)*	*jarum suntik*

T

table	*meh*-juh	*meja*
tablet	bee-*jee* oo-*baht*	*biji ubat*
table tennis	ping-*pong*	*ping-pong*
tail (of animal)	*eh*-kor	*ekor*
tailor	too-*kahng* jah-*hit*	*tukang jahit*

to take (away)	me-*ngahm*-bil [*ahm*-bil]	mengambil [ambil]
(train)	me-*nai*(k)-kee	menaiki [naik]
to take off (depart)	ber-le-*pahs* [le-*pahs*] •	berlepas [lepas] •
	be-*rahng*-kaht [*ahng*-kaht]	berangkat [angkat]
to take photographs	me-*ngahm*-bil fo-to/	mengambil foto/
	gahm-bahr	gambar
to talk (chat)	ber-*chah*-kahp [*chah*-kahp]	bercakap [cakap]
tall	*ting*-gee	tinggi
tampon	*tahm*-pon	tampon
taste	*rah*-suh	rasa
tasty	se-*dahp* • *eh*-nah(k)	sedap • enak
tax	*choo*-kai	cukai
taxi (stand)	(*steh*-sehn) *tehk*-see	(stesen) teksi
tea	teh(h)	teh
teacher	*goo*-roo • *chi*(k)-goo	guru • cikgu (col)
teaching	me-*ngah*-jahr	mengajar
team (sport)	pah-*su*(k)-kahn	pasukan
tear (crying)	air mah-*tuh*	air mata
teeth	*gee*-gee	gigi
telegram	teh-leh-*grahm*	telegram
telephone	teh-*leh*-fon	telefon
to telephone	me-neh-*leh*-fon [teh-*leh*-fon]	menelefon [telefon]
television	teh-leh-*vee*-shen	televisyen
to tell (inform)	mem-be-ree-*tah*-hoo [*tah*-hoo]	memberitahu [tahu]
teller	teh-ler	teler (col)
temperature (fever)	soo-*hoo* bah-*dahn*	suhu badan
(weather)	soo-*hoo* oo-*dah*-ruh	suhu udara
temple		
(Buddhist)	to-*kong* boo-*dah*	tokong Buda
(Chinese)	to-*kong* chee-nuh	tokong Cina
(Hindu)	*koo*-il	kuil
tennis (court)	(pah-*dahng*) teh-*nis*	(padang) tenis
tent	kheh-*mah*(h)	khemah
tent pegs	pah-*koo* kah-*yoo* • pahn-*chahng*	paku kayu • pancang
	kheh-*mah*(h)	khemah
tenth	ke-se-*poo*-lu(h)	kesepuluh
terrible	me-nge-*ree*-kahn [nge-*ree*]	mengerikan [ngeri]
test (exam)	oo-*jee*-ahn (pe-pe-*rik*-sah-ahn)	ujian (peperiksaan)
to thank	ber-te-*ree*-muh *kah*-si(h)	berterima kasih

Thank you.
te-*ree*-muh *kah*-si(h).

Terima kasih.

that	*ee*-too	itu
theatre (play)	*pahng*-gung sahn-dee-*wah*-rah	panggung sandiwara
there (distant)	dee *sah*-nuh	di sana
(nearby)	dee *see*-too	di situ

there is/are ...
dee *sah*-nuh/*see*-too *ah*-duh ...

di sana/situ ada ...

they	me-*reh*-kuh	mereka
thief	pen-choo-*ree*	pencuri
thin	*nee*-pis • *ti*-pis	nipis • tipis
to think	ber-*fee*-kir [*fee*-kir]	berfikir [fikir]
third	ke-*tee*-guh	ketiga
thirsty	hows • dah-*hah*-guh	haus • dahaga
this	*ee*-nee	ini
thought	fee-ki-*rahn*	fikiran
thread	be-*nahng*	benang
throat	te-*kah(k)* • ke-*rong*-kong	tekak • kerongkong
Thursday	*hah*-ree kah-*mis*	hari Khamis
ticket	tee-*keht*	tiket
ticket collector	pe-*moo*-ngut tee-*keht*	pemungut tiket
ticket office	pe-*jah*-baht tee-*keht*	pejabat tiket
tide (low/high)	air (*soo*-rut/pah-*sahng*)	air (surut/pasang)
tiger	hah-*ree*-mow	harimau
tight	ke-*taht* • sem-*pit*	ketat • sempit
time	mah-*suh*	masa

> What time is it?
> *poo*-kul be-*rah*-puh?   Pukul berapa?

timetable	jah-doo-*ahl* wak-too	jadual waktu
tin opener	pem-*boo*-kuh tin	pembuka tin
tired	pe-*naht*	penat
tissues	ti-*soo*	tisu
to	ke	ke
toad	*kah*-tah(k) • *ko*-do(k)	katak • kodok
toast (bread)	(*ro*-tee) bah-*kahr*	(roti) bakar
tobacco	tem-*bah*-kow	tembakau
today	*hah*-ree ee-nee	hari ini
together	ber-*sah*-muh	bersama
toilet paper	*tee*-soo	tisu
toilet	*tahn*-duhs	tandas
tomorrow	eh-*so*(k)	esok
tomorrow afternoon	te-ngah-*hah*-ree/pe-*tahng* eh-so(k)	tengahari/petang esok
tomorrow morning	eh-*so*(k) *pah*-gee	pagi esok
tongue	lee-*dah(h)*	lidah
tonight	mah-*lahm* ee-nee	malam ini
too (excessive)	ter-*lah*-loo	terlalu
too (as well)	*joo*-guh • pun	juga • pun

> Too expensive!
> ter-*lah*-loo mah-*hahl*!   Terlalu mahal!
> Too many/much!
> ter-*lah*-loo bah-nya(k)!   Terlalu banyak!

tool	*ah*-laht	alat
tooth	gee-gee	gigi

tooth (front/back)	gee-gee (de-pahn/be-lah-kahng)	gigi (depan/belakang)
toothache	sah-kit gee-gee	sakit gigi
toothbrush	be-rus gee-gee	berus gigi
toothpaste	oo-baht gee-gee	ubat gigi
torch (flashlight)	lahm-poo soo-lu(h)	lampu suluh
to touch	me-nyen-tu(h)[sen-tu(h)]	menyentuh [sentuh]
tour	ber-ke-lee-ling	berkeliling
tourist	pe-lahn-chong [lahn-chong]	pelancong [lancong]
tourist information	pe-jah-baht	pejabat
office	mah(k)-loo-maht pe-lahn-chong	maklumat pelancong
toward	ke ah-rah(h)	ke arah
towel	too-ah-luh	tuala
tower	me-nah-rah	menara
toxic waste	see-suh boo-ah-ngahn tok-sik	sisa buangan toksik
track (footprints)	ke-sahn je-ja(k)	kesan jejak
(sports)	o-lah(h)-rah-guh	olahraga
(path)	jah-lahn ke-chil • lo-rong	jalan kecil • lorong
traffic	lah-loo-lin-tahs	lalulintas
traffic jam	ke-se-sah-tahn lah-loo-lin-tahs	kesesatan lalu lintas
traffic lights	lahm-poo ee-shah-raht	lampu isyarat
trail (route)	jah-lahn	jalan
train	ke-reh-tuh-ah-pee	keretapi
train station	steh-sehn ke-reh-tuh-ah-pee	stesen keretapi
to translate	men-ter-je-mah(h)-kahn [ter-je-mah(h)]	menterjemahkan [terjemah]
to travel	me-ngem-bah-ruh	mengembara
travel agency	eh-jen-see pe-lahn-cho-ngahn	agensi pelancongan
travel book	boo-koo kem-bah-ruh	buku kembara
travellers cheque	chehk kem-bah-ruh	cek kembara
travel sickness	mah-bu(k) jah-lahn	mabuk jalan
tree	po-ko(k) • po-hon	pokok • pohon
to trek	per-jah-lah-nahn [jah-lahn] • pe-ngem-bah-ruh-ahn [kem-bah-ruh]	perjalanan [jalan] • pengembaraan [kembara]
trip (journey)	per-jah-lah-nahn	perjalanan
trousers	se-loo-ahr pahn-jahng	seluar panjang
truck	lo-ree	lori
true	be-nahr	benar

It's true. be-nahr		Benar.

to trust	per-chah-yuh	percaya
truth	ke-be-nah-rahn	kebenaran
to try (attempt)	men-choo-buh [choo-buh]	mencuba [cuba]
T-shirt	bah-joo tee	baju T
Tuesday	hah-ree se-lah-suh	hari Selasa
tune (song)	lah-goo • nah-duh	lagu • nada
turn	be-lo(k) • poo-sing	belok • pusing

Turn left/right.
beh-*lo(k)* ki-ree/*kah*-nahn

Belok kiri/kanan.

TV	teh-leh-*vee*-shen	*televisyen*
twice	*doo*-uh *kah*-lee	*dua kali*
twin beds	*kah*-til *kem*-bahr	*katil kembar*
twins	*kem*-bahr	*kembar*
type (of product)	je-*nis*	*jenis*
to type	me-*naip* (taip)	*menaip [taip]*
typhoid	tai-*foid*	*tifoid*
typical	bee-*ah*-suh	*biasa*
tyre	*tai*-yahr	*tayar*

U

umbrella	*pah*-yung	*payung*
under	*bah*-wah(h)	*bawah*
to understand	fah-*hahm*	*faham*

I (don't) understand.
sai-yuh *(tee-*dah(k)) fah-*hahm*

Saya (tidak) faham.

underwear	se-loo-*ahr* dah-*lahm*	*seluar dalam*
unemployed	pe-*ngahng*-gur	*penganggur*
unions	per-sah-*too*-ahn se-*ker*-juh	*persatuan sekerja*
universe	ah-*lahm* se-*mes*-tah	*alam semesta*
university	yoo-ni-*ver*-si-tee	*universiti*
unripe	be-*lum mah*-sah(k)	*belum masak*
unsafe	*tee*-dah(k) se-*lah*-maht	*tidak selamat*
until (June)	se-*hing*-guh (joon)	*sehingga (Jun)*
unusual	*loo*-ahr bee-*ah*-suh	*luar biasa*
up	ah-*tahs*	*atas*
uphill (road)	*(jah*-lahn) nai(k) boo-*kit*	*(jalan) naik bukit*
urgent	men-de-*sah(k)* • *pen*-ting	*mendesak • penting*
useful	ber-*goo*-nuh	*berguna*
usual	bee-*ah*-suh	*biasa*

V

vacant	*ko*-song	*kosong*
vacation	*choo*-tee	*cuti*
vaccination	pen-chah-*chah*-rahn	*pencacaran*
valley	*lem*-bah(h)	*lembah*
valuable	ber-*har*-guh	*berharga*
value (price)	nee-*lai*	*nilai*
van	vahn	*van*
vegetables	*sai*-yur-*sai*-yu-rahn	*sayur-sayuran*
vegetarian (food)	*sai*-yu-rahn *sah*-juh	*sayuran saja*
(person)	*(o*-rahng yahng)	*(orang yang)*
	mah-kahn *sai*-yur *sah*-juh	*makan sayur saja*

I'm vegetarian.
sai-yuh *mah*-kahn *sai*-yur sah-*hah*-juh   *Saya makan sayur sahaja.*

vegetation	toom-*bu(h)*-toom-*bu(h)*-hahn	tumbuh-tumbuhan
vein	oo-*raht dah*-rah(h)	urat darah
venereal disease	pe-*nyah*-kit ke-*lah*-min	penyakit kelamin
very	sah-*ngaht* • ah-*maht*	sangat • amat
video cassette	*kah*-seht vi-dee-o	kaset video
view	pe-*mahn*-dah-ngahn	pemandangan
	[*pahn*-dahng]	[pandang]
village	*kahm*-pung • deh-*suh*	kampung • desa
virus	vi-*rus*	virus
visa	*vee*-sah	visa
to visit	me-lah-*waht* [lah-*waht*] •	melawat [lawat] •
	me-*ngoon*-ju-ngee [*koon*-jung]	mengunjungi [kunjung]
vitamin	vi-*tah*-min	vitamin
voice	soo-*ah*-ruh	suara
volcano	*goo*-nung be-*rah*-pee	gunung berapi
volume (sound)	soo-*ah*-ruh	suara
vomit (n/v)	moon-*tah(h)*	muntah
to vote	me-*ngun*-dee [*un*-dee]	mengundi [undi]
vulgar	bee-*ah*-dahb • kah-*sahr*	biadab • kasar

W

wait	*toong*-goo	tunggu
waiter	pe-*lah*-yahn	pelayan
waiting room	*bee*-li(k) me-*noong*-goo	bilik menunggu
to wake up	bah-*ngun* • *bahng*-kit	bangun • bangkit
to walk	ber-*jah*-lahn kah-*kee*	berjalan kaki
wall (inside)	*deen*-ding	dinding
(outside)	tehm-*bo(k)*	tembok
to want	hen-*da(k)* • *ee*-ngin • mow	hendak • ingin • mahu
war	pe-*rahng*	perang
wardrobe	*ahl*-mah-ree	almari
warm	soo-*ahm*	suam
to wash (yourself)	*mahn*-dee	mandi
(something)	men-*choo*-chee [*choo*-chee]	mencuci [cuci]
washing machine	me-*sin* bah-*su(h)*	mesin basuh
watch (for wrist)	jahm tah-*ngahn*	jam tangan
to watch	me-*non*-ton (ton-ton)	menonton [tonton]

Watch out!
ber-hah-*tee*-hah-*tee*!/ah-*wahs*!   *Berhati-hati!/Awas!*

water	air ...	air
boiled	... *mah*-sah(k)	masak
mineral	... ee-*ne*-ruhl	mineral
purified	... u-*lehn*	tulen

water bottle	bo-*tol* air	*botol air*
waterfall	air *ter*-jun	*air terjun*
watermelon	tem-*bee*-kai	*tembikai*
waves	om-*bah(k)*	*ombak*
way	*jah*-lahn	*jalan*

Please tell me the way to ...
to-long be-ree-*tah*-hoo *sai*-yuh   *Tolong beritahu saya*
jah-lahn ke ...?   *jalan ke ...?*

Which way?
jah-lahn *mah*-nuh?   *Jalan mana?*

Way Out.
jah-lahn ke-*loo*-ahr   *Jalan keluar.*

we (incl)	*kee*-tuh	*kita*
(excl)	*kah*-mee	*kami*
weak	le-*mah(h)*	*lemah*
wealthy	kah-*yuh*	*kaya*
to wear	me-mah-*kai* [pah-*kai*]	*memakai [pakai]*
weather	choo-*ah*-chuh	*cuaca*
wedding	per-kah-*wi*-nahn •	*perkahwinan* •
	per-nee-*kah(h)*-hahn	*pernikahan*
wedding cake	kehk per-kah-*wi*-nahn	*kek perkahwinan*
wedding present	hah-dee-ah(h) per-kah-*wi*-nahn	*hadiah perkahwinan*
Wednesday	hah-ree rah-*boo*	*hari Rabu*
(this) week	ming-goo (ee-nee)	*minggu ini*
weekend	hoo-*jung* meeng-goo	*hujung minggu*
to weigh	me-*nim*-bahng [*tim*-bahng]	*menimbang [timbang]*
weight	be-*raht*	*berat*

Welcome.
se-lah-*maht* dah-*tahng*   *Selamat datang.*

You're welcome.
sah-*muh*-sah-*muh*   *Sama-sama.*

welfare	ke-bah-*ji(k)*-kahn •	*kebajikan* •
	ke-se-*jah(h)*-te-rah-ahn	*kesejahteraan*
well (healthy)	si-*haht*	*sihat*
west	bah-*raht*	*barat*
Westerner (col)	o-rahng bah-*raht*	*orang barat*
wet	bah-*sah(h)*	*basah*
what	ah-*puh*	*apa*

What?
ah-*puh*?   *Apa?*

What's he saying?
dee-*uh* chah-*kahp* ah-*puh*?   *Dia cakap apa?*

What is that?
ah-puh too? | Apa tu?

What's your name?
see-*ah*-puh *nah*-muh *ahn*-dah? | Siapa nama anda?

What time is it?
poo-kul be-*rah*-puh se-*kah*-rahng? | Pukul berapa sekarang?

wheel	ro-*duh*	roda
wheelchair	ke-*roo*-see be-*ro*-duh	kerusi beroda
when (past, future)	bee-luh	bila

When?
bee-luh? | Bila?

When does (the train) leave?
bee-luh (ke-reh-tah-*ah*-pee) ber-to-*la(k)*? | Bila (keretapi) bertolak?

Where?
mah-*nuh*? | Mana?

Where's the bank?
bank dee mah-*nuh*? | Bank di mana?

which	yahng	yang
while (currently)	sahm-bil	sambil
white	*poo*-ti (h)	putih
who	see-*ah*-puh	siapa

Who?
see-*ah*-puh? | Siapa?

Who's calling?
see-*ah*-puh yahng teh-*leh*-fon? | Siapa yang telefon?

Who is it?
see-*ah*-puh nee? | Siapa ni?

Who are they?
see-*ah*-puh me-*reh*-kuh? | Siapa mereka?

| whole (all) | se-loo-*ru(h)* | seluruh |
| why | ke-*nah*-puh • me-*ngah*-puh | kenapa • mengapa |

Why is the bank closed?
ke-*nah*-puh bank tu *too*-tup? | Kenapa bank tu tutup?

wide	leh-*bahr*	lebar
wife	ees-te-ree	isteri
wild animal	bee-*nah*-tahng lee-*yahr*/boo-*ahs*	binatang liar/buas
to win	me-*nahng*	menang
wind	*ah*-ngin	angin
window	*ting*-kahp	tingkap

to go window-shopping	me-*lee*-haht-*lee*-haht sah-juh [*lee*-haht]	melihat-lihat saja [lihat]
windscreen	kah-chuh de-*pahn*	kaca depan
wine	wain	wain
wings	sah-*yahp*	sayap
winner	joo-*ah*-ruh • *jo*-hahn • pe-me-*nahng*	juara • johan • pemenang
winter	*moo*-sim se-*joo(k)*	musim sejuk
wire	wah-*yahr*	wayar
wise	bee-ja(k)-*sah*-nuh • *ah*-rif	bijaksana • arif
to wish	hah-*jaht* • *hahs*-raht • ke-ee-ngi-nahn [ee-ngin]	hajat • hasrat • keinginan [ingin]
with	de-*ngah* • ber-*sah*-muh	dengan • bersama
within	dee dah-*lahm*	di dalam
within an hour	dah-*lahm* se-*jahm*	dalam sejam
without	*tahn*-puh	tanpa
without filter	*tahn*-puh *fil*-ter	tanpa filter
woman	wah-*nee*-tah • o-*rahng* pe-*rem*-pwahn	wanita • orang perempuan
wonderful	bah-*gus* se-kah-*lee* • meng-kah-*gum*-kahn	bagus sekali • mengkagumkan
wood (timber)	kah-*yoo* (bah-*la(k)*)	kayu (balak)
woodcarving	oo-ki-*rahn* kah-*yoo*	ukiran kayu
wool	boo-*loo* bee-*ree*-bee-*ree*	bulu biri-biri
word	per-kah-*tah*-ahn	perkataan
work	*ker*-juh	kerja
to work	be-*ker*-juh [*ker*-juh]	bekerja [kerja]
workout (sport)	lah-*ti(h)*-hahn (soo-*kahn*)	latihan (sukan)
work permit	*per*-mit *ker*-juh	permit kerja
world	doo-nee-*uh*	dunia
World Cup	pee-*ah*-luh doo-ni-*uh*	Piala Dunia
worried	ree-*sow* • beem-*bahng* • khoo-*ah*-tir	risau • bimbang • khuatir
worship	pe-*nyem*-*bah(h)*-hahn	penyembahan
worth	nee-*lai* • *hahr*-guh	nilai • harga
wound (injury)	loo-*kuh* (ke-che-de-*rah*-ahn)	luka (kecederaan)
wristwatch	jahm tah-*ngahn*	jam tangan
to write	me-*noo*-lis [*too*-lis]	menulis [tulis]
writer	pe-*noo*-lis	penulis
writing paper	ker-*tahs* *too*-lis	kertas tulis
wrong	sah-*lah(h)*	salah

I'm wrong. (my fault)
sai-yuh sah-*lah(h)*　　　　　　　　　　　　Saya salah.

Y

year (this)	*tah*-hoon *(ee*-nee)	*tahun (ini)*
yellow	*koo*-ning	*kuning*
yes	yah	*ya*
yesterday	se-*mah*-lahm	*semalam*
yesterday afternoon	te-ngah-*hah*-ree/pe-*tahng*	*tengahari/petang*
	se-*mah*-lahm	*semalam*
yesterday morning	*pah*-gee se-*mah*-lahm	*pagi semalam*
yet	be-*lum*	*belum*
not yet	be-*lum* lah-*gee*	*belum lagi*
you (inf)	kah-*moo* • *eng*-kow	*kamu • engkau*
(pol)	*ahn*-dah	*anda*
(pl)	kah-*lee*-ahn	*kalian*
young	*moo*-duh	*muda*
younger (sibling)	ah-*di(k)*	*adik*
youth (collective)	be-*lee*-uh	*belia*
youth hostel	ahs-*rah*-mah be-*lee*-uh	*asrama belia*

Z

zebra	*zeh*-brah	*zebra*
zodiac	*bin*-tahng ke-lah-*hi*-rahn	*bintang kelahiran*
zoo	zoo	*zoo*

A

ada	ah-duh	to have
abang	ah-*bahng*	older brother
ada selsema	ah-duh sel-*se*-muh	(to have a) cold
adapter elektrik	a-*dap*-ter eh-*lehk*-trik	adaptor (electric)
adat	ah-daht	custom (tradition)
adik	ah-*di(k)*	younger (sibling)
agama	ah-*gah*-muh	religion
agensi pelancongan	ah-jen-*see* pe-*lahn*-cho-ngahn	travel agency
ahli politik	ah-lee po-*lee*-tik	politicians
AIDS	ayds	AIDS
air	air	water
air (surut/pasang)	air (*soo*-rut/pah-*sahng*)	(low/high) tide
air masak	air *mah*-sah(k)	boiled water
air mata	air *mah*-tuh	tear (crying)
air mineral (berkarbonat/biasa)	air mi-*ne*-rahl (ber-*kar*-bo-naht/bee-*ah*-suh)	mineral water (with/without gas)
air sejuk	air se-*ju(k)*	cold water
air terjun	air *ter*-jun	waterfall
air tulen	air tu-*lehn*	purified water
ais	ais	ice
ais krim	ais krim	ice cream
akibat	ah-*kee*-baht	result
aktivis	*ahk*-ti-vis	activist
aku	ah-koo	I
alahan	ah-lah-hahn	allergy
alam semesta	ah-*lahm* se-*mes*-tah	universe
alam semulajadi	ah-*lahm* se-moo-luh-*jah*-dee	nature
alamat	ah-lah-maht	address (of house)
alasan	ah-lah-sahn	reason
alat	ah-laht	tool
alat selam	ah-laht se-*lahm*	diving equipment
alat solekan	ah-laht so-*leh(k)*-kahn	make-up
alergi	ah-ler-jee	allergy
Allah	ahl-*luh(h)*	God (Muslim)
almari	ahl-*mah*-ree	wardrobe
almari bagasi	ahl-*mah*-ree bah-*gah*-see	luggage lockers
am	ahm	general
aman	ah-*mahn*	peace
amat	ah-*maht*	very
anak anjing	ah-nah(k) *ahn*-jing	puppy
anak biri-biri	ah-nah(k) bee-*ree*-bee-ree	lamb
anak kapal	ah-nah(k) *kah*-pahl	sailor
anak lelaki	ah-nah(k) le-*lah*-kee	boy • son
anak perempuan	ah-nah(k) pe-*rem*-pwahn	girl • daughter

anak-anak	*ah*-nah(k)-*ah*-nah(k)	child
anda	*ahn*-dah	you (pol)
aneh	ah-*neh(h)*	strange
anggur	*ahng*-gur	grape
angin	*ah*-ngin	wind
anjing	*ahn*-jing	dog
anjing pemandu	*ahn*-jing pe-*mahn*-doo	guide dog
anjuran	*ahn*-joo-rahn	proposal
antara	*ahn*-tah-ruh	between
antara bandar	*ahn*-tah-ruh *bahn*-dahr	intercity
antarabangsa	ahn-tah-rah-*bahng*-suh	international
antibiotik	an-tai-bai-o-tik	antibiotics
anting-anting	*ahn*-ting-*ahn*-ting	earrings
apa	*ah*-puh	what
apa-apa	*ah*-puh-*ah*-puh	anything
apa pun	*ah*-puh pun	any
api	ah-*pee*	fire
arahan doktor bertulis	ah-rah-*hahn* *dok*-tor ber-*too*-lis	prescription
arak	ah-*rah(k)*	beer
arif	ah-*rif*	sensible • wise
arkeologi	*ahr*-kee-o-lo-ji	archaeological
artis	*ahr*-tis	painter (artist)
asap	ah-*sahp*	smoke
asli	*ahs*-lee	indigenous • original
asrama belia	as-*rah*-mah be-*lee*-uh	youth hostel
atap	ah-*tahp*	roof
atas	ah-*tahs*	up
atau	ah-*tow*	or
ATM	ay tee ehm	ATM
atmosfera	*aht*-mos-fe-rah	atmosphere (of planet)
avokado	ah-vo-*kah*-do	avocado
awal	ah-*wahl*	early
ayah	ah-*yah(h)*	father
ayam	ai-yahm	chicken
ayat	ah-*yaht*	sentence (words)

B

babi	*bah*-bee	pig
badan	*bah*-dahn	body
bagaimana	bah-*gai*-mah-nuh	how
bagasi	bah-*gah*-see	luggage • baggage
bagasi yang ditinggalkan	bah-*gah*-see yahng dee-ting-*gahl*-kahn	left luggage
bagus	bah-*gus*	brilliant • cool • fantastic
bagus sekali	bah-*gus* se-kah-*lee*	wonderful
bahagian	bah-*hah*-gee-ahn	part

(di) bahagian bawah	(dee) bah-*hah*-gee-ahn bah-*wah(h)*	(at the) bottom
bahagian penjualan	bah-*hah*-gee-ahn pen-joo-*ah*-lahn	sales department
bahasa	bah-*hah*-suh	language
Bahasa Melayu	bah-*hah*-suh me-*lah*-yoo	Malay
bahaya	bah-*hah*-yuh	dangerous
bahu	bah-*hoo*	shoulders
baik	bai(k)	good • OK
baik hati	bai(k) *hah*-tee	kind (adj)
baju	bah-*joo*	shirt
baju gaun	bah-joo gown	dress
baju renang	bah-joo re-*nahng*	bathing suit • swimsuit
baju sejuk	bah-joo se-*ju(k)*	jumper (sweater)
baju T	bah-joo tee	T-shirt
bakar	bah-kahr	burn
bakul	bah-kul	basket
balasan	bah-lah-*sahn*	reply
baldi	bahl-dee	bucket
bandar	bahn-dahr	city
banduan	bahn-*doo*-ahn	prisoner
bangkit	bahng-kit	to wake up
bangsa	bahng-suh	nationality • race (breed)
bangun	bah-*ngun*	to wake up
bangunan	bah-ngoo-nahn	building
bank	bank	bank
bantal	bahn-tahl	pillow
bantuan	bahn-too-ahn	assistance
banyak	bah-nya(k)	many • much
bapa	bah-*puh*	father
bar	bahr	bar (drinks)
barang antik	bah-rahng ahn-tik	antiques
barang kemas	bah-rahng ke-*mahs*	jewellery
barang-barang	bah-rahng-*bah*-rahng	baggage
barat	bah-*raht*	west
baru	bah-roo	new
baru berlaku	bah-roo ber-*lah*-koo	recent
bas	bahs	bus
bas jarak jauh	bahs jah-*rah(k)* jow(h)	long-distance bus
bas mini	bahs mee-*nee*	minibus
bas (bandar) tempatan	bahs (bahn-dahr) tem-*pah*-tahn	local (city) bus
basah	bah-*sah(h)*	wet
basi	bah-*see*	stale
basikal	bah-*see*-kahl	bicycle
basikal gunung	bah-*see*-kahl *goo*-nung	mountain bike
bateri	bah-te-ree	battery
batu	bah-*too*	rock • stone
batuk	bah-tu(k)	cough • to cough

bau	bow	smell
bawah	bah-wah(h)	under
bawang	bah-wahng	onion
bawang putih	bah-wahng poo-ti(h)	garlic
bayaran	bah-yah-rahn	payment
bayaran pos	bah-yah-rahn pos	postage
bayi	bah-yee	baby
bebas	beh-bahs	free (not bound)
beberapa	be-be-rah-puh	few • several • some
beg	behg	bag
beg sandar	behg sahn-dahr	backpack
beg tangan	behg tah-ngahn	handbag
bekas abu rokok	be-kahs ah-boo ro-ko(k)	ashtray
bekerja [kerja]	be-ker-juh [ker-juh]	to work
bekerja sendiri	be-ker-juh sen-dee-ree	self-employed

Belahlah!	
be-la(h)-la(h)!	Get lost!

belajar [ajar]	be-lah-jahr [ah-jahr]	to learn
belia	be-lee-uh	youth (collective)
belimbing	be-lim-bing	starfruit
belok	be-lo(k)	turn
belum	be-lum	yet
belum lagi	be-lum lah-gee	not yet
belum masak	be-lum mah-sah(k)	unripe
benang	be-nahng	thread
benar	be-nahr	true
bendera	ben-deh-ruh	flag
bentuk	ben-tu(k)	shape
beracun	be-rah-chun	poisonous
berangkat [angkat]	be-rahng-kaht [ahng-kaht]	depart

Berapa?	
be-rah-puh?	How much?
Berapa banyak?	
be-rah-puh bah-nya(k)?	How many? (goods)
Berapa ekor?	
be-rah-puh eh-kor?	How many? (animals)

beras	be-rahs	rice (uncooked)
berasal [asal]	be-rah-sahl [ah-sahl]	to come from (origin)
berat	be-raht	weight • heavy
beratur	be-rah-tur	queue
berawan	be-rah-wahn	cloudy
berbahasa (Melayu)	ber-bah-hah-suh (me-lah-yoo)	to speak (Malay)
berangkat [angkat]	be-rahng-kaht [ahng-kaht]	to take off (depart)
berbeza	ber-beh-zuh	different

B

berburu [buru]	ber-*boo*-roo [*boo*-roo]	to hunt
bercakap [cakap]	ber-*chah*-kahp [*chah*-kahp]	to talk (chat)
berdansa [dansa]	ber-*dahn*-sah [*dahn*-sah]	to dance
berdarah [darah]	ber-*dah*-rah(h) [*dah*-rah(h)]	to bleed
berehat [rehat]	ber-*reh*-haht [reh-*haht*]	to relax • to rest
berenang [renang]	be-re-*nahng* [re-*nahng*]	to swim
berfikir [fikir]	ber-*fee*-kir [*fee*-kir]	to think
bergaduh [gaduh]	ber-gah-*du(h)* [gah-*du(h)*]	to fight
berguling	ber-goo-*ling*	rolling
berguna	ber-*goo*-nuh	useful
berharga	ber-*har*-guh	valuable
berhati-hati	ber-*hah*-tee-*hah*-tee	careful
berhenti [henti]	ber-*hen*-tee [*hen*-tee]	to quit • to stop
berhutang	ber-*hoo*-tahng	to owe
beriman	be-*ree*-mahn	religious
berita	be-*ree*-tuh	news
berjalan kaki	ber-*jah*-lahn kah-*kee*	to walk • to hike
berkabus	ber-*kah*-bus	foggy
berkahwin	ber-*kah(h)*-win	marry
berkata [kata]	ber-*kah*-tuh [*kah*-tuh]	to say
berkeliling	ber-ke-*lee*-ling	tour
berkhayal [khayal]	ber-*khah*-yahl [*khah*-yahl]	to hallucinate
berkhema [khemah]	ber-*keh*-mah(h) [*keh*-mah(h)]	to camp
berkongsi (dengan)	ber-*kong*-see (de-*ngahn*)	to share (with)
berkongsi bilik/dorm	ber-*kong*-see bee-li(k)/dorm	to share a dorm
berlawak [lawak]	ber-lah-*wah(k)* [lah-*wah(k)*]	to joke
berlepas [lepas]	ber-le-*pahs* [le-*pahs*]	to take off (depart)
bermain [main]	ber-*main* [main]	to play (a game, music)
bermalam [malam]	ber-*mah*-lahm [*mah*-lahm]	to stay (overnight)
bermimpi [mimpi]	ber-*mim*-pee [*mim*-pee]	to dream
bernikah	ber-*nee*-kah(h)	to marry
berpeluh [peluh]	ber-pe-*lu(h)* [pe-*lu(h)*]	to perspire
bersama	ber-*sah*-muh	together • with
berselancar [selancar]	ber-se-*lahn*-chahr [se-*lahn*-chahr]	to surf
bersendirian	ber-*sen*-dee-ree-ahn	alone
bersetuju [setuju]	ber-se-*too*-joo [se-*too*-joo]	to agree
bersimpati	ber-sim-*pah*-tee	sympathetic
bertanya [tanya]	ber-*tah*-nyuh [*tah*-nyuh]	to ask a question
bertapis	ber-*tah*-pis	filtered
bertemu [temu]	ber-te-*moo* [te-*moo*]	to meet
berterima kasih	ber-te-*ree*-muh kah-si(h)	to thank
beruntung	be-*roon*-tung	lucky
berus gigi	be-*rus gee*-gee	toothbrush
berus rambut	be-*rus rahm*-but	hairbrush

D I C T I O N A R Y

besar	be-*sahr*	big • large
betina	be-*tee*-nuh	female (animal)
betul	be-*tul*	right (correct)
biadab	bee-*ah*-dahb	vulgar
biara	bee-*ah*-ruh	monastery
biarawan	bee-ah-ruh-*wahn*	monk
biarawati	bee-ah-ruh-*wah*-tee	nun

| *Biarlah.*
bee-*ahr*-lah(h) | | Don't bother. |

Biarlah.	bee-*ahr*-lah(h)	Don't bother
biasa	bee-*ah*-suh	usual • typical
bibir	bee-bir	lips
bijaksana	bee-ja(k)-*sah*-nuh	wise
biji ubat	bee-*jee* oo-*baht*	tablet
bil	bil	bill (account)
bila	bee-luh	when
bila-bila	bee-luh-bee-luh	anytime
bilik	bee-li(k)	cabin • room
bilik air	bee-li(k) air	bathroom
bilik menunggu	bee-li(k) me-*noong*-goo	waiting room
bilik seorang	bee-li(k) se-o-rahng	single room
bilik tidur	bee-li(k) *tee*-dur	bedroom
bilik tukar pakaian	bee-li(k) too-*kahr* pah-kai-*ahn*	changing rooms
bimbang	beem-bahng	worried
binatang	bee-*nah*-tahng	animal
binatang hampir pupus	bee-*nah*-tahng *hahm*-pir poo-*pus*	endangered species
binatang liar/buas	bee-*nah*-tahng lee-*yahr*/boo-ahs	wild animal
bintang	bin-*tahng*	stars (in the sky)
bintang kelahiran	bin-*tahng* ke-lah-*hi*-rahn	zodiac
bir	bir	beer
biru	bee-roo	blue
bising	bee-sing	loud • noisy
bocor	bo-*chor*	leak
bodoh	bo-*do*(h)	idiot • stupid
bogel	bo-*gehl*	nude
bola	bo-luh	ball (for sport)
bola sepak	bo-luh seh-pah(k)	football (soccer)
boleh	bo-*leh*(h)	to be able (can)

| *Boleh.*
bo-*leh*(h) | | Sure. |

(kulit) boneka	(koo-*lit*) bo-neh-*kah*	puppet (leather)
bosan	bo-sahn	bored
bot bermotor	bot ber-*mo*-tor	motorboat
bot	bot	boat
botol	bo-*tol*	bottle • jar

C

botol air	bo-*tol* air	water bottle
buah-buahan	boo-*ah(h)*-boo-*ah*-hahn	fruit
buaian	boo-ai-ahn	hammock
buang air besar	boo-*ahng* air be-*sahr*	to shit
buang air kecil	boo-*ahng* air ke-*chil*	to piss
buat	boo-*aht*	for (purpose)
buatan tangan	boo-*ah*-tahn tah-*ngahn*	handmade
budak	boo-*dah(k)*	child
budak perempuan	boo-*dah(k)* pe-*rem*-pwahn	girl
buka	*boo*-kuh	open
bukan	boo-*kahn*	not
bukit	boo-*kit*	hill
buku	*boo*-koo	book
buku catatan	boo-koo *chah*-tah-tahn	diary • notebook
buku doa	boo-koo do-*ah*	prayer book
buku kembara	boo-koo kem-*bah*-ruh	travel book
buku panduan	boo-koo *pahn*-dwahn	guidebook
buku telefon	boo-koo teh-*leh*-fon	phone book
bulan	*boo*-lahn	moon
bulan (ini)	boo-lahn (*ee*-nee)	(this) month
bulan depan	boo-lahn de-*pahn*	next month
bulan lepas	boo-lahn le-*pahs*	last month
bulan madu	boo-lahn mah-*doo*	honeymoon
bulat	boo-*laht*	round (shape)
(di) bulatan	(dee) boo-*lah*-tahn	(at the) roundabout
bulu biri-biri	boo-*loo* bee-*ree*-bee-*ree*	wool
bumbung	*boom*-bung	roof
bumi	boo-*mee*	earth
bunga	*boo*-nguh	flower
bungkusan	*boong*-ku-sahn	package
bunyi	boo-*nyee*	noise • sound
buruk	boo-*ru(k)*	bad
burung	boo-*rung*	bird
busuk	boo-*su(k)*	rotten
but	boot	boots
but jalan	boot *jah*-lahn	hiking boots
butang	boo-*tahng*	buttons

Bye.		
bai		Goodbye. (inf)

C

cacat	chah-*chaht*	disabled
cadangan	chah-*dah*-ngahn	proposal
cadar	*chah*-dahr	sheet (bed)
cakap	chah-*kahp*	speak
cantik	chahn-*ti(k)*	beautiful • pretty
catur	*chah*-tur	chess

cawan	chah-*wahn*	cup
CD	see dee	CD
cek	chehk	cheque
cek kembara	chehk kem-*bah*-ruh	travellers cheque
cemas	che-*mahs*	nervous
cenderamata	chen-de-ruh-*mah*-tuh	souvenir
cepat	che-*paht*	fast (quick)
cerah	che-*rah(h)*	sunny
cerita	che-*ree*-tuh	story
cermin	cher-*min*	mirror
cermin mata	cher-*min mah*-tuh	glasses (eye)
cermin mata hitam	cher-*min mah*-tuh *hee*-tahm	sunglasses
cerpen	cher-*pehn*	short story
cetakan (karya seni)	cheh-*ta(k)*-kahn (kar-*yah* se-*nee*)	print (artwork)
Cik	chi(k)	Miss
cikgu (col)	*chi(k)*-goo	teacher
cili	*chee*-lee	chilli
cincin	chin-chin	ring (on finger)
cinta	chin-tuh	love
cirit-birit	chi-rit-*bi*-rit	diarrhoea
cium	*chee*-um	kiss
coklat	*chok*-laht	chocolate • brown
comel	cho-*mehl*	cute (baby)
contoh	chon-*to(h)*	example
cuaca	choo-*ah*-chuh	weather
cuak	choo-*ah(k)*	nervous
cucu	choo-choo	grandchild
cukai	choo-*kai*	tax
cukai pendapatan	choo-*kai* pen-dah-*pah*-tahn	income tax
cukai penerbangan	choo-*kai* pe-ner-*bah*-ngahn	airport tax
cukur	choo-kur	to shave
curam	choo-*rahm*	steep (hill)
cuti	choo-tee	vacation • holiday
CV	see vee	resumé

D

dadah	dah-*dah(h)*	drug (illegal)
daerah	dah-*eh*-rah(h)	region
daging	dah-ging	meat
daging babi	dah-ging bah-*bee*	pork • ham
daging lembu	dah-ging *lem*-boo	beef

Dah cukup!		
dah(h) choo-kup!		Enough!

dahaga	dah-*hah*-guh	thirsty
dahsyat	*dah(h)*-shaht	horrible
dahulu	dah-*hoo*-loo	past (before)
dalam	dah-*lahm*	deep • in
damai	dah-*mai*	peace
dan	dahn	and
dapat	dah-*paht*	can (able)
dapur	dah-*pur*	kitchen • stove
darah	*dah*-rah(h)	blood
dari	dah-*ree*	from
daripada	dah-ree-*pah*-duh	from
daripada perak	dah-ree-*pah*-duh peh-*ra(k)*	of silver
darurat	dah-*roo*-raht	emergency
(di) dasar	(dee) dah-*sahr*	(at the) bottom
datang	*dah*-tahng	to come (arrive)
dataran	dah-*tah*-rahn	square
dataran tinggi	dah-*tah*-rahn *teeng*-gee	plateau
datuk	dah-*tu(k)*	grandfather
daun terup	down te-*rup*	playing cards
debunga	de-*boo*-nguh	pollen
dekat	de-*kaht*	near • at
demam	de-*mahm*	fever
demokrasi	deh-mo-*krah*-see	democracy
dengan	de-*ngahn*	with
dengan cepat	de-*ngahn* che-*paht*	quickly
dengan serta-merta	de-*ngahn* ser-*tah*-mer-*tah*	immediately
deodoran	di-o-do-rahn	deodorant
desa	deh-*suh*	village
destinasi	*dehs*-tee-nah-see	destination
dewasa	deh-*wah*-suh	adult
di	dee	at • on (location)
di antara	dee *ahn*-tah-ruh	among
di atas	dee ah-*tahs*	aboard • above • over
di bawah	dee bah-*wah(h)*	below
di belakang	dee be-*lah*-kahng	at the back (behind)
di dalam	dee dah-*lahm*	inside
di depan	dee de-*pahn*	in front of • ahead
di hadapan	dee hah-dah-*pahn*	ahead
di kalangan	dee kah-*lah*-ngahn	among
di samping	dee *sahm*-ping	beside
di sana	dee *sah*-nuh	over there
di sana ada ...	dee *sah*-nuh ah-duh ...	there is/are ...
di sebelah	dee se-be-*lah(h)*	next to
di seberang	dee se-be-*rahng*	over

di sini	dee *see*-nee	here
di situ	dee *see*-too	there (nearby)

Di situ ada ...		
dee *see*-too ah-duh ...		There is/are ...

di tepi	dee te-*pee*	beside
dia	*dee*-uh	he • she
dinding	*deen*-ding	wall (inside)
dingin	dee-*ngin*	cool (temperature)
diperbuat (daripada)	dee-per-*boo*-aht (dah-ree-*pah*-duh)	made (of)
diskaun	*dis*-kown	discount
disko	*dis*-ko	disco
ditinggalkan [tinggal]	dee-*ting*-gahl-kahn [*ting*-gahl]	to be left (behind, over)
doa	do-*ah*	prayer
doktor	*dok*-tor	doctor
doktor gigi	*dok*-tor *gee*-gee	dentist
dokumentari	do-kiu-men-*tah*-ree	documentary
dompet	*dom*-peht	purse
dosa	do-*suh*	sin
dram	drahm	drums
drama	*drah*-mah	play (theatre)
(seni) drama	(se-*nee*) *drah*-mah	drama (arts)
drama sabun	*drah*-mah *sah*-bun	soap opera
dua hari lepas	*doo*-uh hah-ree le-*pahs*	day before yesterday
dua kali	*doo*-uh *kah*-lee	twice
duduk	*doo*-du(k)	to sit
duit	*doo*-it	money
dunia	doo-nee-*uh*	world
duta	doo-*tah*	ambassador

E

(kelas) ekonomi	(ke-*lahs*) ee-ko-*no*-mee	economy (class)
ekor	*eh*-kor	tail (of animal)
eksploitasi	ehks-*ploy*-tah-see	exploitation
elektrik	eh-*lehk*-trik	electricity
emak saudara	e-*mah(k)* sow-*dah*-ruh	aunt
emak	e-*mah(k)*	mother
emas	e-*mahs*	gold
enak	*eh*-nah(k)	tasty
Encik	en-*chi(k)*	Mr
enggan	*eng*-gahn	to refuse
engkau	*eng*-kow	you (inf)
enjin	*ehn*-jin	engine
epal	eh-*puhl*	apple

epilepsi	eh-*pee*-lehp-see	epilepsy
erti	er-*tee*	meaning
esok	eh-so(k)	tomorrow
esok pagi	eh-so(k) *pah*-gee	tomorrow morning

F

faham	fah-*hahm*	to understand
fajar (matahari terbit)	fah-*jahr* (mah-tuh-*hah*-ree ter-*bit*)	dawn (sunrise)
farmasi	*fahr*-mah-see	chemist (pharmacy)
fasih	fah-si(h)	fluent
fikiran	fee-ki-*rahn*	thought
fiksyen	fik-shen	fiction
filem	*fee*-lem	movie • film (camera)
filem pendek	*fee*-lem pehn-*deh(k)*	short film
foto	fo-to	photograph

G

gading	gah-*ding*	ivory
gam	gahm	glue
gam kunyah	gahm koo-*nyah(h)*	chewing gum
gambar	*gahm*-bahr	picture • photograph
gangguan	*gahng*-goo-ahn	harassment
ganja	*gahn*-jah	marijuana
ganjil	*gahn*-jil	strange
garaj	gah-*rahj*	garage
garam	gah-*rahm*	salt
garfu	*gahr*-foo	fork
gatal	gah-*tahl*	itch • horny (col)
gay	geh	gay
gaya	*gah*-yuh	style
gelak	ge-*lah(k)*	laugh
gelansar filem	ge-*lahn*-sahr *fee*-lem	slide (film)
gelap	ge-*lahp*	dark
gemar	ge-mahr	to like
gembira	gem-*bee*-ruh	happy
gemuk	ge-*mu(k)*	fat
gendang	gen-*dahng*	drums
geografi	ji-o-grah-fee	geography
gerai	ge-*rai*	food stall
gereja	ge-*reh*-juh	church
gereja Yahudi	ge-*reh*-juh yah-*hoo*-dee	synagogue
gigi	gee-gee	tooth • teeth
gigitan	gee-gee-tahn	bite (dog, insect)
gila	gee-luh	crazy • delirious

gincu	gin-choo	lipstick
gitar	gee-*tahr*	guitar
gol	gol	goal
goreng	go-*rehng*	fried
gram	grahm	gram
gua	goo-uh	cave
gugur	goo-gur	to fall
gula	goo-luh	sugar
gula-gula	goo-luh-goo-luh	sweets
gunting	goon-ting	scissors
gunung	goo-nung	mountain
gunung berapi	goo-nung be-*rah*-pee	volcano
guru	goo-roo	teacher
gurun pasir	goo-run *pah*-sir	desert

H

haba	hah-*buh*	heat
habis	hah-bis	finished
hadiah	hah-dee-ah(h)	present (gift)
hadiah perkahwinan	hah-dee-ah(h) per-kah-*wi*-nahn	wedding present
haiwan	*hai*-wahn	animal
haiwan terlindung	hai-wahn ter-*leen*-dung	protected species
hajat	hah-*jaht*	to wish
hak asasi manusia	ha(k) ah-*sah*-see mah-*noo*-see-uh	civil rights • human rights
hak sama taraf	hah(k) sah-muh tah-*rahf*	equal opportunity
hakim	hah-*kim*	judge (court)
hamil	hah-*mil*	pregnant
hanya	hah-*nyuh*	only
harga	hahr-guh	price • cost
hari	hah-ree	day
hari Ahad	hah-ree ah-*hahd*	Sunday
hari ini	hah-ree ee-nee	today
hari Isnin	hah-ree ees-nin	Monday
hari jadi/lahir	hah-ree jah-dee/lah-*hir*	birthday
hari Jumaat	hah-ree joo-mah-aht	Friday
hari Khamis	hah-ree kah-*mis*	Thursday
hari Krismas	hah-ree *kris*-muhs	Christmas Day
hari Rabu	hah-ree *rah*-boo	Wednesday
hari Sabtu	hah-ree sahb-too	Saturday
hari Selasa	hah-ree se-*lah*-suh	Tuesday
harian	hah-ree-*ahn*	daily
harimau	hah-ree-mow	tiger
harus	hah-*rus*	must
hasil	hah-sil	result
hasis	hah-sis	hashish

I

hasrat	hahs-raht	to wish
hati	hah-tee	liver
haus	hows	thirsty
helai	he-lai	sheet (of paper)
hendak	hen-da(k)	to want
hendsem	hehnd-sem	handsome (male)
herba	her-bah	herbs
(penagih) heroin	(pe-nah-gi(h)) heh-ro-in	heroin (addict)
hidung	hee-dung	nose
hidup	hee-dup	to live (life) • alive
hijau	hee-jow	green
Hindu	hin-doo	Hindu
hitam	hee-tahm	black
HIV positif	ehch ai vee po-si-tif	HIV positive
homoseksual	ho-mo-sehk-soo-ahl	homosexual
hormat	hor-maht	respect
hospital	hos-pee-tahl	hospital
hospital swasta	hos-pee-tahl swahs-tah	private hospital
hotel	ho-tehl	hotel
hubungan	hoo-bu-ngahn	relationship
hujan	hoo-jahn	rain
hujung minggu	hoo-jung meeng-goo	weekend
hukuman	hoo-ku-mahn	sentence (prison)
huru-hara	hoo-roo-hah-ruh	anarchist
hutan	hoo-tahn	forest
hutan simpan	hoo-tahn sim-pahn	protected forest

I

ibu	ee-boo	mother
ibu bapa	ee-boo bah	parents
ibu mertua	ee-boo mer-too-uh	mother-in-law
idea	ai-deh-ah	idea
ikan	ee-kahn	fish
imigresen	ee-mee-greh-sen	immigration
indah	in-dah(h)	beautiful (scenery) • pretty
informasi	in-for-mah-see	information
ingat	ee-ngaht	to remember
Inggeris	ing-ge-ris	English
ingin	ee-ngin	to want
ini	ee-nee	this
insurans	in-soo-rahns	insurance
istana	ees-tah-nuh	palace
isteri	ees-te-ree	wife
istimewa	ees-tee-meh-wuh	special
itik	ee-ti(k)	duck
itu	ee-too	that
izin	ee-zin	permission

J

jadual perjalanan	jah-*doo*-ahl per-jah-*lah*-nahn	itinerary
jadual waktu	jah-doo-*ahl* wak-too	timetable
jahit	jah-*hit*	to sew
jaket	ja-*keht*	jacket
jalan	*jah*-lahn	avenue • road • street • trail • way
jalan bertol	jah-lahn ber-tol	motorway (tollway)
jalan gunung	jah-lahn *goo*-nung	mountain path
jalan-jalan	jah-lahn-*jah*-lahn	stroll
jalan kecil	jah-lahn ke-*chil*	path • track
jalan keretapi	jah-lahn ke-reh-tah-*ah*-pee	railroad
jalan masuk	jah-lahn mah-su(k)	entrance
jalan pejalan kaki	jah-lahn pe-*jah*-lahn kah-*kee*	footpath
jalan utama	jah-lahn oo-*tah*-muh	road
jam	jahm	clock • hour • watch
jam loceng	jahm *lo*-chehng	alarm clock
jam tangan	jahm tah-*ngahn*	wristwatch
jambatan	*jahm*-bah-tahn	bridge
jangkitan	*jahng*-ki-tahn	infection
janji	*jahn*-jee	promise
jantan	*jahn*-tahn	male (animal)
jantung	*jahn*-tung	heart
jarak	jah-*rah(k)*	distance (length)
jarak panjang	jah-*rah(k)* pahn-jahng	long distance
jarang	jah-*rahng*	rare (uncommon)
jari	*jah*-ree	finger
jarum	*jah*-rum	needle (sewing, syringe)
jarum suntik	*jah*-rum soon-*ti(k)*	syringe
jasa	*jah*-suh	service (assistance)
jatuh	jah-*tuh(h)*	to fall
jauh	jah-*uh(h)*	far
jawapan	jah-*wah*-pahn	reply
jean	jeen	jeans
jenis	je-*nis*	type (of product)
jingga	*jeeng*-gah	orange (colour)
jip	jeep	jeep
jiran	*jee*-rahn	neighbour
johan	*jo*-hahn	winner
jualan murah	joo-*ah*-lahn moo-*ra(h)*	(on) sale
juara	joo-*ah*-ruh	winner
juga	*joo*-guh	also • too
jujur	*joo*-jur	honest

Jum!	Come on!
joom!	

jumlah	joom-*lah(h)*	quantity
jurugambar	joo-roo-*gahm*-bahr	photographer
jurulatih	joo-roo-*lah*-ti(h)	instructor
jururawat	joo-roo-*rah*-waht	nurse
jurutera	joo-roo-te-ruh	engineer
juruwang	joo-roo-*wahng*	cashier
jus	joos	juice
juta	joo-*tuh*	million

K

kaca	*kah*-chuh	glass
kaca depan	*kah*-chuh de-*pahn*	windscreen
kacak	kah-*chah(k)*	handsome (male)
kacang	*kah*-chahng	bean • nut (food)
kad kredit	kahd *kreh*-dit	credit card
kad pengenalan	kahd pe-*nge*-nah-lahn	ID
kad telefon	kahd teh-*leh*-fon	phonecard
kadang-kadang	kah-*dahng*-kah-*dahng*	sometimes
kadar pembayaran	kah-*dahr* pem-bah-*yah*-rahn	rate of pay
kain	kain	material (clothing)
kain lampin	kain *lahm*-pin	nappy
kain pembalut	kain *pem*-bah-lut	bandage
kajipurba	kah-jee-*pur*-buh	archaeological
kakak	kah-*kah(k)*	older sister
kaki	kah-*kee*	foot • leg
kalau	kah-*low*	if
kalian	kah-*lee*-ahn	you (pl)
kambing	*kahm*-bing	goat
(kedai) kamera	(ke-*dai*) ka-me-rah	camera (shop)
kami	*kah*-mee	we (excl)
kampung	*kahm*-pung	village
kamu	kah-*moo*	you (inf)
kamus	*kah*-mus	dictionary
kanan	*kah*-nahn	right (not left)
kanta	kahn-*tuh*	lens
kantung tidur	kahn-*tung tee*-dur	sleeping bag
kapal	*kah*-pahl	ship
kapal terbang	*kah*-pahl *ter*-bahng	aeroplane
kapas	*kah*-pahs	cotton
karya seni	ka-ri-*ah* se-*nee*	artwork
kasar	kah-*sahr*	vulgar
kaset	*kah*-seht	cassette
kaset video	*kah*-seht *vi*-dee-o	video cassette
kasih	kah-*si(h)*	love
kastam	*kahs*-tahm	customs (border)
kasut	*kah*-sut	shoes
kasut but	*kah*-sut boot	boots

katak	kah-tah(k)	frog • toad
katil	kah-til	bed
katil kelamin	kah-til ke-lah-min	double bed
katil kembar	kah-til kem-bahr	twin beds
kaum	kowm	race (breed)
kawan	kah-wahn	friend
kawan-kawan	kah-wahn-kah-wahn	company (friends)
kawasan	kah-wah-sahn	region
kawasan luar bandar	kah-wah-sahn loo-ahr bahn-dahr	countryside
kawasan perkhemahan	kah-wah-sahn per-keh-mah-han	campsite
kaya	kah-yuh	rich (wealthy)
kayu	kah-yoo	puppet (wooden) • wood
ke	ke	to
ke arah	ke ah-rah(h)	toward
keadilan	ke-ah-di-lahn	justice
keagamaan	ke-ah-gah-mah-ahn	religious
kebajikan	ke-bah-ji(k)-kahn	welfare
kebajikan sosial	ke-bah-ji(k)-kahn so-see-ahl	social welfare
kebanggaan [bangga]	ke-bahng-gah-ahn [bahng-guh]	pride
kebenaran	ke-be-nah-rahn	truth
kebiasaan	ke-bee-ah-sah-ahn	habit
kebocoran	ke-bo-cho-rahn	puncture
kebun	ke-bun	garden • farm
kebun botani	ke-bun bo-tah-nee	gardens (botanical)
kecederaan [cedera]	ke-che-de-rah-ahn [che-de-rah]	injury
kecemasan	ke-che-mah-sahn	emergency
kecil	ke-chil	little (small)
kedai	ke-dai	shop
kedai buku	ke-dai boo-koo	bookshop
kedai cenderamata	ke-dai chen-de-ruh-mah-tuh	souvenir shop
kedai dobi	ke-dai do-bee	laundry (shop)
kedai roti	ke-dai ro-tee	bakery
kedai ubat Cina	ke-dai oo-baht chee-nuh	herbalist shop
kedatangan [datang]	ke-dah-tah-ngahn [dah-tahng]	arrivals
kedua	ke-doo-uh	second (in order)
kedua-dua	ke-doo-uh-doo-uh	both
kedutaan	ke-doo-tah-ahn	embassy
keinginan [ingin]	ke-ee-ngi-nahn [ee-ngin]	to wish
kejayaan	ke-jah-yah-ahn	success
keju	keh-joo	cheese
kejutan	ke-joo-tahn	surprise
kek hari jadi	kehk hah-ree jah-dee	birthday cake

272

K

kek lahir	kehk lah-*hir*	birthday cake
kek perkahwinan	kehk per-kah-*wi*-nahn	wedding cake
kekalahan [kalah]	ke-kah-*lah*-hahn [kah-*lah(h)*]	loss
kekasih	ke-*kah*-si(h)	lover
kekuatan	ke-koo-*ah*-tahn	strength
kekurangan	ke-koo-*rah*-ngahn	shortage
kelab (malam)	ke-*lahb* (mah-lahm)	(night)club
kelabu	ke-*lah*-boo	grey
(kelajuan) filem	(ke-*lah*-joo-ahn) *fee*-lem	film (speed)
kelakar	ke-*lah*-kahr	joke • funny
kelapa	ke-*lah*-puh	coconut
kelas kedua	ke-*lahs* ke-*doo*-uh	2nd class
kelas pertama	ke-*lahs* per-*tah*-muh	1st class
kelayakan	ke-lah-*yah(k)*-kahn	qualifications
kelompok	ke-*lom*-po(k)	group
kelengkapan [lengkap]	ke-*leng*-kah-pahn [*leng*-kahp]	equipment
kelewatan	ke-*leh*-wah-tahn	delay
kelmarin lepas	kel-*mah*-rin le-*pahs*	day before yesterday
keluar	ke-*loo*-ahr	exit
keluar bersama	ke-*loo*-ahr ber-*sah*-muh	to go out with
keluarga	ke-*loo*-ahr-guh	family
kemalangan	ke-mah-*lah*-ngahn	accident
kemasukan	ke-mah-*su(k)*-kahn	admission (entry)
kematian	ke-*mah*-tee-ahn	death
kembali	kem-*bah*-lee	return
kembar	kem-*bahr*	twins
kemeja	ke-*meh*-juh	shirt
kemewahan	ke-meh-*wah*-hahn	luxury
kemiskinan	ke-*mees*-ki-nahn	poverty
kemudian	ke-*moo*-dee-ahn	later
kemungkinan	ke-*mung*-ki-nahn	chance
kenal	ke-*nahl*	to know (someone) • to recognise
kenapa	ke-*nah*-puh	why
kencing	ken-*ching*	piss
kencing manis	ken-*ching* mah-*nis*	diabetes
kentang	ken-*tahng*	potato
kentut	ken-*tut*	fart
kenyang	ke-*nyahng*	full (of food)
kepala	ke-*pah*-luh	head
kepanasan [panas]	ke-*pah*-nahs-sahn [*pah*-nahs]	to be hot
kera	ke-*ruh*	monkey
kerajaan	ke-rah-*jah*-ahn	government
keramah-tamahan	ke-rah-*mah(h)*-tah-*mah(h)*-hahn	hospitality
kerana	ke-*rah*-nuh	because

D I C T I O N A R Y

kerani bank	ke-*rah*-nee bank	bank clerk
kerap	ke-*rahp*	often
keras	ke-*rahs*	hard (not soft)
(tempat letak) kereta	(tem-*paht* le-*tah(k)*) ke-*reh*-tuh	car (park)
keretapi	ke-*reh*-tuh-*ah*-pee	train
kerja	*ker*-juh	work
kerongkong	ke-*rong*-kong	throat
kertas	*ker*-tahs	paper
kertas rokok	*ker*-tahs ro-ko*(k)*	cigarette papers
kertas tulis	*ker*-tahs too-lis	writing paper
kerusi	ke-*roo*-see	chair
kerusi beroda	ke-*roo*-see be-*ro*-duh	wheelchair
kesejahteraan	ke-se-*jah(h)*-te-rah-ahn	welfare
kesalahan	ke-*sah*-lah-hahn	mistake
kesan jejak	ke-*sahn* je-*ja(k)*	track (footprints)
kesepuluh	ke-se-*poo*-lu(h)	tenth
kesesatan lalu lintas	ke-se-*sah*-tahn lah-loo-*lin*-tahs	traffic jam
kesilapan	ke-see-lah-*pahn*	mistake
Kesukanan Olimpik	ke-*soo*-kah-nahn o-*lim*-pik	Olympic Games
ketakutan	ke-tah-*ku*-tahn	fear
ketam	ke-*tahm*	crab
ketat	ke-*taht*	tight
ketawa	ke-tah-*wuh*	laugh
ketibaan [tiba]	ke-*tee*-buh-an [*tee*-buh]	arrivals
ketiga	ke-*tee*-guh	third
ketinggian	ke-*teeng*-gee-ahn	altitude
kewarganegaraan	ke-*wahr*-guh-ne-gah-rah-ahn	citizenship
khas	khahs	special
khemah	keh-*mah(h)*	tent
khidmat	*khid*-maht	service (assistance)
khuatir	khoo-*ah*-tir	worried
kicap	kee-*chahp*	soy sauce
kidal	*ki*-dahl	left-handed
kilang	kee-*lahng*	factory
kilogram	*ki*-lo-grahm	kilogram
kilometer	*ki*-lo-mee-ter	kilometre
kini	kee-nee	present (time)
kipas	kee-*pahs*	fan (machine)
kira-kira	kee-ruh-*kee*-ruh	approximately
kiri	*ki*-ree	left (not right)
kita	kee-tuh	we (incl)
kocek	ko-*cheh(k)*	pocket
kodok	ko-do(k)	frog • toad

Malay	Pronunciation	English
kokain	ko-*kehn*	cocaine
kolam renang	ko-*lahm* re-*nahng*	swimming pool
kolej	ko-*lehj*	college
komik	*ko*-mik	comics
kompas	*kom*-pahs	compass
kondom	*kon*-dom	condom
konsert	*kon*-sert	concert
konstipasi	*kons*-tee-pah-see	constipation
kontrasepsi	kon-trah-*sehp*-see	contraceptive
kopi	*ko*-pee	coffee
kos	kos	cost
kosong	*ko*-song	empty • vacant
kotak	ko-*tah(k)*	box (package)
kotak pertolongan	ko-*tah(k)* per-to-*lo*-ngahn	first-aid kit
kotor	ko-*tor*	dirty
kotor kemas	ko-*tor* ke-*mahs*	sleazy (person)
kraftangan	*krahf*-tah-ngahn	handicrafts
kretek	*kreh*-teh(k)	clove cigarettes
krim pelembab	krim pe-*lem*-bahb	moisturising cream
krim pelindung cahaya matahari	krim pe-*leen*-dung chah-*hah*-yuh mah-tah-*hah*-ree	sunblock
kualiti	kwah-lee-*tee*	quality
kuarantin	kwah-*rahn*-teen	quarantine
kuasa	koo-ah-*suh*	power
kuat	koo-*aht*	strong
kubur	koo-*bur*	grave
kucing	koo-*ching*	cat
(penunggangan) kuda	(pe-*nung*-gah-ngahn) koo-duh	horse (riding)
kuil	*koo*-il	temple (Hindu)
kuinin	kui-*nin*	quinine
kuiz	kuiz	game show
kuliah	koo-lee-*ah(h)*	lecture
kulit	*koo*-lit	skin • leather
kulit terbakar	*koo*-lit ter-bah-*kahr*	sunburnt
kumpulan	*koom*-poo-lahn	group (music) • band (music)
kumpulan darah	*koom*-poo-lahn *dah*-rah(h)	blood group
kumpulan rock	*koom*-poo-lahn rok	rock group
kuno	*koo*-no	ancient
kunci	*koon*-chee	key
kuning	*koo*-ning	yellow
kupu-kupu	*koo*-poo-*koo*-poo	butterfly
kurang	*koo*-rahng	less
kurus	*koo*-rus	skinny
kutu	*koo*-too	flea • lice

L

ladang	lah-*dahng*	farm
lagu	lah-*goo*	song • tune
lain	lain	other

| *Lain kali.* | | |
| lain *kah*-lee | Next time. | |

(had) laju	(hahd) lah-*joo*	speed (limit)
lalat	lah-*laht*	fly
lalulintas	lah-loo-*lin*-tahs	traffic
lama	lah-*muh*	long (time) • old
lambat	*lahm*-baht	late (not on time)
lampu	*lahm*-poo	light (electric)
lampu isyarat	*lahm*-poo ee-*shah*-raht	traffic lights
lampu suluh	*lahm*-poo soo-*lu*(h)	torch (flashlight)
langit	lah-*ngit*	sky
langkah	lang-*kah*(h)	step
lanskap	lahns-*kahp*	landscape
lantai	*lahn*-tai	floor (of room)
lapangan terbang	lah-*pah*-ngahn *ter*-bahng	airport
lapar	lah-*pahr*	hungry
lari	lah-*ree*	run
latihan (sukan)	lah-*ti*(h)-hahn (soo-*kahn*)	workout (sport)
laut	lowt	sea
lautan	*low*-tahn	ocean
lawa	lah-*wah*	pretty (adj)
lawak	lah-*wah*(k)	joke • funny
lawan	lah-*wahn*	opposite
layan diri	lah-*yahn* dee-*ree*	self-service
layar	lah-*yahr*	sail
layar perak	lah-*yahr* pe-*rah*(k)	screen (film)
lebar	*leh*-bahr	wide
lebih	le-*bi*(h)	more
lebih baik	le-*bi*(h) bai(k)	better
lebih suka	le-*bi*(h) soo-kuh	to prefer
lelaki	le-*lah*-kee	male • man
lemah	le-*mah*(h)	weak
lembab	*lem*-bahb	humid
lembah	*lem*-bah(h)	valley
lembu	*lem*-boo	cow
lembut	*lem*-but	gentle • soft
lengan	le-*ngahn*	arm (of body)
lensa	*lehn*-sah	lens
lepas	le-*pahs*	ago
lesbian	lehs-*bee*-uhn	lesbian
lesen memandu	leh-*sehn* me-*mahn*-doo	drivers licence
lewat	leh-*waht*	late (not on time)

lidah	lee-*dah(h)*	tongue
lif	lif	lift (elevator)
lihat	lee-*haht*	to see
lilin	lee-lin	candle
limau nipis	lee-mow *nee*-pis	lemon
lisan	lee-*sahn*	oral
logam	lo-*gahm*	metal
lompat	lom-*paht*	jump (across)
loncat	lon-*chaht*	jump (high)
longgar	long-gahr	loose
lori	lo-*ree*	truck
lorong	lo-*rong*	alley • path
luar	loo-ahr	outside
luar biasa	loo-ahr bee-*ah*-suh	unusual
luas	loo-*ahs*	large
luka (kecederaan)	loo-*kuh* (ke-che-de-*rah*-ahn)	wound (injury)
lukisan	loo-*ki*-sahn	painting (picture)
lucu	loo-*choo*	joke • funny
lumpuh kaki	loom-pu(h) kah-*kee*	paraplegic
lumpur	loom-pur	mud
lupa	loo-*puh*	to forget
(garisan) lurus	(gah-*ri*-sahn) loo-*rus*	straight (line)
lusa	loo-suh	day after tomorrow
lutut	loo-*tut*	knee

M

maaf	mah-*ahf*	sorry

Maafkan saya.		
mah-*ahf*-kahn *sai*-yuh		Excuse me.

mabuk	mah-*bu(k)*	to be drunk
mabuk jalan	mah-*bu(k)* jah-lahn	travel sickness
mabuk laut	mah-*bu(k)* lowt	seasick
macam mana	mah-chahm *mah*-nuh	how
mahal	mah-*hahl*	expensive
mahasiswa	mah-*hah*-sis-wah	student (university)
mahkamah	*mah(h)*-kah-mah(h)	court (legal)
mahu	mow	to want
main daun terup	main down te-*rup*	to play cards
main kad	main kahd	to play cards
majalah	mah-jah-*lah(h)*	magazine
majikan	mah-*ji(k)*-kahn	employer
majoriti	mah-*jo*-ree-tee	majority
makan	mah-kahn	eat
makan malam	mah-kahn *mah*-lahm	dinner

makan sayur saja	mah-kahn sah-yur sah-juh	vegetarian
makan tengahari	mah-kahn te-ngah-hah-ree	lunch
makanan	mah-kah-nahn	food
maklumat	mahk-loo-maht	information
makna	mahk-nuh	meaning
maksud	mahk-sud	wish
malam	mah-lahm	night • evening
malam ini	mah-lahm ee-nee	tonight
Malam Krismas	mah-lahm kris-muhs	Christmas Eve
malam semalam	mah-lahm se-mah-lahm	last night
malaria	mah-lah-ree-ah	malaria
malas	mah-lahs	lazy
Malaysia	mah-lay-see-ah	Malaysia
malu	mah-loo	embarrassment • shy
mampu	mahm-poo	can (able)

Mana? mah-nuh?		Where?
mana-mana	mah-nuh-mah-nuh	anywhere
mancis	mahn-chis	matches
mandi	mahn-dee	to bathe/shower • to wash (yourself)
mangga	mang-guh	mango • padlock (col)
manis	mah-nis	sweet (adj)
manuskrip	mah-niu-skrip	script
marah	mah-rah(h)	angry
masa	mah-suh	time
masa depan	mah-suh de-pahn	future
masak	mah-sah(k)	to cook • ripe
masalah	mah-sah-ah-lah(h)	problem
masam	mah-sahm	sour
masih	mah-si(h)	still (yet)
masin	mah-sin	salty
masjid	mahs-jid	mosque
masuk	mah-su(k)	to enter
masyarakat	mah-shah-rah-kaht	society
mata	mah-tuh	eye
matahari	mah-tuh-hah-ree	sun
matahari terbenam	mah-tuh-hah-ree ter-be-nahm	sunset
matahari terbit	mah-tuh-hah-ree ter-bit	sunrise
mati	mah-tee	dead (battery, animal)
mee	mee	noodles

M

meja	*meh*-juh	table
mekanik	me-*ka*-nik	mechanic
mel	mehl	mail
mel biasa	mehl bee-*ah*-suh	surface mail
mel ekspres	mehl ehks-prehs	express mail
mel udara	mehl oo-*dah*-ruh	airmail
melakukan [laku]	me-lah-*koo*-kahn [lah-*koo*]	to do
melaporkan [lapor]	me-lah-*por*-kahn [lah-*por*]	to report
melawat [lawat]	me-lah-*waht* [lah-*waht*]	to visit
melayani [layan]	me-lah-*yah*-nee [lah-*yahn*]	to serve
meletakkan [letak]	me-le-*tah(k)*-kahn [le-*tah(k)*]	to put
melihat [lihat]	me-*lee*-haht [lee-haht]	to look
melihat-lihat saja [lihat]	me-*lee*-haht-*lee*-haht sah-juh [lee-haht]	to go window-shopping
melindungi [lindung]	me-lin-du-ngee [lin-dung]	to protect
melukis	me-*loo*-kis	painting (activity)
memaafkan [maaf]	me-mah-*ahf*-kahn [mah-*ahf*]	to forgive
memakai [pakai]	me-mah-*kai* [pah-*kai*]	to wear
memancing [pancing]	me-*mahn*-ching [*pahn*-ching]	to fish
memandu [pandu]	me-*mahn*-doo	to drive
memangga (col)	me-*mahng*-guh	padlock
membaca [baca]	mem-*bah*-chuh [*bah*-chuh]	to read
membantah [bantah]	mem-*bahn*-tah(h) [*bahn*-tah(h)]	to argue • to protest
membantu [bantu]	mem-*bahn*-too [*bahn*-too]	to help
membatalka [batal]	mem-bah-*tahl*-kah [bah-*tahl*]	to cancel
membawa [bawa]	mem-*bah*-wuh [*bah*-wuh]	to carry • to bring
membayangkan	mem-bah-*yahng*-kahn	imagine
membayar [bayar]	mem-*bah*-yahr [*bah*-yahr]	to pay
membeku [beku]	mem-be-koo [be-koo]	to freeze
membeli [beli]	mem-be-*lee* [be-*lee*]	to buy
membeli-belah [beli]	mem-be-*lee*-be-*lah(h)* [be-*lee*]	to go shopping
membenarkan	mem-be-*nahr*-kahn	to allow
memberahikan [berahi]	mem-be-*rah*-hee-kahn [be-*rah*-hee]	sexy
memberi [beri]	mem-be-*ree* [be-*ree*]	to give
memberitahu [tahu]	mem-be-*ree*-tah-hoo [tah-hoo]	to tell (inform)
membersihkan [bersih]	mem-ber-*si(h)*-kahn [ber-*si(h)*]	to clean
membina [bina]	mem-*bee*-nuh [*bee*-nuh]	to build
membuat [buat]	mem-*boo*-aht [*boo*-aht]	to make • to do
membuat tempahan	mem-*boo*-aht tem-pah-hahn	to make a booking
membuka [buka]	mem-*boo*-kuh [*boo*-kuh]	to open
membunuh [bunuh]	mem-*boo*-nuh(h) [boo-*nuh(h)*]	to kill
memeriksa [periksa]	me-me-*rik*-sah [pe-*rik*-sah]	to check
memikirkan diri sendiri saja	me-mee-*kir*-kahn dee-*ree* sen-dee-*ree* sah-juh	selfish

memilih [pilih]	me-*mee*-li(h) [*pee*-li(h)]	to choose
meminjam [pinjam]	me-*min*-jahm [*pin*-jahm]	to borrow
meminta [minta]	me-*min*-tuh [*min*-tuh]	to ask for something
memisahkan [pisah]	me-mee-*sah*(h)-kahn [pee-*sah*(h)]	to separate
memotong [potong]	me-*mo*-tong [*po*-tong]	to cut
memperbaiki [baik]	mem-per-*bai*-kee	to repair
memulai [mula]	me-moo-*lah*-ee [moo-*luh*]	to kick off
memulakan [mula]	me-moo-*lah*-kahn [moo-*luh*]	to start
mempunyai [punya]	mem-*poo*-nyah-ee [*poo*-nyah]	to have
memutuskan [putus]	me-moo-*tus*-kahn [poo-*tus*]	to decide
menafikan [nafi]	me-nah-*fee*-kahn [nah-*fee*]	to deny
menaiki [naik]	me-*nai*(k)-kee [*nai*(k)]	to ride (horse, bus, bike)
menaip [taip]	me-*naip* (taip)	to type
menandatangani [tandatangan]	me-nahn-duh-*tah*-ngah-nee [tahn-duh-*tah*-ngahn]	to sign
menang	me-*nahng*	to win
menara	me-*nah*-ruh	tower
menarik	me-*nah*-ri(k)	interesting
menarik [tarik]	me-*nah*-ri(k) [*tah*-ri(k)]	to pull
mencampurkan [campur]	men-cham-*pur*-kahn [*chahm*-pur]	to mix
mencari [cari]	men-*chah*-ree [*chah*-ree]	to look for • to search
mencegah	men-che-*gah*(h)	prevent
mencium [cium]	men-*chee*-um [*chee*-um]	to kiss
mencuba [cuba]	men-*choo*-buh [*choo*-buh]	to try (attempt)
mencuci [cuci]	men-*choo*-chee [*choo*-chee]	to wash (something) • to develop (film)
mencuri [curi]	men-*choo*-ree [*choo*-ree]	to steal
mendaki gunung	men-*dah*-kee *goo*-nung	mountaineering
mendalam	men-*dah*-lahm	intense
mendapat [dapat]	men-*dah*-paht [*dah*-paht]	to earn
mendayung	men-*dah*-yung	to row
mendengar [dengar]	men-de-*ngahr* [de-*ngahr*]	to hear • to listen
menderita [derita]	men-de-*ree*-tuh [de-*ree*-tuh]	to suffer
mendesak	men-de-*sah*(k)	urgent
mendidik [didik]	men-dee-*di*(k) [dee-*di*(k)]	to educate
mendung	*men*-dung	cloudy
meneka [teka]	me-ne-*kuh* [te-*kuh*]	to guess
menelefon [telefon]	me-neh-*leh*-fon [teh-*leh*-fon]	to telephone
menemani	me-ne-*mah*-nee	to accompany
menembak [tembak]	me-*nehm*-bah(k) [*tehm*-bah(k)]	to shoot
menempah [tempah]	me-*nehm*-pah(h) [*tehm*-pah(h)]	to order
menentang	me-nen-*tahng*	against (opposed)
menerima [terima]	me-ne-*ree*-muh [te-*ree*-muh]	to accept • to receive

mengadu [adu]	me-ngah-doo [ah-doo]	to complain
mengajar	me-ngah-jahr	teaching
mengakhiri [akhir]	me-ngah-khi-ree [ah-khir]	to end
mengambil [ambil]	me-ngahm-bil [ahm-bil]	to pick up • to take away
mengambil foto/gambar	me-ngahm-bil fo-to/ gahm-bahr	to take photographs
mengandung	me-ngahn-dung	to be pregnant
mengantuk	me-ngahn-tu(k)	sleepy
mengapa	me-ngah-puh	why
mengatur [atur]	me-ngah-tur [ah-tur]	to organise
mengejek	me-ngeh-jeh(k)	to make fun of
mengeksport [eksport]	me-ngehks-port [ehks-port]	to export
mengakui [akui]	me-ngah-koo-ee [ah-koo-ee]	to recognise
mengembara	me-ngem-bah-ruh	to travel
mengerikan [ngeri]	me-nge-ree-kahn [nge-ree]	terrible • horrible
mengeringkan [kering]	me-nge-ring-kahn [ke-ring]	to dry
mengesahkan [sah]	me-nge-sah(h)-kahn [sah(h)]	to confirm (a booking)
mengesyorkan [syor]	me-nge-shor-kahn [shor]	to recommend
mengganggu [ganggu]	meng-gahng-goo [gahng-goo]	to annoy
menggigit [gigit]	meng-gee-git [gee-git]	to bite
menggunakan kembali	meng-goo-nah-kahn kem-bah-lee	to recycle
menghantar [hantar]	meng-hahn-tahr [hahn-tahr]	to send
menghasilkan [hasil]	meng-hah-sil-kahn [hah-sil]	to produce
menghiburkan [hibur]	meng-hee-bur-kahn [hee-bur]	entertaining
menghidu [hidu]	meng-hee-doo [hee-doo]	to smell
menghilangkan [hilang]	meng-hee-lahng-kahn [hee-lahng]	to lose (something)
menghiris [hiris]	meng-hee-ris [hee-ris]	to slice
menghukum [hukum]	meng-hoo-kum [hoo-kum]	to punish
mengikuti [ikut]	me-ngee-ku-tee [ee-kut]	to follow (join in)
mengira [kira]	me-ngee-ruh [kee-ruh]	to count
mengisi [isi]	me-ngee-see [ee-see]	to fill
mengizinkan	me-ngee-zin-kahn	to allow
mengkagumkan	meng-kah-gum-kahn	wonderful
mengulangi [ulang]	me-ngoo-lah-ngee [oo-lahng]	repeat
mengunci [kunci]	me-ngun-chee [koon-chee]	to lock
mengundi [undi]	me-ngun-dee [un-dee]	to vote
mengunjungi [kunjung]	me-ngoon-ju-ngee [koon-jung]	to visit
mengurat	me-ngoo-rut	to chat up
mengurut [urut]	me-ngoo-rut [oo-rut]	to massage
menikmati [nikmat]	me-nik-mah-tee [nik-maht]	to enjoy (oneself)

menimbang [timbang]	me-*nim*-bahng [*tim*-bahng]	to weigh
meninggal [tinggal]	me-*ning*-gahl [*ting*-gahl]	to die (person)
meninggal dunia	me-*ning*-gahl doo-ni-uh	dead (person)
menipu [tipu]	me-*nee*-poo [*tee*-poo]	to lie
menjaga [jaga]	men-*jah*-guh [*jah*-guh]	to look after
menjawab [jawab]	men-*jah*-wahb [*jah*-wahb]	to reply • to answer
menjerit [jerit]	men-je-*rit* [je-*rit*]	to shout
menjual [jual]	men-joo-*ahl* [joo-*ahl*]	to sell
menjumpai [jumpa]	men-*joom*-pah-ee [*joom*-pah]	to find
menolak [tolak]	me-no-*lah(k)* [to-*lah(k)*]	to refuse
menolong [tolong]	me-*no*-long [*to*-long]	to help
menonton [tonton]	me-*non*-ton [*ton*-ton]	to watch
mensyempu [syempu]	men-*shehm*-poo [shem-*poo*]	to shampoo
mentah	men-*tah(h)*	raw (food)
mentega	men-*teh*-guh	butter
menterjemahkan [terjemah]	men-ter-je-*mah(h)*-kahn [ter-je-*mah(h)*]	to translate
(rokok) mentol	(ro-ko(k)) *mehn*-tol	menthol (cigarettes)
mentul	*mehn*-tul	light bulb
menu	*meh*-noo	menu
menukar [tukar]	me-*noo*-kahr [*too*-kahr]	to change
menulis [tulis]	me-*noo*-lis [*too*-lis]	to write
menumpang	me-*noom*-pahng	to hitchhike
menunggang [tunggang]	me-*noong*-gahng [*toong*-gahng]	to ride (bus, car, plane, train)
menunjukkan [tunjuk]	me-*noon*-joo(k)-kahn [*toon*-joo(k)]	to show
menutup [tutup]	me-*noo*-tup [*too*-tup]	to close
menyakitkan	me-*nyah*-*kit*-kahn	painful
menyanyi [nyanyi]	me-*nyah*-nyee [*nyah*-nyee]	to sing
menyedari [sedar]	me-nye-*dah*-ree [se-*dahr*]	to realise
menyediakan [sedia]	me-nye-dee-*ah*-kahn [se-dee-*uh*]	to prepare
menyelam [selam]	me-nye-*lahm* [se-*lahm*]	to dive
menyelamatkan [selamat]	me-nye-*lah*-maht-kahn [se-*lah*-maht]	to save
menyentuh [sentuh]	me-nyen-*tu(h)* [sen-*tu(h)*]	to touch
menyesal [sesal]	me-nye-*sahl* [se-*sahl*]	to regret
menyewa [sewa]	me-*nyeh*-wuh [*seh*-wuh]	to hire (rent)
menyuntikkan [suntik]	me-nyun-*ti(k)*-kahn [sun-*ti(k)*]	to inject
merah	*meh*-rah(h)	red
merah jambu	*meh*-rah(h) jahm-boo	pink
merasuah	me-rah-soo-*ah(h)*	to bribe
merayakan [raya]	me-*rah*-yuh-kahn [*rah*-yuh]	to celebrate
mereka	me-*reh*-kuh	they

merindui [rindu]	me-*rin*-doo-ee [*rin*-doo]	to miss (feel absence)
merokok [rokok]	me-ro-ko(k) [*ro*-ko(k)]	to smoke
merompak [rompak]	me-rom-*pa(k)* [rom-*pa(k)*]	to rob
mesin	me-*sin*	machine
mesin basuh	me-*sin* bah-su(h)	washing machine
mesti	mes-tee	must
mesyuarat	me-*shoo* ah-raht	meeting
meter	*mee*-ter	metre
migraine	*mai*-grehn	migraine
milimeter	mi-li-*mee*-ter	millimetre
minggu	*ming*-goo	week
minggu depan	*ming*-goo de-*pahn*	next week
minggu ini	*ming*-goo ee-nee	this week
minggu lepas	*ming*-goo le-*pahs*	last week
minit	*mi*-nit	minute
minum	*mee*-num	to drink
minuman	mee-nu-*mahn*	drink
minyak	*min*-yah(k)	petrol
minyak masak	*min*-yah(k) *mah*-sah(k)	oil (cooking)
misalan	mi-*sah*-lahn	example
miskin	*mis*-kin	poor
modem	mo-*dem*	modem
mogok	mo-*go(k)*	(on) strike
monyet	mo-*nyeht*	monkey
motosikal	mo-to-*see*-kahl	motorcycle
mual	*moo*-ahl	nausea
muda	*moo*-duh	young
mudah	*moo*-dah(h)	easy
muka	*moo*-kuh	face
mulakan	*moo*-luh-kahn	to begin
mulut	*moo*-lut	mouth
munasabah	moo-*nah*-sah-bah(h)	sensible
mungkin	*moong*-kin	maybe • perhaps
muntah	moon-*tah(h)*	vomit • to vomit
murah	*moo*-rah(h)	cheap
murah hati	moo-*rah(h)* hah-tee	generous
murid	*moo*-rid	student (school)
murni	*moor*-nee	pure
musim	*moo*-sim	season
musim bunga	*moo*-sim *boo*-nguh	spring (season)
musim luruh	*moo*-sim *loo*-ru(h)	autumn
musim panas	*moo*-sim *pah*-nahs	summer
musim sejuk	*moo*-sim se-*joo(k)*	winter
mutu	*moo*-too	quality
muzik	*moo*-zik	music
muzium	moo-*zee*-um	museum

N

naik	nai(k)	to board (ship, etc)
(jalan) naik bukit	(jah-lahn) nai(k) boo-kit	uphill (road)
nama	nah-muh	name
nama keluarga	nah-muh ke-loo-ahr-guh	surname
nama panggilan	nah-muh pang-gi-lahn	nickname
nama pertama	nah-muh per-tah-muh	first name
nanas	nah-nahs	pineapple
nanti	nahn-tee	later
naskhah	nahs-kah(h)	script
nasi	nah-see	rice (cooked)
nasib	nah-sib	luck
negara	ne-gah-ruh	country
nenas	neh-nahs	pineapple
nenek	neh-neh(k)	grandmother
nilai	nee-lai	value (price) • worth
nipis	nee-pis	thin
nombor	nom-bor	number
novel	no-vel	novel (book)
nyamuk (kelambu)	nyah-mu(k) (ke-lahm-boo)	mosquito (net)
nyaris-nyaris	nyah-ris-nyah-ris	almost

O

offside	of-said	offside
OK	oh-kay	OK
oksigen	ok-see-jen	oxygen
olahraga	o-lah(h)-rah-guh	track (sports)
ombak	om-bah(k)	waves
operasi	o-pe-rah-see	operation
operator (telefon)	o-pe-reh-tor (teh-leh-fon)	(telephone) operator
orang	o-rahng	person • people
orang asing	o-rahng ah-sing	foreigner
orang barat	o-rahng bah-raht	Westerner (col)
orang Eropah	o-rahng eh-ro-pah(h)	European
orang gaji	o-rahng gah-jee	servant
orang Islam	o-rahng ees-lahm	Muslim
orang suci	o-rahng soo-chee	saint
orang tua	o-rahng too-uh	parents
orang yang tidak dikenali	o-rahng yahng tee-dah(k) dee-ke-nah-lee	stranger
oren	o-rehn	orange (food, colour)
orgasma	or-gahs-mah	orgasm
orkestra	or-kehs-truh	orchestra
otak	o-tah(k)	brain
otot	o-tot	muscle

P

pada	pah-*duh*	at (time)
pada waktu tengahari	pah-*duh wahk*-too te-ngah-*hah*-ree	in the afternoon
padang pasir	pah-dahng pah-*sir*	desert
padang tenis	pah-dahng teh-*nis*	tennis court
paderi	pah-de-*ree*	priest (Catholic, Protestant)
(yang) paling	(yahng) pah-*ling*	most (the)
pagi	pah-gee	morning
pagi semalam	pah-gee se-*mah*-lahm	yesterday morning
paip	paip	pipe (plumbing)
pakar	pah-*kahr*	specialist
(kedai) pakaian	(ke-*dai*) pah-*kai*-ahn	clothing (store)
paku kayu	pah-*koo* kah-*yoo*	tent pegs
paling penting	pah-ling *pen*-ting	essential
pam	pahm	pump
pameran	pah-*meh*-rahn	exhibition
panas	pah-nahs	hot (temperature) • heat
pancang khemah	pahn-*chahng* kheh-*mah(h)*	tent pegs
panggang	pahng-gahng	roasted
panggung sandiwara	pahng-gung sahn-dee-*wah*-rah	theatre (play)
panggung wayang	pahng-gung *wai*-yahng	cinema
panjang	pahn-jahng	long (measurement) • length
pantai	pahn-tai	beach
pantas	pahn-*tahs*	quick • quickly
papan kekunci	pah-*pahn* ke-*koon*-chee	keyboard
papan markah	pah-*pahn* mahr-*kah(h)*	scoreboard
papan mata	pah-*pahn* mah-tuh	scoreboard
papan selancar	pah-*pahn* se-*lahn*-chahr	surfboard
parlimen	pahr-lee-men	parliament
parti	pahr-tee	party (political)
pas naik	pahs nai(k)	boarding pass
pasar (malam)	pah-sahr (*mah*-lahm)	(night) market
pasaraya	pah-sah-*rah*-yuh	supermarket
pasir	pah-*sir*	sand
(nombor) pasport	(*nom*-bor) pahs-port	passport (number)
pasukan	pah-*su(k)*-kahn	team (sport)
patah	pah-*tah(h)*	broken
patung	pah-tung	statue
payung	pah-yung	umbrella
pecah	pe-chah	break (fracture)
pedang	pe-dahng	sword
pedas	pe-dahs	hot (spicy)
pegas	pe-gahs	spring (coil)

pegawai pengawas stesen keretapi	pe-ngah-wahs steh-sehn ke-reh-tah-ah-pee	stationmaster
peguam	pe-gwahm	lawyer
pejabat maklumat pelancong	pe-jah-baht mah(k)-loo-maht pe-lahn-chong	tourist information office
pejabat pos	pe-jah-baht pos	post office
pejabat tiket	pe-jah-baht tee-keht	ticket office
pejalan kaki	pe-jah-lahn kah-kee	pedestrian
pekak	pe-kah(k)	deaf
pekerja	pe-ker-juh	employee
pekerja pejabat	pe-ker-juh pe-jah-baht	office worker
pekerjaan	pe-ker-jah-ahn	job • occupation
pelabuhan	pe-lah-bu-hahn	port • harbour
pelacur	pe-lah-chur	prostitute
pelajar	pe-lah-jahr	student (school)
pelan	pe-lahn	plan
pelancong [lancong]	pe-lahn-chong [lahn-chong]	tourist
pelarian	pe-lah-ree-ahn	refugee
pelayan	pe-lah-yahn	waiter
pelepasan	pe-le-pah-sahn	departure
pelik	pe-li(k)	strange
peluang	pe-loo-ahng	chance
peluk	pe-lu(k)	hug
pelukis	pe-loo-kis	painter (artist)
pelukis potret	pe-loo-kis po-treht	portrait sketcher
pemain	pe-main	player
pemain muzik	pe-main moo-zik	musician
pemain sukan	pe-main soo-kahn	sportsplayer
pemakaman	pe-mah-kah-mahn	funeral
pemenang	pe-me-nahng	winner
pemandangan [pandang]	pe-mahn-dah-ngahn [pahn-dahng]	scenery • view
pemandu	pe-mahn-doo	guide (person, audio)
pembasmi kuman	pem-bahs-mee koo-mahn	antiseptic
pemberian [beri]	pem-be-ree-ahn [be-ree]	present (gift)
pembuka botol	pem-boo-kuh bo-tol	bottle opener
pembuka tin	pem-boo-kuh tin	can opener
pemeriksaan kembali	pe-me-rik-sah-ahn kem-bah-lee	review
pemetik api	pe-me-ti(k) ah-pee	lighter
pemilik	pe-mee-li(k)	owner
pemimpin [pimpin]	pe-meem-pin [peem-pin]	leader
pemungut tiket	pe-moo-ngut tee-keht	ticket collector
pen	pehn	pen
(penagih) heroin	(pe-nah-gi(h)) heh-ro-in	heroin (addict)

penanaman hutan semula	pe-nah-*nah*-mahn hoo-*tahn* se-*moo*-luh	reforestation
penangguhan	pe-*nahng*-gu-hahn	delay
penat	pe-*naht*	tired
pencacaran	pen-chah-*chah*-rahn	vaccination
pencemaran	pen-che-*mah*-rahn	pollution
pencuri	pen-choo-*ree*	thief
(kaunter) pendaftaran	(*kown*-ter) pen-*dahf*-tah-rahn	check-in (desk)
pendakian tebing batu	pen-dah-*kee*-ahn te-*bing* bah-*too*	rock climbing
pendapat	pen-*dah*-paht	opinion
pendek	*pehn*-deh(k)	short (length, height)
pendidikan	pen-dee-*di*(k)-kahn	education
pendingin udara	pen-*dee*-ngin oo-*dah*-ruh	air-conditioner
penebangan hutan	pe-ne-*bah*-ngahn hoo-*tahn*	deforestation
penerbangan	pe-ner-*bah*-ngahn	flight
penerbit [terbit] (filem)	pe-*ner*-bit [*ter*-bit] (*fee*-lem)	producer (of film)
pengadil	pe-*ngah*-dil	referee
penganggur	pe-*ngahng*-gur	homeless • unemployed
penganut Buda	pe-*ngah*-nut boo-duh	Buddhist
pengarah (filem)	pe-*ngah*-rah(h) (*fee*-lem)	director (of film)
pengembalian wang	pe-ngem-*bah*-lee-ahn wahng	to refund
pengembaraan [kembara]	pe-ngem-*bah*-ruh-ahn [kem-*bah*-ruh]	to trek
pengemis	pe-*nge*-mis	beggar
pengenalan	pe-*nge*-nah-lahn	identification
pengguguran	peng-goo-*goo*-rahn	abortion
penggunting rambut	peng-*gun*-ting *rahm*-but	barber
penghibur jalanan	*peng*-hi-bur *jah*-lah-nahn	busker
penginapan	pe-*ngee*-nah-pahn	accommodation
pengsan	*pehng*-sahn	to faint
pengurus	pe-*ngoo*-rus	manager
pening	pe-*ning*	dizzy
Penipu!	pe-nee-*pool*	Cheat!
penjaga anak	pen-*jah*-guh ah-nah(k)	babysitter
penjaga gol	pen-*jah*-guh gol	goalkeeper
penjagaan anak	pen-jah-*gah*-ahn ah-nah(k)	childminding
penjara	pen-*jah*-ruh	prison
penjual dadah	pen-joo-*ahl* dah-*dah*(h)	drug dealer
penjuru	*pen*-joo-roo	corner
pensyarah	pen-shah-*rah*(h)	lecturer
pentas	pen-*tahs*	stage

penting	pen-ting	important • urgent
penuh	pe-nuh(h)	full
penuh sesak	pe-nuh(h) se-sa(k)	crowded
penulis	pe-noo-lis	writer
penumpang	pe-noom-pahng	passenger
penyakit	pe-nyah-kit	disease
penyakit berak darah	pe-nyah-kit beh-ra(k) dah-rah(h)	dysentery
penyakit kelamin	pe-nyah-kit ke-lah-min	venereal disease
penyakit sengal-sengal tulang	pe-nyah-kit se-ngahl-se-ngahl too-lahng	rheumatism
penyampai	pe-nyahm-pai	presenter (TV, etc)
penyampaian [sampai]	pe-nyahm-pai-ahn [sahm-pai]	presentation
penyanyi	pe-nyah-nyee	singer
penyeluk saku	pe-nye-lu(k) sah-koo	pickpocket
penyembahan	pe-nyem-bah(h)-hahn	worship
penyokong [sokong]	pe-nyo-kong [so-kong]	fan (of a team)
penyunting	pe-nyun-ting	editor
perak	peh-ra(k)	silver
perahu	pe-rah-hoo	boat
perang	pe-rahng	war
perasaan [rasa]	pe-rah-sah-ahn [rah-suh]	feelings
peraturan	pe-rah-tu-rahn	rules
perayaan	pe-rah-yah-ahn	festival
percaya	per-chah-yuh	to trust
percintaan	per-chin-tah-ahn	romance
percuma	per-choo-muh	free (of charge)
perdana menteri	per-dah-nuh men-te-ree	prime minister
perempuan	pe-rem-pwahn	female (human) • woman
pergaduhan	per-gah-du(h)-hahn	fight
pergi	per-gee	to go
(tiket) pergi balik	(tee-keht) per-gee bah-li(k)	return (ticket)

Pergilah!	per-gee-la(h)!	Get lost!

pergunungan	per-goo-nu-ngahn	mountain range
perhentian bas	per-hen-tee-ahn bahs	bus stop
perhimpunan	per-him-pu-nahn	rally (demonstration)
peribadi	pe-ree-bah-dee	personality • private
periuk	pe-ree-u(k)	pot (cooking)
perjalanan	per-jah-lah-nahn	trip • journey
perjalanan [jalan]	per-jah-lah-nahn [jah-lahn]	to trek
perkahwinan	per-kah(h)-wi-nahn	marriage
pernikahan	per-nee-kah(h)-hahn	wedding
perkataan	per-kah-tah-ahn	word

Malay	Pronunciation	English
perlahan	per-*lah*-hahn	slow
perlu	per-*loo*	need
perlumbaan	per-*loom*-bah-ahn	race (sport)
permaidani	per-*mai*-dah-nee	rug
permainan	per-*mai*-nahn	game (board game, sport)
permainan komputer	per-*mai*-nahn kom-*piu*-ter	computer game
permit	per-*mit*	permit
permit kerja	per-*mit* ker-juh	work permit
pernah	per-*nah(h)*	already
perniagaan	per-nee-ah-*gah*-ahn	business
pernikahan	per-nee-*kah(h)*-hahn	wedding
perogolan [rogol]	pe-ro-*go*-lahn [ro-*gohl*]	rape
perpustakaan	per-poos-*tah*-kah-ahn	library
persatuan	per-sah-*too*-ahn se-*ker*-juh	unions
persendirian	per-sen-dee-*ree*-ahn	private
persimpangan	per-*sim*-pah-ngahn	intersection
pertama	per-*tah*-muh	first
pertanyaan	per-*tah*-nyuh-ahn	question
pertemuan	per-te-*moo*-ahn	meeting
pertolongan	per-*to*-lo-ngan	assistance
(kadar) pertukaran	(kah-*dahr*) per-too-*kah*-rahn	exchange (rate)
pertunjukan [tunjuk]	per-toon-*joo(k)*-kahn [toon-*joo(k)*]	performance • show
perut	pe-*rut*	stomach
pesanan	pe-*sah*-nahn	message
pesara	pe-*sah*-ruh	pensioner
pesta	*pehs*-tuh	party (fiesta)
peta	pe-*tah*	map
peta jalan	pe-*tah* jah-lahn	road map
petang	pe-*tahng*	afternoon
petang esok	pe-*tahng* eh-so(k)	tomorrow afternoon
petang ini	pe-*tahng* ee-nee	this afternoon
petang semalam	pe-*tahng* se-*mah*-lahm	yesterday afternoon
petani	pe-*tah*-nee	farmer
peti besi	pe-*tee* be-*see*	safe (vault)
peti sejuk	pe-*tee* se-*ju(k)*	refrigerator
petrol	*peh*-trol	petrol
Piala Dunia	pee-*ah*-luh doo-ni-*uh*	World Cup
pidato politik	pee-*dah*-to po-*lee*-tik	political speech
pil	pil	pill
pilihanraya	pee-lee-*hahn*-rah-yuh	elections
pinggan	*ping*-gahn	plate
pinggang	*ping*-gahng	back (of body)
pinggir bandar	*ping*-gir *bahn*-dahr	suburb
pinggir laut	*ping*-gir lowt	coast
ping-pong	ping-*pong*	table tennis
pintu	*peen*-too	door

pintu masuk	*peen*-too mah-*su(k)*	entrance
pisang	*pee*-sahng	banana
pisau	*pee*-sow	knife
pisau cukur	*pee*-sow *choo*-kur	razor
pisau lipat	*pee*-sow *lee*-paht	penknife
planet	*plah-neht*	planet
plastik	*plahs*-tik	plastic
plug	pluhg	plug (electricity)
PMS	pee em es	premenstrual tension
pohon	*po*-hon	tree
poker	*po*-ker	poker (the game)
poket	*po-keht*	pocket
pokok	*po*-ko(k)	tree
polis	*po*-lis	police
pondok	pon-*do(k)*	mountain hut
popular	po-*piu*-luhr	popular
poskad	pos-*kahd*	postcard
poskod	pos-*kod*	postcode
poster	*pos*-ter	poster
potong	*po*-tong	piece
presiden	preh-*see*-den	president
projektor	pro-*jehk*-tor	projector
Puan	pwahn	Mrs
puisi	poo-*ee*-see	poetry
pulang	poo-*lahng*	to go home
pulau	poo-*low*	island
pun	pun	also • too
puncak	poon-chah(k)	peak (of mountain)
purba	*pur*-buh	ancient
purse	puhrs	purse
pusat membeli-belah	poo-*saht* mem-be-*lee*-be-*lah(h)*	department stores
pusing	poo-sing	turn
pusingan	poo-*si*-ngahn	leg (of a race)
putih	poo-ti(h)	white

radiator	rah-*dee*-ah-tor	radiator
rakaman	rah-*kah*-mahn	recording
raket	rah-*keht*	racquet
ramah-tamah	rah-*mah(h)*-tah-*mah(h)*	outgoing
ramai	rah-*mai*	busy (place, party)
rambut	rahm-but	hair
rancangan	rahn-*chah*-ngahn	program (TV)
rantai	rahn-tai	necklace
rasa	rah-suh	taste
rasisme	rah-*sis*-muh	racism

rehat	reh-*haht*	rest (relaxation)
rendah	ren-*dah(h)*	low
rentak	ren-*tah(k)*	rhythm
republik	ree-*puhb*-lik	republic
resit	re-*sit*	receipt
restoran	rehs-*to*-rahn	restaurant
resume	reh-siu-*meh*	resumé
ribut	ree-*but*	storm
ringan	ri-*ngahn*	light (not heavy)
risau	ree-*sow*	worried
risiko	ree-*see*-ko	risk
roda	ro-*duh*	wheel
(kertas) rokok	(ker-*tahs*) ro-ko(k)	cigarette (papers)
rosak	ro-*sah(k)*	rotten
roti	ro-tee	bread
roti bakar	ro-tee *bah*-kahr	toast (bread)
ruam	roo-*ahm*	rash
ruam bayi	roo-*ahm bah*-yee	nappy rash
ruang	roo-*ahng*	space (area)
ruang tamu	roo-*ahng tah*-moo	lounge (room)
rumah	roo-*mah(h)*	house
rumput	*room*-put	grass
runtuhan	run-*tu*-hahn	ruins
runtuhan bersejarah	run-*tu*-hahn ber-se-*jah*-rah(h)	historical ruins
rusa	roo-*suh*	deer

S

saat	sah-*aht*	second (unit of time)
sabar	sah-*bahr*	patient (adj)
sabun	sah-*bun*	soap
sains	sains	science
saintis	sain-tis	scientist
saiz	saiz	size
sajak	sah-*jah(k)*	poetry
sakit	sah-kit	sick • pain
sakit gigi	sah-kit *gee*-gee	toothache
sakit haid	sah-kit haid	period pain
sakit kepala	sah-kit ke-*pah*-luh	headache
sakit lelah	sah-kit le-*lah(h)*	asthma
sakit perut	sah-kit pe-*rut*	indigestion • stomachache
saku	sah-*koo*	pocket
salah	sah-*lah(h)*	wrong
salah faham	sah-*lah(h)* fah-*hahm*	misunderstanding
sama	sah-muh	same

sambil	sahm-bil	while (currently)
sampah	sahm-pah(h)	rubbish
sampai	sahm-pai	to arrive
sampan	sahm-pahn	boat
sampul surat	sahm-pul soo-raht	envelope
sangat	sah-ngaht	very • intense
sangat baik	sah-ngaht bai(k)	excellent
sangat lemak	sah-ngaht le-mah(k)	rich (food)
sangat ulung	sah-ngaht oo-lung	excellent
sarapan pagi	sah-rah-pahn pah-gee	breakfast
sarung bantal	sah-rung bahn-tahl	pillowcase
satu saja	sah-too sah-juh	just one
sawan babi	sah-wahn bah-bee	epilepsy
saya	sai-yuh	I
sayang	sah-yahng	love
sayap	sah-yahp	wings
sayap kanan	sah-yahp kah-nahn	right-wing
sayap kiri	sah-yahp ki-ree	left-wing
sayuran saja	sai-yu-rahn sah-juh	vegetarian (food)
sayur-sayuran	sai-yur-sai-yu-rahn	vegetables
sebab	se-bahb	because
sebarang	se-bah-rahng	any
sebelum	se-be-lum	before
seberang	se-be-rahng	across
sedap	se-dahp	delicious
sederhana	se-der-hah-nuh	simple
sedia	se-dee-uh	ready
sedih	se-di(h)	sad
sedikit	se-dee-kit	little (amount)
segan	se-gahn	shy
segar	se-gahr	fresh
segiempat	se-gee-em-paht	square (shape)
(tiket) sehala	(tee-keht) se-hah-luh	one-way (ticket)
sehingga (Jun)	se-hing-guh (joon)	until (June)
sejak	se-jah(k)	since
sejarah	se-jah-rah(h)	history
sejuk	se-ju(k)	cold
sekali	se-kah-lee	once
sekali lagi	se-kah-lee lah-gee	once again
sekarang	se-kah-rahng	now • present
sekarang juga	se-kah-rahng joo-guh	right now
sekejap lagi	se-ke-jahp lah-gee	soon
sekolah	se-ko-lah(h)	school
sekolah menengah (SM)	se-ko-lah(h) me-ne-ngah(h)	high school
seks	sehks	sex
seks selamat	sehks se-lah-maht	safe sex
seksisme	sehk-sis-muh	sexism

selalu	se-*lah*-loo	always
selama	se-*lah*-muh	for (length of time)
selama-lamanya	se-*lah*-muh-*lah*-muh-nyuh	forever
selamat	se-*lah*-maht	safe (secure)

Selamat datang.
se-*lah*-maht dah-*tahng* — Welcome.

Selamat hari jadi!
se-*lah*-maht *hah*-ree *jah*-dee! — Happy Birthday!

Selamat jalan.
se-*lah*-maht *jah*-lahn — Goodbye. (speaker staying)

Selamat malam.
se-*lah*-maht *mah*-lahm — Good night.

Selamat pagi.
se-*lah*-maht *pah*-gee — Good morning.

Selamat petang.
se-*lah*-maht pe-*tahng* — Good afternoon.

Selamat tengahari.
se-*lah*-maht te-ngah-*hah*-ree — Good day.

Selamat tinggal.
se-*lah*-maht *ting*-gahl — Goodbye. (speaker leaving)

selatan	se-lah-*tahn*	south
selepas	se-le-*pahs*	after
selesa	se-*leh*-suh	comfortable
selimut	se-*lee*-mut	blanket
selipar	se-*lee*-pahr	sandals
seluar dalam	se-loo-*ahr* dah-*lahm*	underwear
seluar panjang	se-loo-*ahr* pahn-*jahng*	trousers
seluar pendek	se-loo-*ahr* pehn-*de(k)*	shorts (clothes)
seluruh	se-loo-*ru(h)*	whole (all)
semacam	se-*mah*-chahm	similar
semalam	se-*mah*-lahm	yesterday
sembahyang	sem-*bah*-yahng	prayer
sembelit	*sem*-be-lit	constipation
sempadan	*sem*-pah-dahn	border
sempit	*sem*-pit	tight
sempurna	sem-*pur*-nuh	perfect
semua	se-*moo*-uh	all
semua orang	se-*moo*-uh o-*rahng*	everyone
semuanya	se-moo-*uh*-nyuh	everything
semula	se-*moo*-luh	again
semut	se-*mut*	ant
senang	se-*nahng*	easy

D
I
C
T
I
O
N
A
R
Y

seni	se-*nee*	art
seni prasejarah	se-*nee* prah-se-jah-*rah(h)*	prehistoric art
seni tembikar	se-*nee* tem-*bee*-kahr	pottery
seni ukir	se-*nee* oo-kir	sculpture
senibina	se-*nee-bee*-nuh	architecture
seni foto	se-*nee* fo-to	photography
seniman/seniwati	se-*nee*-mahn/	artist
	se-*nee*-wah-tee (m/f)	
sentiasa	*sen*-tee-ah-sah	always
senyap	se-*nyahp*	quiet
senyum	se-*nyum*	to smile
sepasang	se-*pah*-sahng	pair (a couple)
sepi	se-*pee*	quiet
serangan	se-*rah*-ngahn	assault
serangga	se-*rahng*-guh	bug • insect
seratus	se-*rah*-tus	a hundred
sering	se-*ring*	often
serius	see-*ree*-uhs	serious
seronok	se-*ro*-no(k)	fun
serupa	se-*roo*-puh	similar
seseorang	se-se-o-*rahng*	someone
sesuai	se-*soo*-ai	appropriate
sesuatu	se-*soo-ah*-too	something
sesudah	se-*soo-dah(h)*	after
setelah	se-te-*lah(h)*	after
setem	se-*tehm*	stamp
setengah	se-te-*ngah(h)*	half
setengah liter	se-te-*ngah(h)* lee-ter	half a litre
setia	se-*tee*-uh	loyal
setiap	se-*tee*-ahp	each • every
setiap hari	se-*tee*-ahp *hah*-ree	every day
setiausaha	se-*tee*-uh-oo-suh-huh	secretary

Setuju.	se-*too*-joo	Agreed.

siap	see-*ahp*	ready
siapa	see-*ah*-puh	who
siar-siar	see-*ahr*-see-*ahr*	stroll
sibuk	si-*bu(k)*	busy (time)
sihat	si-*haht*	healthy
sikap	see-*kahp*	bad (attitude)
silakan	see-*lah*-kahn	please
simpang jalan	sim-*pahng jah*-lahn	crossroad
sinseh	*sin*-seh(h)	herbalist (person)
sintetik	sin-*teh*-tik	synthetic

sisa	see-suh	rest (what's left)
sisa buangan toksik	see-suh boo-ah-ngahn tok-sik	toxic waste
smir	smir	pap smear
soalan	so-ah-lahn	question
sosialis	so-see-ah-lis	socialist
stadium	stah-dee-um	stadium
standard	stahn-dahrd	standard (usual)
stesen	steh-sehn	station
stesen bas	steh-sehn bahs	bus station
stesen keretapi	steh-sehn ke-reh-tuh-ah-pee	railway/train station
stoking	sto-king	socks
studio	stoo-dee-o	studio
suam	soo-ahm	warm
suami	soo-ah-mee	husband
suara	soo-ah-ruh	voice • volume (sound)
suasana	soo-ah-sah-nuh	environment • atmosphere
subang	soo-bahng	earrings
suci	soo-chee	pure
sudah	soo-dah(h)	already
sudu	soo-doo	spoon
sudut	soo-dut	corner
suhu badan	soo-hoo bah-dahn	temperature (fever)
suhu udara	soo-hoo oo-dah-ruh	temperature (weather)
suka	soo-kuh	to like
suka menerima rasuah	soo-kuh me-ne-ree-muh rah-soo-ah(h)	corrupt (adj)
sukan	soo-kahn	sport
sukar	soo-kahr	difficult
suku	soo-koo	quarter
sundal	soon-dahl	prostitute
sungai	soo-ngai	river
suntikan [suntik]	sun-ti(k)-kahn [sun-ti(k)]	injection
sunyi	soo-nyee	quiet
surat	soo-raht	letter
surat beranak	soo-raht be-rah-nah(k)	birth certificate
surat berdaftar	soo-raht ber-dahf-tahr	registered mail
surat khabar	soo-raht kah-bahr	newspaper
susah	soo-sah(h)	difficult
susu	soo-soo	milk
sutera	soo-te-ruh	silk
syarahan	shah-rah-hahn	lecture
syarikat	shah-ree-kaht	company (business)
syiling	shee-ling	coins

T

tadika	tah-*dee*-kah	kindergarten
tafakur	tah-*fah*-kur	meditation
tahi	tai(k)	shit
tambah	*tahm*-bah(h)	plus

Tahniah!		
tah(h)-nee-ah(h)!		Congratulations!

tahu	tah-hoo	to know (something)
tahun ini	tah-hoon *ee*-nee	this year
tahun depan	tah-hoon de-*pahn*	next year
tahun lepas	tah-hoon le-*pahs*	last year
tak apa	ta(k) *ah*-puh	never mind
takut	tah-*kut*	afraid
tali	tah-*lee*	rope • string
tali kasut	tah-*lee kah*-sut	shoelaces
tali pinggang keledar	tah-*lee peeng*-gahng ke-leh-*dahr*	seat belt
taman negara	tah-*mahn* ne-*gah*-ruh	national park
tampon	*tahm*-pon	tampon
tanah	tah-*nah(h)*	land (ground)
tanaman	tah-*nah*-mahn	plant
tanda	*tahn*-duh	sign
tanda lebam	*tahn*-duh le-*bahm*	bruise
tandas	*tahn*-duhs	toilet
tandas awam	*tahn*-duhs ah-*wahm*	public toilet
tandatangan	*tahn*-duh-*tah*-ngahn	signature
tangan	tah-*ngahn*	hand
tangga	*tahng*-guh	stairs
tanggungjawab	tang-gung-*jah*-wahb	responsibility
tanpa	*tahn*-puh	without
tanpa filter	*tahn*-puh *fil*-ter	without filter
taraf	tah-*rahf*	standard (adj)
taraf kehidupan	tah-*rahf* ke-hee-*du*-pahn	standard of living
tarikh	tah-*rikh*	date (time)
tarikh lahir	tah-*rikh* lah-*hir*	date of birth
taruhan	tah-*ru*-hahn	bet
tasik	tah-*si(k)*	lake
tatabahasa	tah-tah-bah-*hah*-suh	grammar
tawaran	tah-*wah*-rahn	offer
tawar-menawar [tawar]	tah-wahr-me-*nah*-wahr [*tah*-wahr]	to bargain
tayar	tai-yahr	tyre
tebing tinggi	te-*bing ting*-gee	cliff
teduh	te-*du(h)*	shade
teh	teh(h)	tea

telah	te-*lah*(h)	already
tekak	te-*kah*(k)	throat
tekanan	te-*kah*-nahn	pressure
tekanan darah	te-*kah*-nahn *dah*-rah(h)	blood pressure
teks	tehks	subtitles
telanjang	te-*lahn*-jahng	nude
telefon	teh-*leh*-fon	telephone
telefon awam	teh-*leh*-fon *ah*-wahm	phone box
telefon bimbit	teh-*leh*-fon *bim*-bit	mobile phone
telegram	teh-leh-*grahm*	telegram
teler (col)	teh-ler	teller
televisyen	teh-leh-*vee*-shen	television • TV
telinga	te-*lee*-nguh	ear
telur	te-*lur*	egg
teman	te-*mahn*	friend
teman lelaki	te-*mahn* le-*lah*-kee	boyfriend
teman wanita	te-*mahn* wah-*nee*-tah	girlfriend
tembakau	tem-*bah*-kow	tobacco
tembikai	tem-*bee*-kai	watermelon
tembok	tehm-*bo*(k)	wall (outside)
tempahan	tem-*pah*(h)-hahn	reservation
tempat	tem-*paht*	location • place
tempat duduk	tem-*paht doo*-du(k)	seat
tempat letak kereta	tem-*paht* le-*tah*(k) ke-*reh*-tuh	car park
tempat kelahiran	tem-*paht* ke-lah-*hi*-rahn	place of birth
tempat suci	tem-*paht* soo-*chee*	shrine
tempatan	tem-*pah*-tahn	local
temujanji	te-*moo*-jahn-jee	date (appointment)
tenaga nuklear	te-*nah*-guh noo-*klee*-er	nuclear energy
tenang	te-*nahng*	calm
tendangan [tendang]	ten-dah-ngahn [ten-dahng]	kick
tengah malam	te-*ngah*(h) mah-lahm	midnight
tengahari	te-ngah-*hah*-ree	noon
(padang) tenis	(pah-*dahng*) teh-*nis*	tennis (court)
tepat pada masanya	te-*paht* pah-duh mah-*sah*-nyuh	on time
tepi (jalan)	te-*pee* (jah-lahn)	side (of street)
tepi laut	te-*pee* lowt	seaside
terakhir	te-rah-*khir*	last (final)
terang	te-*rahng*	light (not dark)
terbaik	ter-bai(k)	best
terburu-buru	ter-boo-*roo*-boo-roo	in a hurry

Terima kasih.
te-*ree*-muh *kah*-si(h)   Thank you.

terkenal	ter-ke-*nahl*	famous
terlalu	ter-*lah*-loo	too (excessive)
terlalu banyak makan ubat	ter-*lah*-loo bah-nya(k) mah-kahn oo-baht	overdose
terlalu mahal	ter-*lah*-loo mah-*hahl*	rip-off
termasuk	ter-*mah*-su(k)	included
teropong	te-*ro*-pong	binoculars
terpencil	ter-pen-*chil*	remote
terseliuh	ter-se-*lee*-uh(h)	sprain
tersesat [sesat]	ter-*se*-saht [*se*-saht]	lost
terus ke hadapan	te-*rus* ke hah-dah-*pahn*	straight ahead
tetamu	te-*tah*-moo	guest
tetapi	te-*tah*-pee	but
tiada	tee-*ah*-duh	none
tiap-tiap	*tee*-ahp-*tee*-ahp	each • every
tiba	*tee*-buh	to come (arrive)
tidak	*tee*-dah(k)	no
tidak apa-apa	*tee*-dah(k) *ah*-puh-*ah*-puh	nothing
tidak kemas	*tee*-dah(k) ke-*mahs*	sleazy (person)
tidak pernah	*tee*-dah(k) per-*nah*(h)	never
tidak selamat	*tee*-dah(k) se-lah-*maht*	unsafe
tidur	*tee*-dur	to sleep • asleep
tifoid	tai-*foid*	typhoid
tikar	*tee*-kahr	mat
tiket	tee-*keht*	ticket
tikus	*tee*-kus	rat
tilam	tee-*lahm*	mattress
timun	*tee*-mun	cucumber
timur	*tee*-mur	east
tinggal	*ting*-gahl	to live (somewhere)
tinggi	*ting*-gee	tall • high
tingkap	*ting*-kahp	window
tingkat	*ting*-kaht	floor (storey)
tipis	*ti*-pis	thin
tisu	*tee*-soo	toilet paper • tissues
tokong Buda	*to*-kong boo-*dah*	temple (Buddhist)
tokong Cina	*to*-kong *chee*-nuh	temple (Chinese)
tolong	*to*-long	help • please
topeng	*to*-*pehng*	mask (face)
topi	*to*-pee	hat
topi keledar	*to*-pee ke-leh-*dahr*	helmet
trek perbandu	trehk ber-*pahn*-doo	guided trek
tua	*too*-uh	old (person)
tuala	*too*-*ah*-luh	towel
tuala wanita	*too*-*ah*-luh wah-*nee*-tah	sanitary napkins

Tuan	too-ahn	Mr
Tuhan	too-hahn	God (Muslim)
tukang jahit	too-kahng jah-hit	tailor
tukang tenung	too-kahng te-nung	fortune teller
tukang tilik	too-kahng tee-li(k)	fortune teller
tulang	too-lahng	bone
tulen	too-lehn	pure
tuli	too-lee	deaf
tumbuh-tumbuhan	toom-bu(h)-toom-bu(h)-hahn	vegetation
tunangan	too-nah-ngahn	fiance(e)
tunggu	toong-goo	wait
tunjuk perasaan	toon-ju(k) pe-rah-sah-ahn	demonstration
tuntutan bagasi	toon-tu-tahn bah-gah-see	baggage claim
tutup	too-tup	shut

U

ubat	oo-baht	medicine
(kedai) ubat Cina	(ke-dai) oo-baht chee-nuh	herbalist shop
ubat gigi	oo-baht gee-gee	toothpaste
ubat pencegah hamil	oo-baht pen-che-gah(h) hah-mil	the Pill
ubat pencuci perut	oo-baht pen-choo-chee pe-rut	laxatives
ubat tahan sakit	oo-baht tah-hahn sah-kit	painkillers
ubat tidur	oo-baht tee-dur	sleeping pills
ucapan politik	oo-chah-pahn po-lee-tik	political speech
udang	oo-dahng	shrimp
udara	oo-dah-ruh	air
ujian (peperiksaan)	oo-jee-ahn (pe-pe-rik-sah-ahn)	test (exam)
ujian darah	oo-jee-ahn dah-rah(h)	blood test
ujian nuklear	oo-jee-ahn noo-klee-er	nuclear testing
ukiran kayu	oo-ki-rahn kah-yoo	woodcarving
ular	oo-lahr	snake
umum	oo-mum	general
umur	oo-mur	age
undang-undang	oon-dahng-oon-dahng	law
ungu	oo-ngoo	purple
universiti	yu-ni-ver-si-tee	university
untuk	oon-tu(k)	for (purpose)
untuk berseronok	oon-tu(k) ber-se-ro-no(k)	to have fun
urat darah	oo-raht dah-rah(h)	vein
urutan	oo-ru-tahn	massage
utama	oo-tah-muh	main
utara	oo-tah-ruh	north

V

van	vahn	van
virus	vi-*rus*	virus
visa	*vee*-sah	visa
vitamin	vi-*tah*-min	vitamin

W

wain	wain	wine
waktu makan tengahari	*wak*-too *mah*-kahn te-ngah-*hah*-ree	lunchtime
wang	wahng	money
wang tunai	wahng *too*-nai	cash
wanita/perempuan	wah-*nee*-tah/ pe-*rem*-pwahn	woman
wap	wahp	steam
warung	wah-*rung*	food stall
warna	*wahr*-nuh	colour
wartawan	wahr-*tah*-wahn	journalist
wawancara	wah-wahn-*chah*-ruh	interview
wayar	wah-*yahr*	wire

Y

ya	yah	yes
yang	yahng	which
yang berikutnya	yahng be-ree-*kut*-nyah	next
yang lalu	yahng *lah*-loo	past (before)

Z

zakar	zah-*kahr*	penis
zebra	*zeh*-brah	zebra
zoo	zoo	zoo

INDEX

Abbreviations 12
Accommodation 77
    Booking Ahead 78
    Checking In 79
    Checking Out 85
    Finding Accommodation 77
    Laundry 82
    Requests & Complaints 82
Address, Forms of 41
Addresses 61
Adjectives 23
Adverbs 25
Age 47
Ailments 170
Alcohol 154
Allergies 57, 174
Amounts 199
Ancestors 186
Animals 164
Answers 35
Around Town 87
    Bank 89
    Internet 95
    Looking For 88
    Post Office 91
    Sightseeing 96
    Telephone 93
Arrows to Mecca 104
Articles (Grammar) 19
Arts 118
ATM 89

Baby 128
Batik 116, 125
Bank 89
Bargaining 121
Basic Phrases 39

Be, To (Grammar) 29
Beach 160
Beggars 133
Bicycle 74
Blood Type 208
Boat 69
Body Language 53
Body, Parts of the 175
Books 129
Breakfast 135, 136
Breaking the
    Language Barrier 55
Breaking Up 103
Bugs 155, 165
Bus 65
Business 182
Buying Tickets 62

Calendar 189
Camera 130
Camping 155
Can (Grammar) 31
Car 70
Car Problems 73
Casual Language 18
Checking In 79
Checking Out 85
Chemist 176
Children 105, 181
Cigarettes 131
Classifiers (Grammar) 36
Climate 124
Clothing 124
    Women's 52
Coffee 152
Colours 126
Common Interests 109

Communication 55
Comparatives (Grammar) 24
Complaints (Hotel) 82
Computers 95
Condiments 151
Condoms 102
Conjunctions (Grammar) 38
Consonants 17
Conversation 42
Cooking Methods 151
Cost 120, 121
Counting 202
Countries 46
Country, In the 155
    Beach 160
    Camping 155
    Fauna 164
    Flora & Agriculture 165
    Geography 163
    Hiking 157
    Weather 161
Crafts 116
Credit Card 120
Currency 89
Cultural Differences 47
Customs 64, 204
Cycling 74

Dancing 101
Dates (Time) 189
Dating 101, 103
Days 188
Dentist 178
Desserts 145
Diabetes 57
Directions 60
Disabled Travellers 179
Diseases 171
Diving 161

Doctor 167
Drinks 152
    Alcoholic 154
    Non-Alcoholic 152
Drivers (Instructions) 68
Drugs 17

Eating Out 138
Email 182
Emergencies 203
English 55
Essential Verbs (Grammar) 28
Essential Items (Shopping) 122
Exchange Rate 90

Fabrics 125
Family 105
Family History 186
Family Members 107
Family, Travelling with the 181
Fauna 164
Fax 182
Feelings 54
Ferries 69
Festivals 193
Film 130
Film Industry 111
Filming 183
Finding Your Way 59
First Encounters 42
Fish 148
Flora 165
Food 135
    Breakfast 135, 136
    Cooking Methods 151
    Condiments 151
    Eating Out 138
    Eggs 144
    Fish 148

Fruit 149
Market 146
Meat 148
Menu Decoder 141
Noodles 142
Rice Dishes 143
Seafood 148
Self-Catering 146
Staples 147
Sweets 145
Typical Dishes 141
Vegetables 148
Vegetarian &
    Special Meals 136
Forms of Address 41
Forms, Filling in 97
Fractions 200
Fruit 149
Funerals 198
Fungal Infections 127
Future (Time) 191

Gay Travellers 180
Geography 163
Getting Around 59
    Air 63
    Bicycle 74
    Boat 69
    Bus 65
    Buying Tickets 62
    Car 70
    Car Problems 73
    Directions 60
    Finding Your Way 59
    Local Transport 76
    Taxi 68
    Train 66
Going Out 99
Goodbyes 40

Grammar 19
    Adjectives 23
    Adverbs 25
    Answers 35
    Classifiers 36
    Conjunctions 38
    Modals 30
    Negatives 35
    Nouns 20
    Prepositions 37
    Possession 22
    Pronouns 20
    Tense 29
    To Be 29
    To Have 30
    Questions 32
    Question Words 34
    Verbs 26
    Word Order 19
Greetings 40
Groceries 146

Handicapped Travellers 179
Handshakes 53
Have, To (Grammar) 30
Headcoverings (Women) 52
Health 167, 207
    Ailments 170
    Alternative Treatments 175
    At the Chemist 176
    At the Dentist 178
    At the Doctor 167
    Parts of the Body 175
    Special Health Needs 174
    Women's Health 172
Hiking 157
    Hiking Gear 159
History, Family 186
Hobbies 110

Holidays 193
Homestays 57
Hospital 208
Hygeine 127

Illnesses 170
Imperatives (Grammar).......... 32
Insects 165
Internet 95
Interpreter 182
Interests 109
Islam 53, 184

Jewellery 117, 123
Jobs 49

Kites 117

Language Difficulties 55
Letters (Writing) 113
Longer Stays 85
Looking For ...
    Accommodation 77
    Places 88
    Love 102

Mail 91
Main Courses 141
Making Conversation 42
Map 8
Martial Arts 118
Market 146
Materials 125
Meat 148
Meetings 56
Meeting People 39
    Age 47
    Body Language 53
    Breaking the
        Language Barrier 55

Cultural Differences 47
Feelings 54
First Encounters 42
Forms of Address 41
Goodbyes 40
Greetings 40
Homestays 57
Making Conversation 42
Nationalities 46
Occupations 49
Religion 50
Staying in Touch 56
Useful Words & Phrases 44
You Should Know 39
Menu Decoder 141
Mobile Phone 183
Modals (Grammar) 30
Monsoon 162
Music 116, 128
Money 89
Months 189

Nationalities 46
Nightclubs 99, 100
Negatives (Grammar) 35
'No', Ways of Saying 56
Noodles 142
Nouns (Grammar) 20
    Plurals 20
Numbers & Amounts 199
    Cardinal Numbers 199
    Fractions 200
    Ordinal Numbers 200

Occupations 49
Opinions 114

Paperwork 97
Passport 98
Past (Time) 190

Paying (Accommodation) 81
Pharmacy 176
Phone Calls 94
Photography 96, 130
Phrases, Basic 39
Pick-Up Lines 100, 101, 103
Pilgrimage 184
Planes 63
Plants 165
Police 204, 206
Politics 114
Possession (Grammar) 22
Post Office 91
Prayers 104, 184, 192
Prefixes (Grammar) 26
Prepositions (Grammar) 37
Present (Time) 190
Pronouns (Grammar) 20
    Personal Pronouns 20
    Possessive Pronouns 22
Pronunciation 15
    Consonants 17
    Diphthongs 16
    Stress 15
    Transliteration System 15
    Vowels 16
Publications 129
Pythons 166

Quantity 201
Questions (Grammar) 32, 34

Ramadan 102, 193, 195
Religion 50, 184
Religious Festivals 102
Religious Buildings 104
Restaurants 138
Rice Dishes 143
Romance 101, 103
Roots, Tracing Family 186

Seasons 192
Shopping 119
Shop Assistants 121
Sickness 167
Sightseeing 96
Signs 62, 69, 92
Sign Language 179
Sizes 132
Singing 116
Smoking 131
Snacks 145
Social Issues 114
Souvenirs 123, 126
Spices 151
    Spicy Food 44
Sport 111
    Types of Sport 112
Staying in Touch 56
Stationery 129
Streetlife 133
Studying 50
Sunscreen 127
Superlatives (Grammar) 24
Sweets 145
Swimming 160

Taxi 68
Table Manners 51
Tea 153
Telecommunications 93
Telegram 91
Telephone 93
Temples 104, 184
    Etiquette 185
Tense (Grammar) 29
Thank You 58
Tickets 62
Time 84, 187

To Be (Grammar) 29
To Have (Grammar) 30
Toiletries 127
Tops (Spinning) 117
Town, Around 87
Traffic Jams 73
Transliterations
    (Pronunciation) 15
Transport
    Air 63
    Bicycle 74
    Boat 69
    Bus 65
    Buying Tickets 62
    Car 70
    Taxi 68
    Train 66
Transvestites 180
Trekking 157
TV Channels 111
TV Crews 183

Vegetables 148
Vegetarian &
    Special Meals 136
Verbs 26
    Essential Verbs 28
    Modals 30
    Prefixes 26
    To Be 29
    To Have 30
Vowels 16

Walking 158
Want To (Grammar) 31
Water 152
Weather 124, 161
Weddings 197
Weights 133
Wildlife 164
Women's Health 172
Women's Rights 52
Word Order (Grammar) 19
Writing Letters 113

NOTES

Phrasebooks

L onely Planet phrasebooks are packed with essential words and phrases to help travellers communicate with the locals. With colour tabs for quick reference, an extensive vocabulary and use of script, these handy pocket-sized language guides cover day-to-day travel situations.

- handy pocket-sized books
- easy to understand Pronunciation chapter
- clear & comprehensive Grammar chapter
- romanisation alongside script to allow ease of pronunciation
- script throughout so users can point to phrases for every situation
- full of cultural information and tips for the traveller

'...vital for a real DIY spirit and attitude in language learning'
– *Backpacker*

'the phrasebooks have good cultural backgrounders and offer solid advice for challenging situations in remote locations'
– *San Francisco Examiner*

Arabic (Egyptian) • Arabic (Moroccan) • Australian (*Australian English, Aboriginal and Torres Strait languages*) • Baltic States (*Estonian, Latvian, Lithuanian*) • Bengali • Brazilian • Burmese • British (*English, dialects, Scottish Gaelic, Welsh*) • Cantonese • Central Asia (*Kazakh, Kyrgyz, Pashto, Tajik, Tashkorghani, Turkmen, Uyghur, Uzbek & others*) • Central Europe (*Czech, German, Hungarian, Polish, Slovak, Slovene*) • Costa Rica Spanish • Czech • Eastern Europe (*Albanian, Bulgarian, Croatian, Czech, Hungarian, Macedonian, Polish, Romanian, Serbian, Slovak, Slovene*) • East Timor (*Tetun, Portuguese*) • Egyptian Arabic • Ethiopian (Amharic) • Europe (*Basque, Catalan, Dutch, French, German, Greek, Irish, Italian, Maltese, Portuguese, Scottish Gaelic, Spanish, Turkish, Welsh*) • Farsi (Persian) • Fijian • French • German • Greek • Hebrew • Hill Tribes (*Lahu, Akha, Lisu, Mong, Mien, & others*) • Hindi/Urdu • Indonesian • Italian • Japanese • Korean • Lao • Latin American Spanish • Malay • Mandarin • Mongolian • Moroccan Arabic • Nepali • Papua New Guinea • Pidgin • Pilipino (Tagalog) • Polish • Portuguese • Quechua • Russian • Scandinavian (*Danish, Faroese, Finnish, Icelandic, Norwegian, Swedish*) • South-East Asia (*Burmese, Indonesian, Khmer, Lao, Malay, Tagalog Pilipino, Thai, Vietnamese*) • South Pacific (*Fijian, Hawaiian, Kanak languages, Maori, Niuean, Rapanui, Rarotongan Maori, Samoan, Tahitian, Tongan & others*) • Spanish (*Castilian, also includes Catalan, Galician & Basque*) • Sri Lanka • Swahili • Thai • Tibetan • Turkish • Ukrainian • USA (*US English, vernacular, Native American, Hawaiian*) • Vietnamese

COMPLETE LIST OF LONELY PLANET BOOKS

AFRICA Africa on a shoestring • Cairo • Cape Town • East Africa • Egypt • Ethiopia, Eritrea & Djibouti • The Gambia & Senegal • Healthy Travel Africa • Kenya • Malawi • Morocco • Mozambique • Read This First: Africa • South Africa, Lesotho & Swaziland • Southern Africa • Southern Africa Road Atlas • Tanzania, Zanzibar & Pemba • Trekking in East Africa • Tunisia • Watching Wildlife East Africa • Watching Wildlife Southern Africa • West Africa • World Food Morocco • Zimbabwe, Botswana & Namibia

AUSTRALIA & THE PACIFIC Aboriginal Australia & the Torres Strait Islands • Auckland • Australia • Australia Road Atlas • Bushwalking in Australia • Cycling Australia • Cycling New Zealand • Fiji • Healthy Travel Australia, NZ and the Pacific • Islands of Australia's Great Barrier Reef • Melbourne • Micronesia • New Caledonia • New South Wales & the ACT • New Zealand • Northern Territory • Outback Australia • Out to Eat – Melbourne • Out to Eat – Sydney • Papua New Guinea • Queensland • Rarotonga & the Cook Islands • Samoa • Solomon Islands • South Australia • South Pacific • Sydney • Sydney Condensed • Tahiti & French Polynesia • Tasmania • Tonga • Tramping in New Zealand • Vanuatu • Victoria • Walking in Australia • Watching Wildlife Australia • Western Australia

CENTRAL AMERICA & THE CARIBBEAN Bahamas, Turks & Caicos • Baja California • Bermuda • Central America on a shoestring • Costa Rica • Cuba • Dominican Republic & Haiti • Eastern Caribbean • Guatemala • Guatemala, Belize & Yucatán: La Ruta Maya • Havana • Healthy Travel Central & South America • Jamaica • Mexico • Mexico City • Panama • Puerto Rico • Read This First: Central & South America • World Food Mexico • Yucatán

EUROPE Amsterdam • Amsterdam Condensed • Andalucía • Austria • Barcelona • Belgium & Luxembourg • Berlin • Britain • Brussels, Bruges & Antwerp • Budapest • Canary Islands • Central Europe • Copenhagen • Corfu & the Ionians • Corsica • Crete • Crete Condensed • Croatia • Cycling Britain • Cycling France • Cyprus • Czech & Slovak Republics • Denmark • Dublin • Eastern Europe • Edinburgh • England • Estonia, Latvia & Lithuania • Europe on a shoestring • Finland • Florence • France • Frankfurt Condensed • Georgia, Armenia & Azerbaijan • Germany • Greece • Greek Islands • Hungary • Iceland, Greenland & the Faroe Islands • Ireland • Istanbul • Italy • Krakow • Lisbon • The Loire • London • London Condensed • Madrid • Malta • Mediterranean Europe • Milan, Turin & Genoa • Moscow • Mozambique • Munich • The Netherlands • Normandy • Norway • Out to Eat – London • Paris • Paris Condensed • Poland • Portugal • Prague • Provence & the Côte d'Azur • Read This First: Europe • Rhodes & the Dodecanese • Romania & Moldova • Rome • Rome Condensed • Russia, Ukraine & Belarus • Scandinavian & Baltic Europe • Scotland • Sicily • Slovenia • South-West France • Spain • St Petersburg • Sweden • Switzerland • Trekking in Spain • Tuscany • Venice • Vienna • Walking in Britain • Walking in France • Walking in Ireland • Walking in Italy • Walking in Spain • Walking in Switzerland • Western Europe • World Food France • World Food Ireland • World Food Italy • World Food Spain